OXFORD ENGLISH MONOGRAPHS

General Editors

The Faerie Queene and Middle English Romance: The Matter of Just Memory

ANDREW KING

CLARENDON PRESS · OXFORD

OXFORD
UNIVERSITY PRESS

Great Clarendon Street, Oxford OX2 6DP
Oxford University Press is a department of the University of Oxford.
It furthers the University's objective of excellence in research, scholarship,
and education by publishing worldwide in

Oxford New York

Athens Auckland Bangkok Bogotá Aires Calcutta
Cape Town Chennai Dar es Salaam Delhi Florence Hong Kong Istanbul
Karachi Kuala Lumpure Madrid Melbourne Mexico City Mumbai
Nairobi Paris São Paulo Shanghai Singapore Taipei Tokoyo Toronto Warsaw
and associated companies in Berlin Ibadan

Oxford is a registered trade mark of Oxford University Press
in the UK and certain other countries

Published in the United States
by Oxford University Press Inc., New York

British Library Cataloguing in Publication Data
Data available.
Library of Congress Cataloging in Publication Data
Data available
ISBN 0–19–818722–X

1 3 5 7 9 10 8 6 4 2
Typeset in 10.5pt on 12pt Sabon by Kolam Information Services Pvt Ltd, Pondicherry, India
Printed in Great Britain
on acid-free paper by
T.J. International Ltd, Padstow, Cornwall

For my parents

Preface

The purpose of this study is to consider Middle English romance as a literary tradition of considerable thematic and narrative coherence and also to demonstrate that this tradition has made a deep and significant impression on *The Faerie Queene*. Spenser's engagement with Middle English romance—both verse romance and Malory—is a profoundly important aspect of his work, one which needs to be set alongside the mass of existing books which focus on his debts to classical and Italian humanist epic. At the heart of this inquiry into a specific literary tradition is the contention that Spenser's use of Middle English romance was a deliberately meaningful gesture—meaningful to contemporary readers for whom Middle English romance had acquired complex and ambivalent values. I will be concerned to show how the political and cultural values which, in Spenser's perception, Middle English romance possessed in fact had their roots in the medieval period and in the manner in which the tradition developed in association with historical and hagiographical writings. Two aspects of the native medieval romance tradition deserve special emphasis. One is the tendency of Middle English verse romance and Malory, in common with historical writings and saints' lives, to locate the narrative events in a recognizably English landscape. The other characterizing tendency of the native romance tradition is the interest which writers show in two basic narrative-patterns: the orphaned, exiled, or displaced male youth of noble birth but impoverished upbringing, and the female figure of virtue who is treacherously slandered and consequently outcast. Both of these aspects of Middle English romance, I will argue, reflect an interest in self-understanding or identity, either the historically derived identity of a region or the nation or an individual character's progress towards deeper self-knowledge. Not only is the development of this tradition in the medieval period of great interest in its own right; its assimilation by Spenser in Protestant England involves a fascinatingly complex recovery of medieval heritage in order to gain 'prophetic' authority for the Reformation. However, Spenser stands apart from the most influential authors of English Protestant historiography and apology, such as Foxe and Bale, in his developed anxiety concerning the invocation of providence in relation to a concept of nationhood

The binding concept of this monograph is revealed in its Spenserian subtitle, the 'matter of just memory'. In relation to Middle English romance, memory describes the traditional aspect of romance—how romances rework and develop the same basic stories and characters. Memory also applies to Middle English romance's interest in regional or national history and origins, as well as individual characters' gradual recalling of their innate identities. *The Faerie Queene* too becomes, as Spenser himself describes it, 'matter of iust memory' (II.Proem.1) by recollecting earlier medieval texts and by participating in native romance's interest in national identity and historical consciousness. And although Spenser describes Eumnestes, the figure of memory, as a 'man of infinite remembrance' with 'incorrupted' historical records (II.ix.56), he also notes that the records in Eumnestes' chamber 'were all worme-eaten, and full of canker holes' (II.ix.57). This tension will become crucial as we explore Spenser's response to Middle English romance in the light of Protestant historiography as well as Elizabethan imperialism. If earlier romance can be 'remembered' in a way that is distinctly advantageous to Reformation England, as it is in Book I, then it is equally true that the admitted creativity or subjectivity of memory threatens the sense, represented with assurance in Middle English romance, that English history reveals the guiding force of providence.

In the course of writing this book I have incurred many debts which I am delighted to acknowledge. Professor Helen Cooper supervised this work in its earlier form, as a doctoral thesis, with remarkable wit, kindness, and erudition. It is hard for me to speculate what shape this work would have taken without the benefit of her scholarly expertise and personal support— though I have no doubt that it would have been a less pleasing shape. My examiners for the thesis, Dr Richard McCabe and Dr Rosalind Field, provided stimulating criticism in relation to that work, and they have generously maintained a helpful interest in its transformation into a book. I am also greatly indebted to Professor Anne Hudson, Professor Douglas Gray, and

Dr Malcolm Parkes, who all provided a formative influence and constructive criticism in relation to this topic at an early stage. Two of my undergraduate instructors at the University of Toronto, Professor John Leyerle and Professor James Carscallen, guided me towards postgraduate study at Oxford and have kindly maintained a supportive interest in my work. My thanks go also to Dr Glenn Black and Dr Dennis Kay for reading sections of this work and offering insightful criticism which has, I hope, led me to strengthen my position. The two anonymous readers of Oxford University Press offered detailed, helpful reactions which became fundamental to my final revision, and I am also very grateful to Ms Sophie Goldsworthy at the Press for her patience in dealing with my several queries. The Bodleian Library, University of Oxford kindly granted permission for the reproduction on the dustjacket cover of the woodcut from f.ii.r of *Syr Beuis of Hampton* (1585), S.Seld.d.45(2). Mr Patrick Carter kindly solved many computer problems for me.

My sincere thanks to various corporations and individuals who have provided financial or academic support: the Association of Commonwealth Universities; the Social Sciences and Humanities Research Council of Canada; the Provost and Fellows of Oriel College, Oxford; the Centre for Reformation and Renaissance Studies at the University of Toronto; Dalhousie University and the Killam Foundation; the Bodleian Library; the University Library, Cambridge; my uncle, Dr Peter Duncan; and my parents.

Contents

Abbreviations

AS	*Arthurian Studies*
BJRL	*Bulletin of the John Rylands Library*
BM	British Museum
BN	Bibliothèque Nationale
CFMA	Classiques Français du Moyen Age
CE	*College English*
CR	*The Chaucer Review*
CS	Camden Society
CUL	Cambridge University Library
EETS	Early English Text Society ('Original Series', unless otherwise stated)
—os	Original Series
—es	Extra Series
—ss	Supplementary Series
ELH	*English Literary History*
ELR	*English Literary Renaissance*
G-J	*Gütenberg-Jährbuch*
HLQ	*Huntingdon Library Quarterly*
JEGP	*Journal of English and Germanic Philology*
JMH	*Journal of Medieval History*
JWCI	*Journal of the Warburg and Courtauld Institutes*
MÆ	*Medium Ævum*
MH	*Medievalia et Humanistica*
MLN	*Modern Language Notes*
MLR	*Modern Language Review*
MP	*Modern Philology*
NM	*Neuphilologische Mitteilungen*
NQ	*Notes and Queries*
n.s.	new series
OED	Oxford English Dictionary
PBA	*Proceedings of the British Academy*
PHFCAS	*Proceedings of the Hampshire Field Club and Archaeological Society*
PMLA	*Publications of the Modern Language Association*
PQ	*Philological Quarterly*
RMS	*Reading Medieval Studies*
RS	Rolls Series
SATF	Société des anciens textes Français

SB	*Studies in Bibliography*
SCJ	*Sixteenth Century Journal*
SP	*Studies in Philology*
SS	*Spenser Studies*
STC	*A Short-Title Catalogue of Books Printed in England, Scotland, & Ireland, And of English Books Printed Abroad 1475–1640*, ed. A. W. Pollard and G. R. Redgrave, rev. and enlarged W. A. Jackson, F. S. Ferguson, and Katherine F. Pantzer. 2nd edn. 2 vols. London, 1976, 1986.
STS	Scottish Text Society
TLF	Textes littéraires Français
TRHS	*Transactions of the Royal Historical Society*
Variorum	*The Works of Edmund Spenser: A Variorum Edition*, ed. Edwin Greenlaw, Charles Grosvenor Osgood, and Frederick Morgan Padelford. 10 vols. Baltimore, 1932–49.

I

Approaching Spenser's Medievalism

The chamber of Eumnestes, or Memory, which Arthur and
Guyon visit is graphically bookish:

> ... all was hangd about with rolles,
> And old records from auncient times deriu'd,
> Some made in books, some in long parchment scrolles.[1]

If *The Faerie Queene* is 'matter of iust memory' (II.Proem.1), then
according to this representation of Memory it is composed from
earlier books, or self-consciously aware of its origins in previous
historical and literary traditions. This point is vividly realized
when Arthur and Guyon each read a book relevant to their
individual lineages: for Arthur 'An auncient booke, hight *Briton
moniments*', and for Guyon 'another booke, / That hight *Antiquitie of Faerie* lond' (II.ix.59, 60). The matter of these books
becomes the matter of *The Faerie Queene* in the following
Canto, where the two knights' books become the same book
which we are reading. Matter can designate either a physical
substance or the subject or sense of a text;[2] Spenser combines
both senses, the physical and the textual, in a very medieval view
of the creation of work as an almost physical thrusting together or
regurgitation of different volumes.[3] Crucially, the matter of the
books which Arthur and Guyon read, or which *The Faerie
Queene* itself remembers, relates to native literary and historical
traditions—Arthurian history and faerie romance mirroring

---

[1] Edmund Spenser, *The Faerie Queene*, ed. A. C. Hamilton (London and New
York, 1977), II.ix.57.

[2] As in the Man of Law's narrative—'And turne I wole agayn to my matere'
(II.322); Geoffrey Chaucer, *The Riverside Chaucer*, gen. ed. Larry D. Benson, 3rd
edn. (Boston, 1987).

[3] Laȝamon describes his sources in physical terms: he 'leide þeos boc ·] þa leaf
wende. / he heom leofliche bi-heold' (Caligula, 24–5; he 'laid those books out and
turned the leaves; he looked at them affectionately'). The creation of his own work,
the *Brut*, appears to be a physical act of compression: he 'þa þre boc · þrumde to are'
(Caligula, 28; he 'condensed/compressed those three books into one'); Laȝamon, *Brut*,
ed. G. L Brook and R. F. Leslie, EETS 250, 277 (London, 1963, 1973).

English history. In this context, it is interesting to consider how Spenser's earlier work, *The Shepheardes Calender*, is also the matter, in both the textual and physical senses, of a remembered native literary tradition.

Like the Redcrosse Knight, who is a changling found and raised by a ploughman (1.x.65–6), and like numerous orphaned or socially displaced heroic youths in Middle English romance whom we will later consider, *The Shepheardes Calender* is left, as it were, on our doorstep by Immerito: 'As child whose parent is unkent'.[4] And although Immerito instructs his book to declare itself illegitimate, 'base begot with blame' ('To His Booke.', 14), the conventions of the foundling story suggest that this creature's apparent baseness or rusticity masks legitimacy of birth and perhaps even an innate nobility: Redcrosse, for instance, springs 'from ancient race/Of *Saxon* kings' (1.x.65). E. K.'s 'Epistle' to *The Shepheardes Calender* discusses the text's language in the same metaphorical terms, concerned with birth and legitimacy. Immerito 'hath *laboured* to restore, as to theyr rightfull *heritage* such good and *naturall* English words, as have ben long time out of use and almost cleare *disherited*' (84–6; my emphases). The chasteness of the 'Mother tonge' ('Epistle', 87–8) appears to be at stake.[5] Or, from another perspective, Immerito in his labouring becomes the mother who gives birth to, or confers legitimacy on, an offspring comprised of 'naturall English words'. The metaphors employing the terms of birth and legitimacy in both Immerito's address and E. K.'s 'Epistle' draw attention to the Eclogues' 'ancestral' roots in earlier English literature, offsetting the powerful Virgilian associations concomitant with pastoral poetry in the Renaissance. Like Redcrosse and other orphaned heroes who, we will explore in later chapters, gradually remember or come to terms with their true nativity and identity, *The Shepheardes Calender* involves the reader in a process of recollecting an earlier native literary tradition from which it is sprung; in that process, according to the expectations created by the foundling narrative,

---

[4] 'To His Booke.', 2; *The Yale Edition of the Shorter Poems of Edmund Spenser*, ed. William A. Oram et al. (New Haven and London, 1989).

[5] The metaphor of legitimacy conferred through birth resurfaces in E. K.'s 'Epistle' at 108–14. Cf. Sidney's epistle to his sister in *The Old Arcadia* where Sidney wishes 'to cast out in some desert of forgetfulness this child which I am loath to father'; Sir Philip Sidney, *The Countess of Pembroke's Arcadia (The Old Arcadia)*, ed. Katherine Duncan-Jones (Oxford and New York, 1994).

the non-native pastoral traditions become by implication 'illegitimate', false parents who now must be discarded. The signs which prompt that recollection are contained in the work's matter in both senses, physical and textual. Like the foundling youth who possesses a signet ring or some token from his true parents, *The Shepheardes Calender* gives the appearance of deriving from an earlier time. For example, its archaic and dialectal diction necessitated the inclusion of a 'Glosse' to each Eclogue. In a passage such as this—

> Syker thou speakes lyke a lewde lorrell,
>   of Heaven to demen so:
> How be I am but rude and borrell,
>   yet nearer wayes I knowe.
> To Kerke the narre, from God more farre,
>   has bene an old sayd sawe.

> (*Julye*, 93–8)

—Spenser inscribes his work into the linguistic past, as if it were not so much a new work as an old book which he has discovered in Eumnestes' chamber and which he now presents to us.[6] Not surprisingly, the language of *The Shepheardes Calender* confused early humanist readers.[7] The complex visual appearance of the work may also have seemed confusing, though it too seeks to establish the work's pedigree, or legitimacy. The apparatus of woodcuts, 'Arguments', and 'Glosses' suggests, like the archaic language, that *The Shepheardes Calender* is an older work and that it has here been given editorial treatment, such as one would accord a classical text.[8] *The Shepheardes Calender*

---

[6] Concerning the 'medieval' element in Spenser's language, see further: 'Archaism' by Noel Osselton and 'Language, General, and Resources Exploited in Rhyme' by Barbara M. H. Strang in A. C. Hamilton (gen. ed.), *The Spenser Encyclopedia* (Toronto, 1990). The following scholarship considers *The Shepheardes Calender* in terms of its indebtedness to Middle English and early Tudor genres, works, and traditions: Helen Cooper, *Pastoral* (Ipswich, 1977), 152–65; Anthea Hume, *Edmund Spenser* (Cambridge, 1984), 13–56; John N. King, *Spenser's Poetry and the Reformation Tradition* (Princeton, 1990), 14–46. Furthermore, John N. King, *English Reformation Literature* (Princeton, 1982), 18 observes that the 'newness' of *The Shepheardes Calender* has distracted from its debt to native literary traditions rooted in the Middle Ages.

[7] Sir Philip Sidney, *A Defence of Poetry*, ed. Jan Van Dorsten (Oxford, 1973), 64.24–7. Ben Jonson, *Timber, Or Discoveries*, in *Ben Jonson's Literary Criticism*, ed. James D. Redwine, Jr. (Lincoln, Nebraska, 1970), 19.

[8] Ruth Samson Luborsky, 'The Illustrations to *The Shepheardes Calender*', *SS* 2 (1981), 3–53 argues that Spenser was to some degree responsible for the contents

assumes the dignity of a Latin or Greek text, and in doing so the prestige and legitimacy of the classical tradition are transferred to the medieval native literary tradition embodied in Spenser's work.

The Shepheardes Calender announces itself as the 'matter of iust memory', rooted in native literary traditions, in other ways. For one, the title of the work recalls *The Kalender of Shepherdes*, a popular encyclopaedic almanac which was printed with remarkably little change from the late fifteenth to the seventeenth century.[9] Like *The Kalender of Shepherdes*, Spenser's work is set in black letter type, which in 1579 would give an immediate visual impression of native literature.[10] Furthermore, *The Shepheardes Calender* pays homage to Chaucer, who is invoked as Tityrus, the pseudonym which Virgil adopted for himself in his *Eclogues*.[11] Like the 'edited' appearance of the *Calender*, Chaucer's assumption of Virgil's identity is a backward perspective which rewrites medieval native literature as noble rather than bastardized, as a

of the woodcuts. The fact that the complex appearance and organization of *The Shepheardes Calender* remained the same in the four quarto editions that succeeded the 1579 first edition and also in the 1611 folio, despite changes in printers, suggests at the least the significance of this layout and, furthermore, its authorial determination. The Renaissance editions of the *Aeneid* generally included a complex apparatus of commentary that embodied over a thousand years of response to the text; principal editions and translations are described in Giulano Mambelli, *Gli annali delle edizioni virgiliane* (Florence, 1954). Sannazaro's *Arcadia*, in Francesco Sansovino's illustrated edition (Venice, 1571) provided a model for the appearance of *The Shepheardes Calender*; see S. K. Heninger, Jr., 'The Typographical Layout of Spenser's *Shepheardes Calender*', in Karl Josef Höltgen et al. (eds), *Word and Visual Imagination* (Erlangen, 1988), 33–71. As a precedent for *The Shepheardes Calender*, Robert Crowley's three separate quarto editions of *The Vision of Pierce Plowman* (1550) contained a Preface, summary and marginal notes which sought to illuminate obscure language and sense and to interpret the work as a proto-Reformation attack on the Church; see King, *English Reformation Literature*, 331–2.

⁹ *The Kalender of Shepherdes*, ed. H. Oskar Sommer, 3 vols. (London, 1892); *The Kalender & Compost of Shepherds*, ed. G. C. Heseltine (London, 1930). See Appendix II, 176–7 in *Kalender*, ed. Heseltine for a list of the English editions of the *Kalender* to 1656. The *Kalender* is a translation of the French *Kalendrier des bergier* (1493) of Guy Marchant. When I refer to the *Kalender* as a native work, I mean that it would *appear* native, and medieval, to Elizabethan readers, in contrast to Italian literature. See further: Cooper, *Pastoral*, 152.

¹⁰ Colin Burrow, *Edmund Spenser* (Plymouth, 1996), 12–13 is possibly misleading when he argues that black letter type would have appeared archaic in 1579; a cursory look through some of the microfilms of the STC immediately corrects that impression. See further: Malcolm Parkes, *Pause and Effect* (Aldershot, 1992), 54.

¹¹ In *June* 81–96, Colin, or Spenser, proclaims his great respect for Chaucer; see also *Februarie*, 91–101. The 'Romish Tityrus' in *October*, 55–60, is Virgil.

foundling whose disguised birth has finally been discovered to the degradation of his erstwhile classical foster-parents. Why should a work which is self-promotional, marking the arrival of the 'new Poete', create the sense of being a much older work, now discovered and brought to light? Part of the reason must lie in the context of the Elizabethan interest in native antiquities and the support which this research gave to Protestant reform. Piers, one of Spenser's shepherds, recalls by name *Piers Plowman* and the tradition of anti-ecclesiastical satire associated with Langland's work, such as *Pierce the Ploughman's Crede, Mum and the Sothsegger,* the pseudo-Chaucerian *Plowman's Tale,* and a number of Reformation texts based on the ploughman figure.[12] The pre-Reformation texts were interpreted in the Protestant era as the embodiment of a native tradition of enlightened religion which had opposed the illegitimate sovereignty of Rome. At the same time, writers of the Edwardian Reformation and later, such as Robert Crowley, William Baldwin, and Luke Shepherd, were inspired by a native tradition of language, style, and content in the composition of new works.[13] The positioning of *The Shepheardes Calender* in the past associates it with the 'prophetic' character of the proto-Reformation works. The remembered legitimacy of *The Shepheardes Calender* indicates not simply a literary pedigree, but also a religious one.

The 'prophetic' relationship of pre-Reformation literature to Protestant doctrine will be important when we consider how the

[12] Redcrosse connects *The Faerie Queene* as well to the *Piers Plowman*-tradition when we learn that Redcrosse was raised by a ploughman and 'brought..vp in ploughmans state to byde' (i.x.66). Spenser's connections with Langland are the subject of: A. C. Hamilton, 'The Visions of *Piers Plowman* and *The Faerie Queene*', in William Nelson (ed.), *Form and Convention in the Poetry of Edmund Spenser* (New York and London, 1961), 1–34; Judith H. Anderson, The *Growth of a Personal Voice* (New Haven, 1976). On the *Piers*-tradition, see also: Helen C. White, *Social Criticism in Popular Religious Literature of the Sixteenth Century* (New York, 1944), 1–40; Anne Hudson, 'Epilogue: The Legacy of *Piers Plowman*', in John A. Alford (ed.), *A Companion to Piers Plowman* (Berkeley, 1988), 251–66; *The Piers Plowman Tradition*, ed. Helen Barr (London and Rutland, Vermont, 1993). Just as 'Piers' recalls the Langland tradition, 'Colin Clout' recalls Skelton's poem of that name, also perceived as proto-Protestant. The etymology of the name signifies rustic poverty; see John Skelton, *The Complete English Poems*, ed. John Scattergood (Harmondsworth, 1983), 466.
[13] See further King, *English Reformation Literature*, passim; King, *Spenser's Poetry and the Reformation*, 20–31.

memory of older romances operates in Book I and why Spenser makes Arthur his central hero. In addition to the ploughman-texts, there was a wider historical tradition in the sixteenth century which is contextual to the memorial character of both *The Shepheardes Calender* and *The Faerie Queene*. The activities of Matthew Parker, John Bale, William Camden, John Dee, John Stow, Robert Cotton, and the circle of the Elizabethan Society of Antiquaries (founded *c.* 1586) in seeking out, studying, lending, and preserving medieval manuscripts and other monuments provide a significant backdrop to the concerns of this study.[14] The driving force behind this antiquarian scholarship was 'the spirit of nationalism',[15] the desire to use historiography to promote the greatness of the English Protestant nation. John Bale's *Scriptorum Illustrium Maioris Brytannie... Catalogus* (Basle, 1557–9) is a strong witness to the sense that some six-teenth-century Protestant Englishmen had of an important native tradition which had preceded them and which could support their present concerns.[16] William Camden, whom Spenser possibly met, produced in his *Britannia* (1586) a monument to native antiquarian interest which was more representative than exceptional.[17] And the historian John Stow, best remembered today for his *Survey of London* (1598), had a keen interest in earlier English literature; he edited Lydgate (1559), Chaucer (1561), Skelton (1568), and *Certaine Worthye Manuscript*

---

[14] See further: Robin Flower, 'Laurence Nowell and the Discovery of England in Tudor Times', *PBA* 21 (1935), 47–73; T. D. Kendrick, *British Antiquity* (London, 1950); Levi Fox (ed.), *English Historical Scholarship in the Sixteenth and Seventeenth Centuries* (Oxford, 1956); C. E. Wright, 'The Elizabethan Society of Antiquaries and the Formation of the Cottonian Library', in Francis Wormald and C. E. Wright (eds), *The English Library before 1700* (London, 1958), 176–212; Fritz Levy, *Tudor Historical Thought* (San Marino, 1967); May McKisack, *Medieval History in the Tudor Age* (Oxford, 1971); Kevin Sharpe, *Sir Robert Cotton, 1586–1631* (Oxford, 1979); James P. Carley, 'The Manuscript Remains of John Leland, "The King's Antiquary"', *TEXT* 2 (1985), 111–20; J. D. Alsop and Wesley M. Stevens, 'William Lambarde and Elizabethan Polity', *Studies in Medieval and Renaissance History* n.s. 8 (1986), 231–65; David R. Carlson, 'The Writings and Manuscript Collections of the Elizabethan Alchemist, Antiquary, and Herald Francis Thynne', *HLQ* 52 (1989), 203–72; Stan A. E. Mendyk, '*Speculum Britanniae*' (Toronto, 1989).

[15] Sharpe, *Cotton*, 24.

[16] Bale regards Langland as a prophet: 'In hoc opere erudito, præter similitudines varias & iucundas, propheticè plura predixit, que nostris diebus impleri vidimus' (474; from a microfilm copy). See further King, *English Reformation Literature*, 66, 68.

[17] Spenser praises Camden in *The Ruines of Time* as 'the nourice of antiquitie, / And lanterne unto late succeeding age' (169–70).

Poems of Great Antiquitie (1597), the last work dedicated to Spenser.[18] These men were part of a literary and historical movement which provided an academic context for Spenser's own interest in the memorial records of the native literary tradition. Indeed, Spenser's description of Eumnestes' chamber, cited at the beginning of this chapter, might suggest an encounter with an antiquarian in his library of manuscripts. A letter from John Dee to Lord Burghley, from October 1574, asking for an introduction to the Keeper of the Records of Wigmore Castle, provides an historical reflection of Spenser's depiction of Eumnestes' chamber, and both texts present a serious desire to preserve and study manuscripts, albeit in the face of a general neglect:

For that at my late being there, I espied an heap of old papers and parchments, obligations, acquittances, accounts, &c. (in tyme past belonging to the abbey of Wigmor) and there to lye rotting spoyled and tossed in an old decayed chappel, not committed to any mans special charge: but thre quarters of them, I understand, to have byn taken away, by diuerse (either taylors or other) in tymes past. Now my fantasie is, that in some of them will be some mention made of Noble men and Jentlemen of those dayes. Whereby (eyther for chronicle, or pedigree) some good matter be collected out of them by me (at my leysor) by the way of a recreation.[19]

What this antiquarian background does not prepare us for, however, is Spenser's use of specifically romance texts in the same spirit of literary 're-formation'. Whereas Chaucer, Skelton, Wyclif, and the *Piers Plowman*-tradition were all perceived as adaptable to Protestant historical revision, the romances were typically singled out in the late sixteenth century, and indeed earlier, as degenerate, 'monkish' literature.[20] The ingenuity and

---

[18] The dedication reads: 'To the worthiest Poet Maister Ed. Spenser' ([A.8.v]; microfilm of STC 21499). The title-page identifies the editor as I.S. which is very probably Stow. See further: H. R. Woudhuysen, *Sir Philip Sidney and the Circulation of Manuscripts, 1558–1640* (Oxford, 1996), 123–4.

[19] Cited from McKisack, *Medieval History*, 72–3.

[20] Both Roger Ascham and Thomas Nashe famously denounced native romance with reference to the tradition's perceived monastic associations: Roger Ascham, *English Works*, ed. William Aldis Wright (Cambridge, 1904), 231; Thomas Nashe, *The Works of Thomas Nashe*, ed. Ronald B. McKerrow, rev. F. P. Wilson, 2nd edn., 5 vols. (Oxford, 1958), I.11. See also the citation from Arthur Dent's *The Plaine Mans Path-Way to Heaven* (1601) in Louis B. Wright, *Middle-Class Culture in Elizabethan England* (Chapel Hill, 1935), 232. See further: R. S. Crane, 'The Reading of an Elizabethan Youth', *MP* 11 (1913–14), 269–71; Robert P. Adams, '"Bold Bawdry

significance of Spenser's rebuttal of these criticisms will be central
to this exploration of his reception of native romance.

The historian who most powerfully enabled the Elizabethan
resuscitation of earlier native literature on the grounds of its
proto-Reformation spirit was John Foxe.[21] Foxe's *Actes and
Monuments*, or *Book of Martyrs* (first English pub., 1563), presented the Reformation as the re-emergence of the true Apostolic
Church in Britain, founded by Joseph of Arimathea in AD 63 at
the instigation of the Apostle Philip:

> our church was, when this church of theirs [i.e., the Roman Catholic
> Church] was not yet hatched out of the shell, nor did yet ever see any
> light: that is, in the time of the apostles, in the primitive age, in the time
> of Gregory I, and the old Roman church, when as yet no universal pope
> was received publicly, but repelled in Rome.
>
> (1.9)

Like Eumnestes, Foxe has historical records which prove the
legitimacy of the ancient British Church:

> In witness whereof we have the old acts and histories of ancient time to
> give testimony with us, wherein we have sufficient matter for us to shew
> that the same form, usage, and institution of this our present reformed
> church, are not the beginning of any new church of our own, but the
> renewing of the old ancient church of Christ.
>
> (1.9)

Foxe's arguments allow medieval texts and monuments to be 'reformed' to justify the present position, even in the case of a writer
as remote as Ælfric.[22] His technique is analogous to the backward perspective embodied in the language and appearance of
The Shepheardes Calender: the 'truth' which is required now can

---

and Open Manslaughter'': The English New Humanist Attack on Medieval
Romance', *HLQ* 23 (1959–60), 33–48; Velma Bourgeois Richmond, *The Legend of
Guy of Warwick* (New York and London, 1996), 175–6.

[21] See further: Frances A. Yates, *Astraea* (London, 1975), 42–51; Patrick Collinson,
'Truth, Lies and Fiction in Sixteenth-Century Protestant Historiography', in Donald
R. Kelley and David Harris Sacks (eds), *The Historical Imagination in Early Modern
Britain* (Cambridge, 1997), 37–68; David Loades (ed.), *John Foxe and the English
Reformation* (Aldershot, 1997).

[22] John Foxe, *The Acts and Monuments of John Foxe*, ed. George Townsend, 8
vols. (London, 1843–9), v.280. The Old English character typeface used for the
Ælfrician extract must have been cast especially for this work. Foxe praises Wyclif,
Chaucer, and Gower as English Christian heroes who opposed Rome in the spirit of
true religion; I.xxii–xxiii, 93.

be written into the past, giving it an objective and 'prophetic' authority. From another perspective, relevant to both *The Shepheardes Calender* and Book I of *The Faerie Queene*, the Church of England may be seen figuratively as a foundling. This rustic, potentially bastardized child was discovered and adopted by St Augustine of Canterbury under the aegis of Rome in 597. But since then, she has discovered her true parentage, the Apostolic founders, and in that discovery achieved a greater nobility than her foster-parents could offer her. Foxe's view of the earlier antiquity of the British Church is upheld in *The Faerie Queene*:

> ...and after him good *Lucius*,
> That first receiued Christianitie,
> The sacred pledge of Christes Euangely;
> Yet true it is, that long before that day
> Hither came *Ioseph* of *Arimathy*,
> Who brought with him the holy grayle, (they say)
> And preacht the truth, but since it greatly did decay.
>
> (II.x.53)

'Yet true it is' and 'they say' indicate Spenser's awareness, echoed by some notable contemporaries, of the problematic nature of the historiography of ancient Britain—not only the Arthurian history but also the historical writings concerning the early Church. In Book I, however, he will use the narrative-patterns of native romance to give credibility and force to the metaphor of the British Church as a foundling whose innate nobility is finally revealed.

Even more so than *The Shepheardes Calender*, *The Faerie Queene* presents a complex relationship with the past, or complex acts of memory. A good demonstration of this fact is the great irony which lies at the heart of *The Faerie Queene* and the work's engagement with Middle English romance. The most famous literary reaction to Middle English popular romances is Chaucer's burlesque imitation, *The Tale of Sir Thopas*, a work to which Harold Bloom's phrase 'the anxiety of influence' has an especially apt relevance. *Sir Thopas* satirizes the tendency of some Middle English verse romances to descend to awkward, jilting rhythms, banal vocabulary, meaningless rhymes, and absurd narrative and imagery.[23] Spenser was faced with the dilemma of reconciling his great admiration for Chaucer with an interest in

[23] Helen Cooper, *Oxford Guides to Chaucer* (Oxford, 1989), 299–309.

native romance literature which Chaucer himself did not share.
His ingenious response is a deliberate, 'Chaucerian' misreading of
Sir Thopas. Sir Thopas' dream-vision of an 'elf-queene' inspires
him, rather abruptly, to devote his life to seeking her love:

> 'An elf-queene wol I love, ywis,
> For in this world no womman is
>   Worthy to be my make
>   In towne;
> All othere wommen I forsake,
> And to an elf-queene I me take
>   By dale and eek by downe!'
>   (VII.790–6)

Spenser can hardly have failed to register the ludicrous elements
in the scene.[24] And yet this is the passage which supplies the
momentum and the possibility for narrative closure in *The Faerie
Queene*, Arthur's quest for Gloriana. Arthur tells Redcrosse and
Una of his dream-vision of 'a royall Mayd':

> Most goodly glee and louely blandishment
>   She to me made, and bad me loue her deare,
>   For dearely sure her loue was to me bent,
>   As when iust time expired should appeare.
>   But whether dreames delude, or true it were,
>   Was neuer hart so rauisht with delight,
>   Ne liuing man like words did euer heare,
>   As she to me deliuered all that night;
> And at her parting said, She Queene of Faeries hight.
>   (I.ix.14)

Arthur's quest for Gloriana is involved with the poem's deepest
level of meaning, a point which I will be developing later in
relation to Book II. Beyond that, the resonances of Elizabeth, 'a
royall Mayd', should make this moment in the poem profoundly
serious. Even so, the scene recalls Chaucer's parody of native
romance.[25] Spenser's praise of Chaucer as the 'well of English

---

[24] Henryson's *Schir Thomas Norny*, Drayton's *Nimphidia* and also his Eighth
Eclogue in *Idea*, the *Shepheardes Garland* are imitations of *Sir Thopas* which replicate
the burlesque humour of the original.

[25] In addition to the close parallels between the two scenes, another passage in the
1590 text of *The Faerie Queene* mentions Thopas by name: 'Till him Chylde *Thopas*
to confusion brought' (III.vii.48.4). 'Ollyphant', mentioned in the same stanza and
featuring in III.xi.3–6 of both the 1590 and the 1596 editions, also derives from *Sir*

vndefyled' (IV.ii.32) threatens to sound insincere when the work upon which he draws is *Sir Thopas*.[26]

If Spenser's admiration for Chaucer cannot be questioned, then neither can his own lively irony. Spenser's subversively 'serious' reading of *Sir Thopas* disarms Chaucer's irony and his criticism of native romance. At the same time, Spenser makes blatantly clear his own interest in the native literary tradition which Chaucer has chosen to reject. Throughout *The Faerie Queene*, Spenser draws upon the same romances which Chaucer had satirized, and in a few instances even named, in *Sir Thopas*:

> Men speken of romances of prys,
> Of Horn child and of Ypotys,
> Of Beves and sir Gy,
> Of sir Lybeux and Pleyndamour—
> But sir Thopas, he bereth the flour
> Of roial chivalry!
>
> (VII.897–902)

This catalogue refers to three romances—*Bevis of Hampton, Guy of Warwick*, and *Lybeaus Desconus*—which were highly popular in the medieval period and sixteenth century, surviving in a number of manuscripts and printed editions. All three romances have made a strong impact upon *The Faerie Queene* and will feature prominently in this study.

In putting Sir Thopas at the heart of *The Faerie Queene*, Spenser encounters head-on what should be one of the greatest obstacles to his use of native romance—the disparagement of his 'master', Chaucer. The other great obstacle was the fact that Foxe and other Protestant apologists had not included native romance in the canon of proto-Reformation literature; quite the reverse, in fact. But the native romance tradition had also developed in such a way that it offered considerable potential to be adapted into the concerns of Spenser's poem. The history of that development must now be addressed.

Thopas, VII.807–9. See further: John A. Burrow, '*Sir Thopas* in the Sixteenth Century', in Douglas Gray and E. G. Stanley (eds), *Middle English Studies Presented to Norman Davis* (Oxford, 1983), 69–91.

[26] Or else, given that Chaucer was rightly perceived in the fifteenth and sixteenth centuries as a writer who had enriched the English language through the importation of French and Latinate words, Spenser's praise of 'English vndefyled' has an ironic appropriateness in relation to his supposed admiration of *Sir Thopas*, the one work in which Chaucer does limit himself to a fairly Anglo-Saxon and pedestrian vocabulary.

2

Middle English Romance: Tradition, Genre, Manuscripts, and Prints

(I) THE MEDIEVAL PERIOD

> Herknet to me, gode men—
> Wiues, maydnes, and alle men—
> Of a tale þat Ich you wile telle,
> Wo-so it wile here and þer-to duelle.[1]

From the thirteenth to the fifteenth century, romances in English were continuously written, copied, adapted, read, and heard.[2] The evidence both of the texts themselves and of their presentation in surviving manuscripts testifies to the appeal of these narratives across a broad social spectrum. The evidence of surviving texts and manuscripts is limited, however, in its ability to indicate their full contemporary appeal. Many manuscripts containing romances did not survive because they would have been small, perishable, unbound booklets which were read to extinction.[3] Since some Middle English romances survive in only one copy, it is a necessary conclusion that we have lost not only textual witnesses to known romances but also entire romances

---

[1] *Havelok*, ed. G. V. Smithers (Oxford, 1987), 1–4.

[2] On the romance tradition in general, J. Burke Severs (gen. ed.), *A Manual of the Writings in Middle English, 1050–1500: Fascicule 1*, 'Romances' (New Haven, 1967) is an indispensable guide, offering plot-summaries, sources, and the manuscripts and early printed editions for each romance. A more recent bibliography is Joanne A. Rice, *Middle English Romance: An Annotated Bibliography, 1955–1985* (New York, 1987).

[3] The booklet as the basic unit from which larger manuscript-books might be produced is a central tenet of P. R. Robinson, 'A Study of Some Aspects of the Transmission of English Verse Texts in Late Medieval Manuscripts', B.Litt. thesis (University of Oxford, 1972). See also two articles by John J. Thompson: 'Collecting Middle English Romances and Some Related Book-Production Activities in the Later Middle Ages', in Maldwyn Mills, Jennifer Fellows, and Carol Meale (eds), *Romance in Medieval England* (Cambridge, 1991), 17–38 (18–19, 23); 'Looking Behind the Book: MS Cotton Caligula A.ii, Part 1 and the Experience of its Texts', in Jennifer Fellows et al. (eds), *Romance Reading on the Book* (Cardiff, 1996), 171–87 (180).

now unknown to us.[4] Chance survivals of manuscript fragments signify the alarming ease with which texts were lost through use, misuse, or wilful destruction.[5] Furthermore, the evidence of mixed dialect forms in extant texts helps to reconstruct a picture of the stages of transmission which must lie behind a surviving copy. On the basis of such an approach, it has been calculated that at least five manuscripts must have existed for the alliterative *Morte Arthure*; all that survives is a single manuscript and the influence of the work in the Winchester MS of Malory's *Morte Darthur*.[6] The widespread popularity and influence of the romances are also demonstrated by the evidence of contemporary visual arts, antiquarian and regional texts, and genealogies which in some form represent heroes and situations from romances.[7]

I have begun by using the term romance as if it were a definite genre, but that assumption is problematic.[8] The question of genre in relation to Middle English romance is not a concern for medievalists alone, for the picture which emerges of generic complexity is a significant background to understanding the romance mode in *The Faerie Queene*. To approach an historically recovered sense of the nature of Middle English romance we must first consider how the texts which we designate romances form a

[4] In *Sir Thopas*, 'Pleyndamour' (VII.900) may be a Chaucerian invention (considering the comic appeal of its hyperbole) but it may just as easily refer to the hero of a lost romance.

[5] British Library MS Sloane 1044 is a one-leaf fragment from an early fifteenth-century copy of *Guy of Warwick*; Gray's Inn MS 20 is a mid fourteenth-century fragment of *Sir Isumbras*. See further: Gisela Guddat-Figge, *Catalogue of Manuscripts Containing Middle English Romances* (Munich, 1976), 213, 217–18. The famous story of how Bishop Percy in the eighteenth century rescued from the fire the large mid seventeenth-century Folio MS, since bearing his name, affords a glimpse of what must have been a common fate for manuscripts such as this one containing romances. See further: Gillian Rogers, 'The Percy Folio Manuscript Revisited', in Mills, Fellows, and Meale (eds), *Romance in Medieval England*, 39–64.

[6] *The Thornton Manuscript*, intr. D. S. Brewer and A. E. B. Owen (London, 1975), pp. x–xi.

[7] The best illustration of this point is the copiously informative study by Richmond, *Legend of Guy of Warwick*, which focuses on all manifestations of this legend. Havelok, Bevis, and Arthur also had adjunctive manifestations, and these will be mentioned with discussion of those texts below.

[8] See further: Paul Strohm, '*Storie, Spelle, Geste, Romance, Tragedie*: Generic Distinctions in the Middle English Troy Narratives', *Speculum* 46 (1971), 348–59; Paul Strohm, 'The Origin and Meaning of Middle English *Romaunce*', *Genre* 10 (1977), 1–28; John Finlayson, 'Definitions of Middle English Romance', *CR* 15 (1980), 44–62, 168–81.

viable tradition. Confronting the romances in the 'home territory'
of the manuscripts is crucial. From that perspective we can also
consider the likely readership of romance and the contemporary
perceptions of its kind and worth

How did the Middle English texts commonly designated
romances form part of a native literary tradition, beginning
c. 1225 with *King Horn?* With a few exceptions, the verse
romances are not authorial texts, meaning not only that they
are anonymous but also that they often reflect a composite and
layered process of creation. This state of affairs precludes the
notion of tradition familiar from Chaucer onwards, and overlapping chronologically with the romance tradition, of known
authors finding inspiration as well as encountering their own
creative anxiety when faced with the literary achievements of
their predecessors. The absence of closely defined and authoritative texts may seem to militate against the concept of literary
tradition. However, the lack of authorial and textual definition
allowed a luxuriant condition of intertextual influence and cross-
fertilization, a constant imitation and borrowing of plots, themes,
diction, and favourite scenes each time a romance was 'copied' or
newly 'composed'. It is often impossible, and for our purposes
insignificant, to determine the direction of influence among and
the chronological sequence of individual romances (and related
texts) or of the multiple versions of a single romance within this
nexus of intertextuality.[9] What is significant is the realization that
romance was never stagnant, neither textually nor generically. A
romance could incorporate influences from other romances or
from other kinds of writings, such as historical writings and
hagiography, and it is inaccurate to think of such additions as
deviations from a 'pure' form of the text. Jennifer Fellows' comments regarding the transmission of native verse romance are
pertinent:

---

[9] Older editions of Middle English romances that use the method of recension to
deal with a complicated history of revision, such as *The Romance of Sir Beues of
Hampton*, ed. Eugene Kölbing, EETS ES 46, 48, 65 (London, 1885, 1886, 1894),
represent impressive and dedicated scholarship, but the cumbersomeness of the scholarly apparatus reflects the artificiality of the approach in relation to the conditions in
which the romance circulated and was constantly revised. The parallel text edition of
Jennifer Fellows, '*Sir Beves of Hampton*: Study and Edition', 5 vols., Ph.D. thesis
(University of Cambridge, 1980) is truer to the historical conditions of the text.

... scribes are not *trying* to transmit accurate reproductions of an archetype—their alterations are deliberate and constructive; they are not only verbal, but often extend to transpositions, reworkings, introductions, omissions of entire episodes. Scribal activity can no longer be separated from authorial intention, because the scribes themselves have authorial status.[10]

This state of affairs, even though Spenser was possibly unaware of it, was involved in the growth of a romance tradition whose generic flexibility would impact on *The Faerie Queene*. There is a need to understand further the characteristics of that tradition before evaluating its large-scale influence on Spenser's work.

The sense of a native *tradition* of romance is evident in passages which give catalogues of heroes not forming part of the present text, yet still related through the works known to the readers and audience. *The Laud Troy Book* begins:

> Off Beuis, Gy, and of Gauwayn,
> Off kyng Richard, & of Owayn...
> Off Hauelok, Horne, & of Wade...
> Here dedis ben in remembraunce
> In many faire Romaunce.[11]

---

[10] Jennifer Fellows, 'Editing Middle English Romance', in Mills, Fellows, and Meale (eds), *Romance in Medieval England*, 5–16 (7; her emphasis). Derek Pearsall, 'The Uses of Manuscripts: Late Medieval English', *Harvard Library Bulletin* 4 (1994), 30–6 (31) also argues that 'each act of copying was... an act of recomposition, and not an episode in a process of decomposition from an ideal form'. In addition to the creative interaction of scribes, the public performance of a romance by a *disour* could be an act of transmission involving substantial changes in the text, and it is inappropriate to think that such changes were degenerate. A debate continues concerning the 'public performance' of romances, with an increasing tendency to regard the references to oral performance in the texts as part of a self-conscious artistry, analogous to Spenser's archaisms. Nevertheless, I agree with the view of most scholars that various forms of public reading or performance did occur, as an alternative to private reading from a book, and these performances might have induced changes in the text as it later came to be written down anew. See further: Dieter Mehl, *The Middle English Romances of the Thirteenth and Fourteenth Centuries* (London, 1968), 7–13, 166–7; Guddat-Figge, *Catalogue*, 33; Derek Pearsall, 'Middle English Romance and its Audiences', in Mary-Jo Arn and Hanneke Wirtjes, with Hans Jensen (eds), *Historical & Editorial Studies in Medieval & Early Modern English for Johan Gerritsen* (Groningen, 1985), 37–47 (41); Carol Fewster, *Traditionality and Genre in Middle English Romance* (Cambridge, 1987), 30; Andrew Taylor, 'The Myth of the Minstrel Manuscript', *Speculum* 66 (1991), 43–73; Geraldine Barnes, *Counsel and Strategy in Middle English Romance* (Cambridge, 1993), 19–22.

[11] *The Laud Troy Book*, ed. J. Ernst Wülfing, EETS 121, 122 (London, 1902, 1904), 15–26. A similar catalogue occurs in *Richard Coeur de Lion*, 5–20, 6725–41 (*Der Mittelenglische Versroman über Richard Löwenherz*, ed. Karl Brunner, Wiener

(Concerning Bevis, Guy, Gawain, King Richard, Ywain, Havelok, Horn, and Wade—their deeds are remembered in many pleasant romances.)

Interestingly, the hero of this romance, Hector, is a classical figure, and he is elevated in stature through favourable comparison with great native heroes; as in *The Shepheardes Calender*, the classical is here ancillary to the native, a reversal of the relationship which one might consider normal. The narrator appeals to the audience's recollection of familiar heroes, inviting them to hold this tradition in their minds as a contextual pantheon in which to place the forthcoming narrative. Even when romances do not give a catalogue of names, they do typically make an appeal to the audience's knowledge of other heroes. Thus *Guy of Warwick*:

> Therfore schulde men mekely herke
> And thynke gode allwey to wyrke
> And take ensawmpull be wyse men,
> That haue before thys tyme ben:
> Well feyre aventurs befelle them
> (And sythen scheweyd to mony men).[12]

The textual instability and lack of authorship in the native romance tradition place a strong emphasis upon the role of the listener or reader, frequently addressed throughout the course of the narrative, to hold this amorphous tradition 'in remembraunce'. The native tradition truly is the 'matter of iust memory', and in hearing the exploits of any hero the audience is invited to bring to that experience their memories of other heroes, or indeed of other versions of the exploits of this same hero. Given the cross-currents of influence and shared story-patterns, the reader or listener cannot escape memorial contextualization, or a placing of the present work alongside other romances 'in remembraunce'. Sometimes the narrator makes the invitation to

Beiträge zur englischen Philologie 42 (Vienna and Leipzig, 1913). The catalogue of romance heroes in *Sir Thopas* (VII.897–902), cited in the Introduction, is a parody which nonetheless relies upon and enforces the sense of a known tradition. Furthermore, texts which are critical of romance provide lists of individual romances; despite the negative context of these citations of heroes, they too provide evidence of a recognized canon of romances—the likely tendency of any reader to associate whatever romance he or she is reading with comparable texts. See, for example, *Cursor Mundi*, ed. Richard Morris, EETS 57, 59, 62, 66, 68, 99, 101 (London, 1874, 1875, 1876, 1877, 1878, 1892, 1893), Trinity MS, 1–28.

[12] *The Romance of Guy of Warwick: The Second or 15th-Century Version*, ed. Julius Zupitza, EETS ES 25, 26 (London, 1875, 1876), 5–10.

memorial contextualization explicit; before Bevis of Hampton encounters a dragon, we are reminded:

> Swich bataile dede neuer non
> Cristene man of flesch ne bon,
> Of a dragoun þer be side,
> Þat Beues slouȝ þer in þat tide,
> Saue sire Launcelet de Lake,
> He fauȝt wiþ a fur drake,
> And Wade dede also,
> & neuer kniȝtes boute þai to,
> & Gij a Warwik, ich vnder-stonde,
> Slouȝ a dragoun in Norþ-Homberlonde.
>
> (A-text, 2599–608)

(No Christian man of flesh and bone ever accomplished such a battle as Bevis did then in slaying the dragon—except Sir Lancelot de Lake, who fought with a fire-drake [i.e., a dragon], as also did Wade. But no more than those two knights—and Guy of Warwick, I understand, slew a dragon in Northumberland.)

Alternatively, a silent transposition of details from one romance to another might jog the reader's memory and sense of tradition, even if this is not the redactor's intent; such is the case with the repetition of details from Bevis' dragon-fight in *Sir Degare*.[13] In some cases, such as *Sir Eglamour of Artois*, an entire romance is created from such memories, and it powerfully reinforces a sense of tradition. The editor of *Sir Eglamour* stresses the aspect of memory in the work:

The writer seems ... to have been playing a game of 'that reminds me' with his memories of medieval romance, much as Chaucer did in *Sir Thopas*, though in solemn and naïve earnestness.[14]

The sense of a tradition derives from the intertextual play of the romances, but that is a reflection of the coalescence of the

[13] See Nicolas Jacobs, '*Sir Degarre, Lay le Freine, Beues of Hamtoun* and the "Auchinleck Bookshop"', *NQ* 29 (1982), 294–301 (297–300); Nicolas Jacobs 'The Second Revision of *Sir Degarre*: The Egerton Fragments and its Congeners', *NM* 85 (1984), 95–107 (101–4). A similar instance of transposed details relating to a specific scene occurs in *Lybeaus Desconus*, recalling *Guy of Warwick*, when the hero's fight with a giant involves a mock 'baptism' as the hero is knocked into a river; see further the commentary to 1333–62 in *Lybeaus Desconus*, ed. M. Mills, EETS 261 (London, 1969).

[14] *Sir Eglamour of Artois*, ed. Frances E. Richardson, EETS 256 (London, 1965), p. xxxix.

romances in the memories of the people who copied, heard, and recited them. The tradition derives from and sustains the notion of the romances as the 'matter of iust memory'.

The larger manuscript-anthologies which contain Middle English romances, such as the Auchinleck MS, CUL MS ff.2.38, and the Lincoln Thornton MS, can be likened, somewhat fancifully, to Eumnestes' chamber.[15] As 'books of memory', they are really miniature libraries which contain most of the available forms of vernacular writing, not only romance but also historical writings, saints' lives, exempla, sermons, and fabliaux.[16] Just as an audience might bring a knowledge of other romances to bear on their reception of a particular one, so other romances are collected together in the 'memory' of these manuscript-anthologies. And perhaps even more significantly, romances are joined with other kinds of texts; as a model of memory, that joining implies a wider memorial contextualization than other romances in the process of hearing or reading a romance. This analogy of subjective, individual reception, shaped by existing memories, is reflected in the manuscript-anthologies by the way in which items have often been adjusted in order to achieve an homogeneous tone for the collection. The generic definition and textual purity of an item copied into an anthology could count for less compared with the desire or habit of making a book with a certain amount of warp and weft, binding its items together.

Admittedly, the creation of a manuscript-anthology might not be the work of one editorial intelligence; and the choice and arrangement of its items could be dictated by arbitrary and accidental factors, such as what was available for copying, rather than the deliberate editorial judgement of a 'compiler'.[17] Nevertheless,

---

[15] These three manuscripts exist in facsimile: *Thornton*, intr. Brewer and Owen; *The Auchinleck Manuscript*, intr. Derek Pearsall and I. C. Cunningham (London, 1977); *Cambridge University Library MS Ff.2.38*, intr. Frances McSparran and P. R. Robinson (London, 1979). All three manuscripts appear to have attained their roughly present shape as collections in the medieval period.

[16] The book was frequently used as a metaphor for memory in the Middle Ages. This is a major concern of Mary J. Carruthers, *The Book of Memory*, Cambridge Studies in Medieval Literature 10 (Cambridge, 1990), e.g. 16–45, 160–1. See also: Phillipa Hardman, 'A Mediaeval Library "*in Parvo*"', *MÆ* 47 (1978), 262–73.

[17] See further Guddat-Figge, *Catalogue*, 37; John J. Thompson, 'The Compiler in Action: Robert Thornton and the "Thornton Romances" in Lincoln Cathedral MS 91', in Derek Pearsall (ed.), *Manuscripts and Readers in Fifteenth-Century*

some manuscripts which combine Middle English romances with other kinds of narrative and practical texts demonstrate, unlike a modern edited anthology of romances, that the reception of romances is affected by the memorial contextualization manifested in the manuscript; these romances are changed or nuanced to conform to an overall theme for the collection or organized into loose sections which speak as much of generic relationship as of separation.[18] In discussing 'Rate's Miscellany', Bodleian Library MS Ashmole 61, Lynne S. Blanchfield makes the valuable observation that items have been selected and revised to create an overall tone of family piety, and in this context strict generic distinctions between romance and other kinds of writing, such as homiletic and historical writings, cease to be a consideration:

The juxtaposition of such a varied selection of narrative types—yet homogeneous in tone and 'colouring'—suggests that Rate [i.e., the compiler] himself was unaware of, or unconcerned about, any generic difference between, for example, *Sir Eustace* and *Sir Isumbras*, or *Sir Corneus* and *Sir Cleges*, or *Lybeaus* and *King Edward*. What is strongly suggested by the nature of the compilation is that he chose texts according to their content and *mode*—predominantly the romance mode—in order that they might work together as a compilation

England (Cambridge, 1983), 113–24 (117); Julia Boffey and John J. Thompson, 'Anthologies and Miscellanies: Production and Choice of Texts', in Jeremy Griffiths and Derek Pearsall (eds), *Book Production and Publishing in Britain 1375–1475* (Cambridge, 1989), 279–315 (300); Thompson, 'Collecting Middle English Romances', in Mills, Fellows, and Meale (eds), *Romance in Medieval England*; Thompson, 'Looking Behind the Book', in Fellows et al. (eds), *Romance Reading on the Book*, 180. Furthermore, amateur scribes tended to preserve groupings of texts as found in exemplars rather than rearrange them to fit the copyist's own pattern; this point is established by the links between clusters of items in surviving manuscripts. See *CUL MS Ff.2.38*, intr. McSparran and Robinson, p. vii.

[18] Thompson, 'Looking Behind the Book', in Fellows et al. (eds), *Romance Reading on the Book*, 180–2 notes that the scribe of MS Cotton Caligula A.ii has attempted to standardize the visual appearance of the three romances by Thomas Chestre, to indicate the cohesiveness of this unit within the collection. For a critique of the scholarship that sees the organization of manuscript-anthologies as reflecting generic definition, see A. S. G. Edwards, '"The Whole Book": Medieval Manuscripts in Facsimile', *Review* 2 (1980), 19–29. I believe that I avoid Edwards' criticisms because my primary emphasis is on the homogeneity of the collections, reflecting the strong relationships between 'genres', or even a breakdown of generic classification altogether; as a secondary emphasis, I do accept that the organization of some manuscripts reflects a rough determination of different kinds of writing.

providing a comprehensive policy of pastoral care for both the spiritual and temporal needs of its readers.[19]

Thorlac Turville-Petre's account of the Auchinleck MS similarly indicates that the volume reflects a purposeful and idiosyncratic treatment of its exemplars, drawing its historical, hagiographical, and romance texts into a common centre through a nearly ubiquitous emphasis on English national interests.[20] Manuscript-anthologies, such as Ashmole 61, the Auchinleck MS, the Lincoln Thornton MS, and CUL MS FF.2.38, present romance in a context of other items, sometimes loosely organized into sections but equally often intermingled, with titles and colophons which suggest a lack of concern with precise generic boundaries.[21]

The evidence of the manuscripts suggests the artificiality of narrow generic definition; the impression which the manuscripts give is of the amorphousness of romance and its compatibility with, or even transformation into, narrative writings of a different emphasis.[22] A romance such as *Guy of Warwick* could be seen

---

[19] Lynne S. Blanchfield, 'Rate Revisited: The Compilation of the Narrative Works in MS Ashmole 61', in Fellows et al. (eds), *Romance Reading on the Book*, 208–22 (218). See also her 'The Romances in MS Ashmole 61: An Idiosyncratic Scribe', in Mills, Fellows, and Meale (eds), *Romance in Medieval England*, 65–87 (68).

[20] Thorlac Turville-Petre, *England the Nation* (Oxford, 1996), 108–41.

[21] See further *Thornton MS*, intr. Brewer and Owen, p. ix; Guddat-Figge, *Catalogue*, 37–42; *Auchinleck MS*, intr. Pearsall and Cunningham, p. viii; *CUL MS Ff.2.38*, intr. McSparran and Robinson, p. vii; Thompson, 'Compiler in Action', in Pearsall (ed.), *Manuscripts and Readers*, 114–20; Boffey and Thompson, 'Anthologies and Miscellanies', in Griffiths and Pearsall (eds), *Book Production and Publishing*, 300; John Finlayson, '*Richard, Coer de Lyon*: Romance, History, or Something in Between?', *SP* 87 (1990), 156–80; Rosalind Field, 'Romance as History, History as Romance', in Mills, Fellows, and Meale (eds), *Romance in Medieval England*, 163–73; Thompson, 'Collecting Middle English Romance', in ibid., 19–20. Guddat-Figge, *Catalogue*, 39 notes that *Richard Coeur de Lion*, judged today as a romance, appears in the context of romances in three manuscripts, but it also appears in manuscripts which are collections of historical writings, in one case (College of Arms MS 58) intercalated within an historical account of the reign of Richard I. Furthermore, Robert of Sicily, a 'homiletic' romance, is placed among romances of a more chivalric kind in CUL MS FF.2.38, but in Oxford Trinity College MS D.57 it is given the hagiographic title 'Sancti Cicilie Vita Roberti' (ibid., 40–1). See further: Strohm, 'Generic Distinctions', 354–6. The intermingling of the modes of romance and history is a ubiquitous theme in Antonia Gransden's two-volume survey: *Historical Writing in England c.550–c.1307* (Ithaca, N.Y., 1974); *Historical Writing in England ii: c.1307 to the Early Sixteenth Century* (Ithaca, N.Y., 1982).

[22] Finlayson, 'Definitions of Middle English Romance' attempts to apply strictly a generic definition of romance to the texts commonly considered romances, those treated in Fascicule 1 of *A Manual of the Writings in Middle English*. He concludes that at least half of the texts 'do not in any way meet the paradigms proposed' (178).

from the perspective of a homiletic, quasi-hagiographic work, or a chivalric romance full of exciting adventures, or an historical narrative of patriotic bias. This tripartite reading is also possible for *Richard Coeur de Lion*, and at least two of the three perspectives apply variously to *Bevis of Hampton, Of Arthour and of Merlin, Havelok, Sir Isumbras, Emaré*, and others. Which perspective takes precedence will be influenced by the 'memory' which the manuscript represents—the context of items, titles, and organization, if any—as well as the memory and perception of the reader or listener who will, like the manuscript, compare, conflate, and perhaps confuse the new romance within the context of previously acquired narratives. The notion of the manuscript-anthology as an analogue for the collection and transformation of texts in the human memory suggests that the contextualization of romances in manuscripts both reflected and incited a sense that romance could combine with the modes of historical writings and/or pious and hagiographical narratives which depicted God's special providence in human affairs. Most importantly, the sense of generic blending which is derived from the manuscripts is reflected in the texts themselves, a theme which will be developed in the textually oriented chapters which follow.

If a strict definition of romance as a genre is inappropriate in relation to the texts under discussion, then an understanding of the term romance which *will* serve is required. Works such as *Havelok, Bevis of Hampton, Sir Isumbras, Sir Triamour*, and Malory's *Le Morte Darthur* will be termed romances for convenience, even though some of these would have been considered in the medieval period as historical writings. On the other hand, a work such as John Hardyng's *Chronicle* will be termed historical writing, though its graphic verse narrative and acceptance of fabulous events make it close in spirit to *Guy* or *Le Morte Darthur*. What we label texts is not important, once we have accepted that Middle English narratives were hybrids which could present in various proportions the sense of romance, history, and hagiography. What is important is to derive a sense of what romance and history mean as modes of narrative discourse, for these two critical terms in particular will be used to evaluate the character of native 'romances'.[23]

[23] In formulating an account of romance as a mode, I recognize the significance of important theoretical studies, such as Eric Auerbach, *Mimesis*, tr. Willard R. Trask

Many of the characteristics which are usually advanced in definition of the romance mode—the depiction of an exclusively aristocratic lifestyle, a large proportion of magic and marvels, idealized characters and events, lack of narrative specificity, especially as regards time and place—are more suited to the great exemplars of French romance, such as the works of Chrétien de Troyes, than to the Middle English romances. The French *chanson de geste*, which recognizes an historical and political framework for its characters, is in that respect closer to the romance mode in Middle English romance. The world of the native romance mode is idealized only in the sense that its characters and actions tend to be heightened expressions of good and evil, beauty and ugliness. However, it is not an unfallen or paradisal world, and its political struggles and injustices must have enforced a strong sense of connection between the narrative world and the real world of its contemporary readers. The romance mode in English does offer magic and marvels, but not to the same extent as French and Italian texts. Instead, the native romance mode allows a greater representation of everyday life, not just in the political struggles at the centre of the narratives but in detailed passages such as the fight in the streets of London in *Bevis of Hampton*, the smithy at work in *Sir Isumbras*, the economic transactions of the Parisian market in *Octavian*, and *Havelok*'s evocative descriptions of working-class activity in Lincoln. Furthermore, time is felt as a pressure in the native romance mode, a feature which also brings it closer to a sense of realism. But time—for example, the time which is running out when lovers seek to be reunited before death or before an enforced marriage to another person—is never allowed to defeat heroic ambition, and this fact is where romance becomes romance and not realism. The most defining characteristic of the romance mode in the native tradition is that God's providence and grace are interactive qualities which assist the heroes, effecting their victories and the works' narrative closure. Since the narrative centres on the hero's quest, it is concerned with development

(Princeton, 1953), 123–42; Northrop Frye, *Anatomy of Criticism* (Princeton, 1957); Northrop Frye, *The Secular Scripture* (Cambridge, Mass., 1976); Patricia A. Parker, *Inescapable Romance* (Princeton, 1979). At the same time, I have evolved my characterization from the tendencies of Middle English romance, not from French courtly romance (Auerbach), Shakespeare (Frye), or Italian interlaced romance (Parker).

and growth towards perfection, and the hero's personal fulfilment is also the manifestation of God's providence working
through the world to complete his creation. The magical and
supernatural elements in native romance usually fulfil a didactic
role (and thus lose their sense of mystery) by being open manifestations of God's grace.[24] A modern Christian theologian's
description of providence could also be a description of the
mimetic mode of numerous Middle English romances. Providence implies that

Being overcomes the nothing into which it has gone in creation...the
movement is toward realization of potentialities-of-being, and the overcoming of dissolution, frustration, annihilation.[25]

In this view, providence is the ongoing process or completion of
the inital act of creation, and history, when presented as romance,
is a movement from nothing towards fulfilment. Middle English
romances cannot be precisely linked to late classical and patristic
learned traditions of providence, but in general they variously
reflect the two dominant understandings of providence in the
Middle Ages: the Boethian model in which the erratic turning of
fortune's wheel is contained within the larger workings of providence; and the Augustinian doctrine which places a primary
emphasis on God's interactive, re-creative providence, shaping
human events according to the projected fulfilment of his plan.[26]
Because of this providential force, narrative closure is indeed
strong in the native romance mode, in distinction to the *entre-
lacement* of the French (thirteenth-century prose) and Italian
romances,[27] and it represents the achievement of God's will
through the lives of the protagonists. At this point, there is

[24] In Middle English versions of the Breton *lai* and in fifteenth-century prose
romances (excluding Malory) which are fairly direct translations of earlier French
prose romances, magic is often mysteriously self-contained and not attributed to
God's intervention. My characterization applies to Middle English verse romance
outside of the Celtic and directly French models.
[25] John Macquarrie, *Principles of Christian Theology*, 2nd edn. (New York, 1977),
243.
[26] Boethius, *The Consolation of Philosophy*, tr. V. E. Watts (Harmondsworth,
1969), IV–V; 116–69 (esp. IV.iv; 135–6); St Augustine, *Concerning The City of God
against the Pagans*, tr. Henry Bettenson, intr. John O'Meara (Harmondsworth, 1984),
V.xii.11; 196.
[27] See further Parker, *Inescapable Romance* and Colin Burrow, *Epic Romance*
(Oxford, 1993), passim.

nowhere further for the narrative to go, except through the virtuous characters' death and heavenly transcendence; the world of the romance has reached its full perfection.

The value in this romance mode placed upon God's assistance marks the similarity of native romance to hagiography.[28] The conjunction of romance, history, and saints' lives in manuscripts gives an understanding of the difference between the native romance mode and continental models. Thorlac Turville-Petre's comments are cogent:

> Critics are inclined to define texts in terms of genre—romance, chronicle, saint's life, devotional work—but the Auchinleck chronicle [i.e., the *Anonymous Short Metrical Chronicle*], like the contents of the volume as a whole, recognises no such barriers. Despite their variety of genres, the texts of the manuscript have a shared perception of social roles and functions, and a shared concept of England, the state of its present and the contributions of its past.[29]

Perhaps because of the rationalization of the miraculous as the manifestation of God's providence, and also because of patriotic desire, native romance texts also intermingle with the historical mode.[30] The historical mode is created in texts through a specificity of detail which is not only particularizing but also accessible

---

[28] On the relationship between romance and hagiography in Middle English, see: Ojars Kratins, 'The Middle English *Amis and Amiloun*: Chivalric Romance or Secular Hagiography?', *PMLA* 81 (1966), 347–54; Kathryn Hume, 'Structure and Perspective: Romance and Hagiographic Features in the Amicus and Amelius Story', *JEGP* 69 (1970), 89–107; Margaret Hurley, 'Saints' Lives and Romance Again: Secularization of Structure and Motif', *Genre* 8 (1975), 60–73; David N. Klausner, 'Didacticism and Drama in *Guy of Warwick*', *MH* n.s. 6 (1975), 103–19; Diana T. Childress, 'Between Romance and Legend: "Secular Hagiography" in Middle English Literature', *PQ* 57 (1978), 311–22; Margaret Bradstock, '*Sir Gowther*: Secular Hagiography or Hagiographical Romance or Neither?', *Australasian University Modern Language Association* 59 (1983), 26–47; Andrea Hopkins, *The Sinful Knights* (Oxford, 1990); Jennifer Fellows, 'St George as Romance Hero', *RMS* 19 (1993), 27–54; Jocelyn Wogan-Browne, '"Bet...to rede on holy seyntes lyves...": Romance and Hagiography Again', in Carol Meale (ed.), *Readings in Medieval English Romance* (Cambridge, 1994), 83–97. *The South English Legendary* (thirteenth-century) is an important context for the development of the native romance tradition, particularly because of its emphasis on English saints and history; see further J. A. W. Bennett, *Middle English Literature*, ed. and completed Douglas Gray (Oxford, 1986), 60–1.

[29] Turville-Petre, *England the Nation*, 112.

[30] Field, 'Romance as History', in Mills, Fellows, and Meale (eds), *Romance in Medieval England*, 163 notes that the pretension to historicity is a quality of much Anglo-Norman and Middle English romance which distinguishes it from the Continental traditions, more concerned with ethics and psychology.

to contemporary readers through its reference to the English landscape or historical experience. The identification of known localities and precise dates contains a rhetorical argument that these events 'actually happened', since we are given the details which could be examined for confirmation.[31] At the same time, that specificity can create the sense of time as a more detrimental force than would obtain in a text where the romance mode dominated over the historical. Our ability to go to the actual places where historical events occurred, such as Bosworth Field, both enforces the reality of that occurrence and also emphasizes that we are cut off in time from those events; we have arrived too late. 'Too late' should never occur for the heroes of romance, however much of a threat it may seem. The interest in the native romances considered in the following chapters lies largely in the mixture of romance and historical modes in different proportions in single texts. In those texts, God's interactive grace and providence, a prominent feature of hagiography, is the putatively objective force which authorizes the blending of romance and history. The picture which emerges is of a real nation, England, especially blessed by God as it struggles to overcome enemies within and without.

The history of the readership of native romance from the thirteenth to the sixteenth century is important for judging Spenser's strategy in incorporating the tradition in *The Faerie Queene*.[32] The earliest native romances were in Anglo-Norman, the language of the ruling class; and complementary historical works, such as Geoffrey of Monmouth's *Historia regum Britanniae* (*c*. 1135) were in Latin.[33] From the thirteenth century

---

[31] See chapter 3 below for Robert Mannyng's attempts to confirm the historicity of Havelok through an examination of the 'evidence' given in the romance. In the discussion of the texts in the following chapters, I will develop at length native romance's tendency to link the action of the heroes to surviving features of contemporary England.

[32] Studies of the social class of the readership of romance are Pearsall, 'Romance and its Audiences', in Arn and Wirtjes (eds), *Historical & Editorial Studies*; Kate Harris, 'Patrons, Buyers and Owners: The Evidence for Ownership and the Rôle of Book Owners in Book Production and the Book Trade', in Griffiths and Pearsall (eds), *Book Production and Publishing*, 163–99; Carol M. Meale, 'Patrons, Buyers and Owners: Book Production and Social Status', in ibid., 201–38; Carol M. Meale, '"gode men / Wiues maydens and alle men": Romance and its Audiences', in Meale (ed.), *Readings in Medieval English Romance*, 209–25.

[33] See further: Susan Crane, *Insular Romance*, (Berkeley, 1986) 1–6.

onwards, the favoured language for romance was increasingly English, suggesting a broadening social spectrum for native romance readership. The 'prologue' to *Of Arthour and of Merlin* (*c.* 1250–1300) in the Auchinleck MS (*c.* 1330) indicates a shift in romance readership and the gaining prominence of English:

> Of Freynsch no Latin nil y tel more
> Ac on I[n]glisch ichil tel þerfore:
> Riȝt is þat I[n]glische vnderstond
> Þat was born in Inglond.
> Freynsche vse þis gentil man
> Ac euerich Inglische Inglische can,
> Mani noble ich haue yseiȝe
> Þat no Freynsche couþe seye,
> Biginne ichil for her loue
> Bi Ihesus leue þat sitt aboue
> On Inglische tel mi tale.[34]

(I will not speak in French or Latin but in English. It is fitting that one born in England understands English. A particular gentleman may use French, but every Englishman knows English. I have seen many nobly born people who could not speak French. Therefore, for the love of her who by Jesus' leave [or 'by dear Jesus'] sits above, I will tell my story in English.)

It would be wrong to assume from this passage that romance readership was narrowly lower middle-class; the size and character of the Auchinleck MS made it an expensive book, whether owned individually or even corporately. The inclusion here of so many works not only in English but interested in content about England as a nation speaks of an English readership for native romance with considerable financial means.[35] A roughly contem-

---

[34] *Of Arthour and of Merlin*, ed. O. D. Macrae-Gibson, EETS 268, 279 (London, 1973, 1979), Auchinleck MS, 19–29. *Richard Coeur de Lion* similarly begins with a justification for writing in English rather than French (21–8).

[35] In addition to the facsimile, *Auchinleck MS*, intr. Pearsall and Cunningham, important studies of the manuscript include: Laura Hibbard Loomis, 'The Auchinleck Manuscript and a Possible London Bookshop of 1330–1340', *PMLA* 57 (1942), 595–627; A. J. Bliss, 'Notes on the Auchinleck MS', *Speculum* 26 (1951), 652–8; Timothy A. Shonk, 'A Study of the Auchinleck MS: Bookmen and Bookmaking in the Early Fourteenth Century', *Speculum* 60 (1985), 71–91; A. S. G. Edwards and Derek Pearsall, 'The Manuscripts of the Major Poetic Texts', in Griffiths and Pearsall (eds), *Book Production and Publishing*, 257–78 (257–8); Turville-Petre, *England the Nation*, 108–41.

porary manuscript, British Library MS Harley 2253, contains
the Middle English romance of *King Horn* along with items in
Anglo-Norman and Latin.[36] This manuscript provides evidence that Middle English romance was of interest to someone
who also read Latin and Anglo-Norman, in other words, an
educated, possibly clerical person, or someone from the rural
gentry.[37] *Kyng Alisaunder* (early fourteenth-century) addresses
itself repeatedly to 'lewed and lered', a designation which suggests a socially broad reception including laical and clerical
readers.[38]

Interest in the native verse romances remained strong in the
fifteenth century, despite the growth of a new tradition largely
inspired by Chaucer as well as suited to an increasing tendency
to private reading. This tradition consisted of larger romances
(with an increase in prose) pretending to a greater sophistication
and courtliness: the romances of Caxton and Lydgate, *The
Laud Troy Book*, *Partonope of Blois*, and, with qualifications,
Malory. It would be presumptuous, however, to imagine that
readers could not straddle the interests of the two traditions,
and educated and broadly middle-class interest in native
verse romance remained intact well into the sixteenth century.[39]

[36] *Facsimile of British Museum MS. Harley 2253*, intr. N. R. Ker, EETS 255
(London, 1965). On the date of the manuscript, see pp. xxi–xxii. On its likely readership, see Turville-Petre, *England the Nation*, 192–221. The presence of macronic
lyrics indicates a readership of bilingual and trilingual capabilities.

[37] Other manuscripts argue that romance was the choice reading of people whose
intellectual and linguistic capabilities could reach higher. The Lincoln Thornton MS
has a number of Latin theological items, such as prayers, antiphons, collects, tracts,
and psalms, in addition to a large body of romances; Guddat-Figge, *Catalogue*, 45. See
also her catalogue entries for National Library of Scotland MS Adv. 19.3.1 and
Cambridge Trinity College MS O.2.13.

[38] *Kyng Alisaunder*, ed. G. V. Smithers, EETS 227, 237 (London, 1952), 2, 213,
598, 1713, 2969, 8017. *Kyng Alisaunder* survives in four manuscripts, including the
Auchinleck MS, and a printed edition of *c.* 1525. See further: Mehl, *Middle English
Romances*, 229.

[39] Derek Pearsall, 'The English Romance in the Fifteenth Century', *Essays &
Studies* n.s. 29 (1976), 56–83 (64) is perhaps guilty of seeing too sharp a divide in
the fifteenth century between the two traditions. Malory's blending of the native
popular tradition with Continental sources, discussed in due course, suggests that
romance readers could maintain an interest in both traditions and that popular
romance adapted itself to changing patterns of readership rather than entered a period
of stagnation and decline. Furthermore, Naples Bibliotheca Nazionale MS XIII. B29
(dated 1457) contains *Bevis of Hampton*, *Lybeaus Desconus*, and *Sir Isumbras* as well
as Chaucer's *The Clerk's Tale* and a poem by Lydgate; see the entry in Guddat-Figge,
Catalogue.

Denunciations of romance in the medieval period frequently conflate the two traditions, and these diatribes attest more to the continued popularity of both old and new romances rather than a waning interest or radically different reading patterns.[40] Furthermore, the career of Robert Thornton, the fifteenth-century compiler of two manuscript-anthologies containing romances, indicates the appeal of the so-called popular tradition to a member of the rural gentry in the late Middle Ages.[41]

The general scholarly consensus with regard to the medieval period is that the readership of native romance was broad, remarkably so in comparison to France, where romance, tending to ethical concerns and psychological introspection, was more intimately associated with court life.[42] The opening lines from *Havelok* which preface this chapter are eloquently reflective of an address to a socially wide group, incidentally represented by both genders. Of course, the highest and most educated classes, the nobility and the court, would have read (or at least would have had the option of reading) romances in French until about the mid fourteenth century, and after that English romances of the 'Chaucerian' tradition. The lowest classes, who would be illiterate, could provide an audience for public recitations or readings of romance, a form of dissemination which existed side by side with its written counterpart.[43] Carol Meale authoritatively summarizes the range of physical forms in which people of almost all social levels encountered romance:

Romance manuscripts as a group exhibit great diversity, representing most levels of production. Some are copied on paper, some on parchment;

---

[40] See G. K. Owst, *Literature and Pulpit in Medieval England* (Oxford, 1961), 10–13.

[41] See: *Thornton MS*, intr. Brewer and Owen; George R. Keiser, 'Lincoln Cathedral Library MS 91: Life and Milieu of the Scribe', *SB* 32 (1979), 158–79; George R. Keiser, 'More Light on the Life and Milieu of Robert Thornton', *SB* 36 (1983), 111–19; Edwards and Pearsall, 'Manuscripts of Major Poetic Texts', in Griffiths and Pearsall (eds), *Book Production and Publishing*, 257–8.

[42] See further: Albert C. Baugh, 'The Middle English Romance: Some Questions of Creation, Presentation, and Preservation', *Speculum* 42 (1967), 1–31 (12–13); Mehl, *Middle English Romances*, 6, 13; Pearsall, 'Middle English Romances', in Arn and Wirtjes (eds), *Historical & Editorial Studies*, 42.

[43] Guddat-Figge, *Catalogue*, 48. On literacy in the Middle Ages, with particular reference to its rise in the fifteenth century, see M. B. Parkes, 'The Literacy of the Laity', in David Daiches and Anthony Thorlby (gen. eds), *Literature and Western Civilization* (London, 1973), 555–77.

some are clearly professionally produced, others the work of amateur scribes; some are decorated, some plain.[44]

That view, combined with a realization that romance in various forms could also reach below the level of literacy, indicates its broad appeal.

(II) ROMANCE IN PRINT IN THE LATE MIDDLE AGES AND SIXTEENTH CENTURY

The printing of Middle English romance in the sixteenth century is also indicative of its popularity, and that evidence is particularly important in relation to Spenser.[45] The sixteenth century represents a significant period in the history of the native romance tradition as a whole, and studies which cease investigation with the end of the fifteenth century omit a busy and complex phase in the revision, readership, and response to these texts. The bridge from Middle English romance in fifteenth-century manuscripts to sixteenth-century printed books is a solid one, without break or sudden transition, where continuity and shared influence deserve stronger emphasis than any sense of change. The evidence suggests a fairly strong interest in native verse romance until *c.* 1570 and after that a decline in interest due to perceptions of the verse romances as inferior on moral, social, and literary grounds. This basic picture has some complicating factors, however, such as the evidence of the quality of the prints and their texts, the continued reading and copying of romance in manuscript in the sixteenth century, and the mutation of the romances into new forms, literary and otherwise.

William Caxton did not print the 'popular' verse romances. Of his prose romances, *Le Morte Darthur* and *The Foure Sonnes of Aymon* retained the greatest appeal throughout the sixteenth and into the seventeenth century.[46] Wynkyn de Worde, Caxton's

[44] Meale, 'Romance and its Audiences', in Meale (ed.), *Readings in Medieval English Romance*, 213.

[45] I am not disallowing the possibility that Spenser encountered Middle English romances in medieval manuscripts; indeed, I wish to explore that possibility later. But the printing of romance is significant to indicate a milieu in which romances were still widely known.

[46] First printed in 1490, *The Foure Sonnes of Aymon* was reprinted possibly five times in the sixteenth century, the latest edition in 1554 (STC 1007–11.5). Malory's

assistant and successor, realized the desirability of the popular native romances in print.[47] De Worde published three editions of *Bevis of Hampton*, two editions of a shorter version of *Of Arthour and of Merlin*,[48] two editions of *Richard Coeur de Lion*, two editions of *Ipomedon*, and at least one edition each of *Guy of Warwick*, *Sir Eglamour of Artois*, *Sir Torent of Portyngale*, *Octavian*, *Sir Tryamour*, *Sir Degare*, and *The Squire of Low Degree*.[49] Richard Pynson, who was contemporary with de Worde, also printed Middle English verse romances, and in a few cases he offers us the earliest known printed edition of a particular romance.[50] The history of the printing of native verse romance from the beginning of printing in England until de Worde's death in 1535 is largely the history of these two men. Another period of fairly intense activity in the publication of native romance occurred in the 1550s and 1560s; William Copland (d. 1568/9),

Morte Darthur is more significant for our purposes; first printed by Caxton in 1485, it was reprinted by Wynkyn de Worde in 1498 with three later editions in the sixteenth century (the latest in 1578), and it continued to be printed in the seventeenth century (STC 801–5). Both *Paris and Vienne* and *Blanchardine and Eglantine* were printed in rewritten versions in the late sixteenth and early seventeenth centuries (STC 17201, 3125). Large prose romances introduced by other printers, such as *Valentine and Orson* and *Huon of Bourdeaux*, were still being printed in the mid and later sixteenth century. Studies relevant to Caxton's activities as a printer of romance are: N. F. Blake, 'William Caxton: his Choice of Texts', *Anglia* 83 (1965), 289–307; N. F. Blake, 'Caxton Prepares his Edition of the *Morte Darthur*', *Journal of Librarianship* 8 (1976), 272–85; Carol M. Meale, 'Caxton, de Worde, and the Publication of Romance in Late Medieval England', *Library* 6th ser. 14 (1992), 283–98; A. S. G. Edwards and Carol M. Meale, 'The Marketing of Printed Books in Late Medieval England', *Library* 6th ser. 15 (1993), 95–124.

[47] On Wynkyn de Worde, see further: Henry R. Plomer, *Wynkyn de Worde and his Contemporaries* (London, 1925); N. F. Blake, 'Wynkyn de Worde: the Later Years', *G-J* (1972), 128–38; A. S. G. Edwards, 'From Manuscript to Print: Wynkyn de Worde and the Printing of Contemporary Poetry', *G-J* (1991), 143–8; Meale, 'Caxton, de Worde and Publication of Romance'. See also 'Handlist of Publications by Wynkyn de Worde, 1492–1535', Appendix I, in H. S. Bennett, *English Books and Readers 1475 to 1557*, 2nd edn. (Cambridge, 1969), 239–76.

[48] See further: O. D. Macrae-Gibson, 'Wynkyn de Worde's *Marlyn*', *Library* 6th ser. 2 (1980), 73–6.

[49] *Bevis*, STC 1987 (1500), STC 1987.5 (c. 1500), STC 1988.6 (1533?). *Arthour and Merlin*, STC 17841 (1510), STC 17841.3 (1529). *Richard*, STC 21007 (1509), STC 21008 (1528). *Ipomedon*, B-version, STC 5732.5 (c. 1522), STC 5733 (c. 1527). *Guy*, STC 12541 (1497?). *Eglamour*, STC 7541 (1500). *Torent*, STC 24133.5 (1510?). *Octavian*, STC 18779 (1505?). *Tryamour*, STC 24302 (c. 1530). *Degare*, STC 6470 (1512–13). *Squire*, STC 23111.5 (1520?).

[50] The case with STC 24133, *Torent* (1505?); STC 24301.5, *Tryamour* (1503?); and STC 11721, *Generides* (1504?).

who was an original member of the Stationers' Company founded in 1556, was the leading printer of romances in this second generation.[51]

The sixteenth-century prints of verse romance which have survived offer a picture, albeit of limited accuracy, of the romances which were most popular and which Spenser probably knew. In general, this approach reinforces the underlying notion of the continuity of Middle English romance between the medieval and Renaissance periods, at least up to *c.* 1570. The romances which will be isolated in the literary study of the following chapters as the most popular and influential in the medieval period are, significantly, the same texts which were favoured by sixteenth-century printers and readers. For instance, *Bevis of Hampton* and *Guy of Warwick* (both *c.* 1300) were two of the most influential of Middle English romances, adapted and imitated in later romances of the fourteenth and fifteenth centuries; indeed, their popularity remained strong until well into the seventeenth century. Eight or more editions of *Bevis* were printed before 1600, with several printings after that date.[52] *Guy* had at least four editions in the sixteenth century; later, the romance continued to be a presence in a variety of Renaissance rewritings and adaptations.[53] The fact that *Guy* and *Bevis* are both found in the earliest manuscript to contain a substantial collection of Middle English romances, the Auchinleck MS (*c.* 1330), is evidence of the remarkable longevity of the tradition. After *Guy*

[51] Further notes on the lives and the works of the printers will be found in: E. Gordon Duff, *A Century of the English Book Trade* (London, 1905); F. C. Francis, *Robert Copland* (Glasgow, 1961); H. S. Bennett, *English Books & Readers 1475–1557*, 2nd edn. (Cambridge, 1969), 178–97; Edwards and Meale, 'Marketing of Printed Books', 118–19.

[52] STC 1987–96. There were three Elizabethan editions: STC 1988.8 (1560?), STC 1989 (1565?), STC 1990 (*c.* 1585). *Bevis* is the sole instance of a Middle English verse romance which continued to be printed in its medieval text after *c.* 1570; the latest appearance of Bevis (as a relic of medieval and Renaissance readership rather than a scholarly edition) was 1711. See further: Jennifer Fellows, '*Bevis redivivus*: The Printed Editions of *Sir Bevis of Hampton*', in Fellows et al. (eds), *Romance Reading on the Book*, 251–68 (254).

[53] STC 12540–2. The latest surviving edition is *c.* 1565. On Renaissance reworkings of the Guy-legend, see Richmond, *Legend of Guy of Warwick*, 163–236. Two other early romances which were printed in the sixteenth century were *Of Arthour and of Merlin* (STC 17841 (1510); STC 17841.3 (1529)) and *Richard Coeur de Lion* (STC 21007 (1509); STC 21008 (1528)). Like *Guy* and *Bevis*, these two works deal with native 'history' and offer a patriotic understanding of national identity.

and *Bevis*, the most significant, intertextually related romances of the native tradition were those designated the 'Eustace–Constance–Florence–Griselda' group.[54] *Sir Isumbras*, *Sir Eglamour of Artois*, *Sir Triamour*, *Octavian*, *Sir Torent of Portyngale*, and *Sir Degare* will feature prominently in the following chapters, both as some of the most influential romances of the tradition and also as works whose impact on Spenser is noteworthy. It is interesting to note their popularity with printers and readers in the sixteenth century: four editions of *Sir Isumbras*,[55] six editions of *Sir Eglamour*,[56] four editions of *Sir Tryamour*,[57] two editions of *Sir Torent of Portyngale*,[58] one edition of *Octavian*,[59] and four editions of *Sir Degare*.[60] I will offer shortly reasons why more romances than these were likely to have been known in the sixteenth century, but this list as it stands is undoubtedly impressive.

What were the condition of the texts and the quality of their presentation in the printed editions? Rather than offering a degenerate or corrupted text, printers such as de Worde, Pynson, and later William Copland took pains to present a lucid, consistent text. Nicolas Jacobs' detailed study of the transmission of *Sir Degare* has demonstrated that the sixteenth-century prints of that romance 'show evidence of a conscious attempt to clear up the worst of the mess'.[61] Other romances in print demonstrate the concern of the work's first printer, usually de Worde, to present a text of clarity, consistency, and even literary quality. For example,

---

[54] See Lillian Herlands Hornstein, 'Eustace–Constance–Florence–Griselda Legends', in Severs (gen. ed.), *Manual*, 120–32. The description of these romances as a group is a modern scholarly tool and not a judgement that the medieval reader would have applied in any strict sense.

[55] STC 14280.5–14282. Two of these are Elizabethan: STC 14281 (*c.* 1560); STC 14282 (1565?).

[56] STC 7541–7544.5. Possibly two Elizabethan: STC 7543 (*c.* 1555?); STC 7544.5 (*c.* 1565?).

[57] STC 24301.5–24303.3. Two of them Elizabethan: STC 24303 (1561?); STC 24303.3 (1565).

[58] STC 24133–24133.5.

[59] STC 18779.

[60] STC 6470–6472.5. Two of them Elizabethan: STC 6472 (1560); STC 6472.5 (1565?).

[61] Nicolas Jacobs, *The Later Versions of Sir Degarre*, MÆ Monographs, n.s. 18 (Oxford, 1995), 64. The 'mess' to which Jacobs refers is the deterioration of the text in fifteenth-century scribal transmission. Jacobs thinks it probable that the revision of the text for the press was instigated by de Worde (85).

an early printed edition of *Guy of Warwick* contains substantial revisions which are most likely to have been carried out as the work was prepared for the press.[62] Once a romance was in print, later editions could incorporate small and sometimes larger scale revisions; indeed, the same printer might produce different editions of the same romance with considerable textual variations. On the whole, romance in print was textually stable, but printing did not create a rigidly fixed text, and in this respect romance in print represents a continuity with the scribal transmission of the works in the medieval period. Jennifer Fellows' study of the printed editions of *Bevis of Hampton* has determined this interesting fact. In the case of *Bevis*, she found that the fragment which survives of de Worde's text (*c.* 1500) bears a relation to the text of later editions, such as Copland's prints. Pynson's edition of *c.* 1503, however, is a textual anomaly in which entire lines or even couplets have been rewritten to clarify a meaning which might otherwise have been obscured due to archaic or dialectal language.[63]

Orthography and morphology were generally revised in all editions as the romances went through successive printings. The edition of *Bevis* which most closely precedes *The Faerie Queene*, Thomas East's print of *c.* 1585 (STC 1990), no longer has linguistic features which were present in the texts of medieval

[62] Richmond, *Legend of Guy of Warwick*, 169–76. Richmond notes: 'Early printed texts of long romances show great efforts to make manageable sections through shortening and divisions. Copland's edition [of *Guy*] runs to 7976 lines; this is brief when compared with 11,976 in the second or fifteenth-century version' (172). See further: Gavin Bone, 'Extant Manuscripts Printed by W. de Worde with Notes on the Owner, Roger Thorney', *Library*, 4th ser. 12 (1932), 284–306 for de Worde's modernization and correction of the text of Lydgate's *Siege of Thebes*.

[63] For example, *Bevis of Hampton*: STC 1987 (1500), f. 5.v, 10, reads: 'He toke for wyles and slewe a gryce.' Pynson recast the couplet to avoid the last word. Thus STC 1988 (1503?), f. 6.r, 26, reads: 'And for a wyle a Pygge he slewe.' See further: Fellows, 'Bevis redivivus', in Fellows et al., (eds), *Romance Reading on the Book*, 252–4. Fellows also notes that Copland's second edition of *Bevis* (STC 1989; 1565) does not appear to have been set up from his first (STC 1988.8; *c.* 1560); she thinks it likely that these differences derive ultimately from a common original, a lost de Worde print (254), though the possibility that later printers turned to manuscripts in search of better texts cannot be ruled out. In her 'Editing Middle English Romance', in Mills, Fellows, and Meale (eds), *Romance in Medieval England*, 10, f. 21, Fellows also finds 'quite substantial differences between Copland's two printings of *Syr Tryamour*'. See further: Lotte Hellinga, 'Manuscripts in the Hands of Printers', in J. B. Trapp (ed.), *Manuscripts in the First Fifty Years After the Invention of Printing* (London, 1983), 3–11.

manuscripts and the earliest prints: the-*en* form of the present infinitive, the *y*-prefix of the past participle, and the plural noun form ending in-*en*. All of these linguistic features occur in *The Faerie Queene*, and Spenser may have gathered them from earlier printed versions or manuscripts of romance, if not from Chaucer, Lydgate, and other Middle English literature. But the printers of Middle English romance were not, unlike Spenser, interested in the deliberate cultivation of archaism for literary effect. They were trying to keep their texts intelligible, in order to sell copy to as wide a readership as possible.[64] Nevertheless, the continued appearance in the printed romances of arcane technical words relating to chivalry and arms, such as 'troncheon', 'falchion', 'stoure', and 'doughty',[65] in conjunction with the woodcuts of a generally 'medieval' character, would have made the appearance of the romances in print seem insular if not old-fashioned to a reader from the 1570s onwards. Despite small and occasionally larger changes, the printed editions did offer the sixteenth-century reader a genuine confrontation with medieval literature, justifying the extension of the study of native romance into the Renaissance. Comparing corresponding passages from two versions of *Sir Eglamour*, the Lincoln Thornton MS (*c.* 1430–40) and an Elizabethan print by John Walley (?1570; STC 7544) provides a view of essential continuity:

> 'Sir, sen ȝe sall on huntynge fownde,[a]
> I sall ȝow gyffe twa gud grewhundis,
> Are donnede[b] als any doo;
> Als I ame trewe gentyllwoman,
> Þer es no beste on erthe þat ranne
> On fote þay will hym to.
> And a gud swerd I sall gyff the,
> Was fonden in the Grekkes see—

---

[64] Reformation doctrine also instigated changes in romance texts, though not drastically or consistently. In the Bodleian Library copy of Pynson's print of *Bevis* (1503?; STC 1988), the word 'Pope' has twice been manually erased (f. 62.v, 4, 10). In later prints, the text is emended to read 'bishop'. Jacobs, *Later Versions of Degarre*, 104–5, notes the change from 'Masses' to 'masques' in the Percy Folio MS of *Sir Degare*. On the other hand, some printed versions of romance belonging to the Protestant era retain these words: *Sir Tryamour*, pr. W. Copland (1561?), f.152.v, 32 ('Pope'); *Sir Degore*, pr. J. King (1560), ff. 138.v, 2 ('masse'), 143.v, 3 ('masse of the trynite'), 143.v, 7 ('The preest in hys masse for him he prayed').

[65] See, e.g., *Bevis*, pr. East: STC 1990 (*c.* 1585), f. 109.r.23, 32, 33; f. 117.v.5; ff. 102.r.2, 104.v.1, and passim; f. 102.r.8,10 respectively.

Of þam knawe I no moo:
And ȝe hafe happe to heue it wele
Þar es no helme of iryn ne stele
Þat ne it will cleue it in two.'
(Lincoln MS, 259–70)

ᵃ 'set out, go';   ᵇ 'dusky'.

Syr yf you be on huntynge founde
I shall you gyue a good greyhounde
    That is dunne as a doo
For as I am a trewe gentylwoman
There was neuer dere that he at ran
    That myght scape him fro
Also a swerde I gyue the
That was founde in the see
    Of suche knowe I no mo
If ye haue happe to kepe it wele
There is no helme of yron and stele
    But it wolde carue in two.
(STC 7544)⁶⁶

The physical quality and textual value of the prints used to be condemned by medievalists and editors reluctant to acknowledge the historical importance of Middle English romance reception in the sixteenth century or to recognize the overlap between romance in manuscript and in print. Recent scholarship has revised that judgement, offering the basis for a more complex picture of the history of romance readership and book production up to *c.* 1570:

The casual near-dismissal of the romances by H. S. Bennett . . . as 'little quarto volumes' which were cheap to issue and buy, and suitable for an audience of schoolboys who had mastered the alphabet, is sweepingly

⁶⁶ Both passages are cited from *Eglamour*, ed. Richardson; the passage from the Elizabethan print appears in Appendix II, 136 of Richardson's edition. See further ibid., pp. xiv–xx for a useful discussion of the textual tradition of this romance both in its 'early' form in fourteenth- and fifteenth-century manuscripts and its 'late' form in sixteenth- and seventeenth-century printed books and manuscripts. For my own purposes, I have made numerous line-by-line comparisons of romances in early printed editions against edited texts based on medieval manuscripts; the impression of essential continuity is strong. Compare further the extract from Thomas East's print of *Bevis* (*c.* 1585; STC 1990), quoted below in chapter 6, with the fifteenth-century version of *Bevis*, the lower of the two texts in *Bevis*, ed. Kölbing (1885, 1886, 1894), 2420–594, based on Manchester Chetham's Library MS Mum. A.6.31 (olim 8009).

general in its assumption as to who actually read such books; it also fails to take into account features of lay-out and book design which, contrary to implication, reveal that a good deal of care was taken to present the texts advantageously to an ever-growing public. Many of these 'small and cheap' editions contained woodcut illustrations, decorative line-filling ornaments and borders, and attractive grotesque or cadel initials of a type which were used extensively by continental printers.[67]

Jennifer Fellows points out that many of the woodcuts which adorn Richard Pynson's print of *Bevis of Hampton* (1503?; STC 1988) are sufficiently specific in their correspondence to the details of the text that they must have been made especially for this edition.[68] Bespoke illustrations do not fit with a view of the printers producing the romances as cheaply as possible. Nor is the fact that the verse romances were produced in quarto format an indication of cheapness. Caxton produced his large prose romances, such as Malory, in folio editions, but de Worde was inconsistent in retaining this format for such works. Where he did print the prose romances in folio, his reason was surely a practical one, considering the length of these works, and not necessarily an indication of the literature's perceived social and literary status. Carol Meale points out that de Worde used the quarto format for both the native verse romances and some of the newer prose romances:

From de Worde's press it was possible to buy copies of, say, *Richard Coeur de Lion* and *Sir Degare*, Henry Watson's translations of *Oliver of Castille* and *Valentine and Orson* or Copland's of *Helyas*, and a reprint of *Paris and Vienne*...all in the same format: of the romances which de Worde published, only *Melusine* and the reprints of Caxton's *Four Sons of Aymon*...the *Histories of Troy*...and the *Morte Darthur*...are in folio.[69]

The quarto format of romances in print may suggest that they are intended for private reading: these prints are less 'public' or family-orientated than a large manuscript such as Auchinleck. But quarto format is not a certain indication of less prestige, in terms of the putative literary quality of the work or the social status of the intended readership.

[67] Meale, 'Caxton, de Worde, and the Publication of Romance', 290.
[68] Others are more general and appear in other romances and more than once in the same romance. See Fellows, '*Bevis redivivus*', in Fellows et al. (eds), *Romance Reading on the Book*, 252, and pl. 11.
[69] Meale, 'Caxton, de Worde, and the Publication of Romance', 291–2.

Two judgements concerning the readership of native romance in the sixteenth century are highly significant. The first point is that the surviving records of printed editions can only be regarded as an imperfect list of what romances went to press. Although the printed editions of romance were not necessarily cheap, 'thow-away' books, their popularity ensured their physical deterioration on a massive scale.[70] The fact that so many prints survive in fragments—and might so easily have perished altogether—illustrates just how arbitrary and imprecise is our knowledge of what was printed and of how often it was printed. Certainly, more Middle English romances reached print than those that survive—both more editions of romances already known to have been printed and also editions of romances for which no evidence survives of a history in print.[71]

The second point relating to Middle English romance in the sixteenth century is the insight that romances were still read in medieval manuscripts as well as produced in contemporary manuscripts. Thomas Lodge, for example, must have read *Gamelyn*, a source for his *Rosalynde* (1590), in manuscript.[72] The frequent annotations by sixteenth- and seventeenth-century hands in the large medieval manuscript-anthologies containing romances indicate that Lodge was not an exception.[73] John Stow owned Lambeth Palace MS 306, which contains the romance

[70] Bennett, *English Books & Readers 1475–1557*, 149–50. H. S. Bennett, *English Books & Readers 1558–1603* (Cambridge, 1965), 168–9 gives a striking example of how 'the commoner the book, the more likely it is that it will disappear'; the principle applies to romance literature.

[71] See Meale, 'Caxton, de Worde, and the Publication of Romance', 286, f. 10 for romances that only survive in fragments or that do not survive at all in printed editions but which from other evidence are known to have been printed.

[72] C. S. Lewis, *English Literature in the Sixteenth Century Excluding Drama* (Oxford, 1954), 423. On Lodge's associations with Spenser, see: William Wells (ed.), *Spenser Allusions in the Sixteenth and Seventeenth Centuries 1580–1700*, Texts and Studies 68–9 (1971–2), 33, 43, 50. Spenser may allude to Lodge as Alcon in *Colin Clouts Come Home Againe*, 394–5.

[73] *Thornton*, intr. Brewer and Owen, p. viii; *Auchinleck*, intr. Pearsall and Cunningham, pp. x–xvi; *CUL MS Ff.2.38*, intr. McSparran and Robinson, p. xvii. On f. 101.v of Auchinleck, a sixteenth-/seventeenth-century reader has added lines concerning Guy of Warwick. *Arthour and Merlin* in the same MS has been annotated and even textually amended with some care by a reader of *c.* 1600; see *Arthour and Merlin*, ed. Macrae-Gibson, II.39–40, 266–7. On f. 161.r of CUL Ff.2.38 a sixteenth-/seventeenth-century hand has written 'Guy Earl of Warwik' at the head of that text, a title which would enable the reader to locate the work more easily. See further: Guddat-Figge, *Catalogue*, 168, 193–4, 204, 206, 228–31, 264.

Lybeaus Desconus.[74] Furthermore, Middle English romances were still being copied in manuscript in the sixteenth century and later, for example Bodleian Library MSS Douce 261, Ashmole 45, and Greaves 60, British Library MS Harley 6223, and the seventeenth-century Percy Folio MS.[75] One of these books, MS Ashmole 45, is a reasonably high quality manuscript from *c.* 1520–30 containing the signature of the 'Spenserian' poet William Browne (1591–1643).[76] MS Douce 261 dates from 1564 and contains exclusively Middle English romances, with coloured illustrations. The texts of at least three of these romances—*Sir Isumbras, Sir Degare,* and *Sir Eglamour*—appear to have been copied from the printed versions of William Copland, an occurrence which emphasizes the continuity of manuscript-culture in the era of print and its competitive relationship with the press.[77]

The continued reading of Middle English romance in medieval manuscripts in the sixteenth century is particularly significant in relation to Spenser since it allows the possibility that Spenser encountered the romances in this form. Romances in print are deprived of their manuscript 'home'—the context of other romances, historical works, saints' lives, and other kinds of writing—which can adjust a reader's perception of a work's generic and thematic value. Just as *The Shepheardes Calender* presents the sense of being an earlier, 'edited' text, so too *The Faerie Queene* might be likened to a manuscript-anthology, particularly in terms of its structure. The Books of *The Faerie Queene*— relatively separate narrative units compared to the Books of the *Aeneid* or the Cantos of *Orlando Furioso*—recall the sequences of individual, juxtaposed romances, separated usually by spacing and titles, in manuscript-anthologies such as Auchinleck and the Lincoln Thornton MS. Even as *The Faerie Queene* competes with Virgilian Books and Ariostan Cantos, its quite different

[74] *Lybeaus*, ed. Mills, 2.

[75] All of these MSS are described in Guddat-Figge, *Catalogue*.

[76] See further: Carol M. Meale, ' "Prenes: engre": An Early Sixteenth-Century Presentation Copy of *The Erle of Tolous*', in Fellows et al. (eds), *Romance Reading on the Book*, 221–36.

[77] See further: A. I. Doyle, Elizabeth Rainey, and D. B. Wilson, *Manuscript to Print* (Durham, 1975); Mary A. Rouse and Richard H. Rouse, 'Backgrounds to Print', in their *Authentic Witnesses* (Notre Dame, 1991), 449–66; Woudhuysen, *Sidney and Circulation of Manuscripts*, 11–25.

structure seems to recall the experience of reading a book like the
Auchinleck MS; like that book, *The Faerie Queene* contains a
number of romances as well as other intercalated genres, such as a
chronicle of British history (II.x.5–68; III.iii.27–50; III.ix.33–51),
a topographical description of the rivers of England and Ireland
(IV.xi.24–43), Ovidian myths, such as Venus and Adonis portrayed on the wall coverings of Castle Joyous (III.i.34–8), the
fabliau of the Squire of Dames (III.vii.53–61), and the exemplum
of Malbecco (III.x), in addition to complaints, lyrics, and
prayers.[78]

The topic of Middle English romance readership in the sixteenth century raises the question of whether Spenser's first readers, his intended audience, were in a position to recognize his
assimilation of the tradition. Does the presence of Middle English
romance in *The Faerie Queene* have a deliberate rhetorical value
as opposed to belonging to the poet's own antiquarian interest?
Native romance does appear to wane in popularity after *c.* 1570.
Apart from *Bevis*, none of the native verse romances is printed in
its medieval text after that date, though *Guy of Warwick*
remained popular in rewritings and adaptations that testify, perhaps even more so than the printing of the old text, to a widespread continued interest in this native hero. The romance
traditions which became increasingly popular in the last quarter
of the sixteenth century were classical and Continental: translations of Hellenistic romances such as Heliodorus' *Ethiopica* by
Thomas Underdowne (1569, rev. 1587) and *Clitophon and Leu-
cippe* by William Burton (1597), of Italian romances such as
Orlando Furioso by John Harrington (1591) and *Gerusalemme
Liberata* by Edward Fairfax (1600), and of Spanish and Portug-
ese romances such as *Amadis of Gaul* by Anthony Munday
(1590, 1595; but known to English readers prior to those dates
through the French version) and Diego Ortuñez de Calahorra's
The Mirrour of Princely Deedes and Knighthood by Margaret
Tyler (1578). Elizabethan romance writers such as Sidney and
Robert Greene created works strongly influenced by these rather

---

[78] In '"Well Grounded, Finely Framed, and Strongly Trussed Up Together": The
"Medieval" Structure of *The Faerie Queene*', *RES* (forthcoming), I consider in greater
detail the medieval antecedents to the structure of *The Faerie Queene*, adding there in
addition to manuscript-anthologies the possible influences of *compilatio* and story-
collections, especially *The Canterbury Tales*.

than the native romances.[79] However, like the 'division' in the
fifteenth century between the popular verse romances and the
new post-Chaucerian tradition, it would be dangerous to assume
that readers' interests could not include both traditions. Bevis,
Guy, and Arthur at least were famous, quasi-historical figures
whom everyone knew; George Puttenham praises these three in
The Art of English Poesie (1589).[80] Guy of Warwick, furthermore, was reckoned to be an ancestor of the earl of Leicester,
whose brother Ambrose was earl of Warwick.[81] Richard Lloyd's
A Briefe Discourse of . . . the Nine Worthies (1584) replaces Godfrey of Bouillon, one of the traditional nine as recounted by
Caxton in the preface to *Le Morte Darthur*, with Guy of Warwick. And *Bevis of Hampton* was incorporated by Richard Johnson into his account of St George in the very popular *The Seven
Champions of Christendom* (1596, with additions in 1608 and
1616)—after Spenser borrowed from *Bevis* for his account of St
George.[82] The full description given of both Bevis and Guy in
Michael Drayton's *Poly-Olbion* (1613, 1622), furthermore, supports the supposition that these heroes and the romance tradition
which they epitomized were still widely known in the early
seventeenth century.[83] Thomas Nashe's consideration of native
romance as 'worne out absurdities' may have reflected the viewpoint of many of Spenser's readers, but they also, like Nashe,
would have grown up with and would know well the romances.[84]

[79] See further Henry Thomas, 'English Translations of Portuguese Books Before
1640', *Library*, 4th ser. 7 (1926), 1–30; Wright, *Middle-Class Culture*, 377–83; John J.
O'Connor, *Amadis de Gaule and Its Influence on Elizabethan Literature* (New
Brunswick, N.J., 1970); John Simons, 'Robert Parry's *Moderatus*: A Study in Elizabethan Romance', in Fellows et al. (eds), *Romance Reading on the Book*, 237–50.
[80] George Puttenham, *The Arte of English Poesie*, ed. Gladys Doidge Willcock and
Alice Walker (Cambridge, 1936), 1.xix.
[81] On documents associating Robert Dudley with his legendary ancestor, see Richmond, *Legend of Guy of Warwick*, 189–91.
[82] Spenser's use of Bevis in Book I will be discussed in chapter 6. On Johnson's use of
Bevis, see Fellows, 'St George', 36–42, 48–53. Both Johnson's and Spenser's utilization
of *Bevis* in their descriptions of St George's slaying of the dragon suggests Bevis' fame
as the other great English dragon-slayer.
[83] Michael Drayton, *Poly-Olbion*, vol. 4, in *The Works of Michael Drayton*, ed. J.
William Hebel et al. (Oxford, 1961): Bevis, II.231–384, and pp. 46–7; Guy, XIII.327–
52 and p. 286. See also Richmond, *Legend of Guy of Warwick*, 202–8 for the
frequency with which references to Guy of Warwick were made in Renaissance drama.
[84] Nashe, *Works*, ed. McKerrow, 1.26.

The conclusion must be that Spenser's incorporation of native romance came at a time when that borrowing would be recognized; the setting of *The Faerie Queene*, its language, characters, and events would be compellingly familiar, not necessarily in terms of precise borrowings but rather as the narrative and linguistic world of the native romances. At the same time, Spenser's assimilation of native romance occurred at a point in the development of English romance and literature which would make that borrowing polemical, or at least enigmatic, similar to his use of demotic language and rustic native characters in *The Shepheardes Calender*. E. K.'s defence in the 'Epistle' of Spenser's language anticipates a hostile reaction to what might seem a retrogressive step for a 'new Poete'. *The Faerie Queene* no more duplicates the *Orlando Furioso* than *The Shepheardes Calender* reproduces Virgil's *Eclogues*. Both of Spenser's creations are deeply involved in native traditions.

The evidence of the manuscripts has provided a starting point for understanding the romances as a native tradition in which many texts are concerned with historical self-definition under the aegis of God's providential care. And the evidence of prints and manuscripts revealed strands of continuity which allowed this tradition to impinge on *The Faerie Queene*. Now we turn to the texts.

3

The Matter of Just Memory:
Providential History in
Middle English Romance

King Horn, Havelok, Of Arthour and of Merlin, Richard Coeur de Lion, Sir Bevis of Hampton, and *Guy of Warwick* together cover the period *c.* 1225–1300, though the story-matter of these romances also recurs in later and substantially different versions.[1] *Horn* and *Havelok* appear together in one manuscript, Bodleian Library MS Laud Misc. 108, as well as separately in various manuscripts, and the other romances all appear in the Auchinleck MS in addition to surviving in other manuscripts in different contexts. Both of these two manuscripts, furthermore, contain other kinds of texts which provide a framework of historical and Christian didactic concerns relevant to the romances. The intertextuality of these romances—their overlapping of themes and narrative patterns—and their generic ambiguity are reflected in the physical evidence of their collection and contextualization in manuscripts such these.

(I) *KING HORN, HORN CHILDE*, AND *HAVELOK*: ENGLISH
HEROES AND ENGLISH HISTORY

King Horn (*c.* 1225) successfully answers the questions of why Middle English romance was so popular and what kind of satisfaction its readers sought.[2] *Horn* is an energetic, moral tale which

---

[1] *King Horn* is retold about a hundred years after its first appearance in English as *Horn Childe*, discussed in this chapter. In the fifteenth century, through the intermediary stage of a French romance, the Anglo-Norman romance of *Horn et Rimenild* became in English *King Ponthus*. Havelok's career features in a number of historical works, such as an interpolation in one of the manuscripts of Robert Mannyng's *Story of England* and in the prose *Brut*. *Of Arthour and of Merlin, Bevis, Guy*, and *Richard* all exist in fifteenth-century copies with substantial revisions.

[2] *Horn* survives in three manuscripts. *King Horn*, ed. Rosamund Allen (New York and London, 1984) is the modern critical edition, but the visual presentation of its text

shows divine providence overcoming the evil ambitions of individual human characters. In that vision, the narrative is marked
by a sense of movement towards completion. Narrative closure
and providential fulfilment are one and the same, a goal which is
only reached at the work's end and which necessitates that ending
because of its unsustainability as narrative. The providential
momentum towards completion is anticipated in the depiction
of characters who tend to be perfect in the etymological sense of
'created through'. For example, Horn is described thus:

> Fairer ne miste non beo born…
> Fairer nis non thane he was:
> He was bright so the glas,
> He was whit so the flur,
> Rose red was his colur.
> In none kingeriche
> Nas non his iliche.
>
> (10–8)

(No one born could be better looking… No one was more handsome
than he was; he was as radiant as glass, as white as a flower. His
complexion was red like a rose. His like was not in any kingdom.)

Characters are rarely complex or partially developed: in relation
to two of Horn's companions, the narrator informs that 'Athulf
was the beste, / And Fikenylde the werste' (27–8). But the ideal-
istic depiction of the characters does not make their world ir-
relevant to a reader, contemporary or otherwise, who seeks in the
text a reflection of his or her own experiences. Despite Horn's
appearance, great physical prowess, and personal moral perfection, he becomes a victim of savage injustice who must struggle
painfully to regain what is rightfully his. Providence is depicted as
a gradual, slow, and mysterious righting of justice—not a facile
deus ex machina. Horn's efforts to regain his 'baronage' would
have had a particular relevance to the Anglo-Norman and later
English barony who faced increasingly the loss of their own
power.[3] Furthermore, placenames in the poem such as 'Yrlonde'
(1004), 'Suddenne' (143), and 'Westernesse' (157) help to render

is somewhat cumbersome. I have chosen to cite the romance from the anthology *Of
Love and Chivalry*, ed. Jennifer Fellows (London and Rutland, Vermont, 1993).

[3] Crane, *Insular Romance*, 8.

its world more concrete and tangible.[4] And the destruction of churches by seafaring pagans (35–66) augments the work's historical sense and accessibility through its probable reference to the Danish invasions of England.[5] The world of *Horn* is at once in the process of becoming a place of perfectly realized justice and a society whose ills expose the need for a general cure. Put another way, it is English history 'remembered' not according to Sidney's 'bare *Was*'[6] but through the shaping influence of religious belief.

Remembering English history in a way that leads to the fulfilment of justice might be thought wishful thinking; Henry James usefully defines romance as 'the beautiful circuit and subterfuge of our thoughts and *desires*'.[7] However, God's providence is, from a medieval perspective, the objective and real force which allows for an entirely credible depiction of the real world achieving, at the end, social justice and moral perfection. Providence, in other words, is not the author's manipulation of events, but a force which is in fact 'out there' and in which the romance encourages belief. The importance of God's providential care emerges in the emphasis placed upon Horn's Christianity and the paganism of his enemies:

> Horn was in paynes honde,
> With his feren of the londe.
> Muchel was his fairhede,
> For Jhesu Crist him makede.
>
> (81–4)

(Horn and his companions were in the hands of the pagans. His beauty was great because Jesus Christ made him.)

Horn's beauty, which is explained in the preceding passage as the image of Christ in man, prevents the pagans from killing him:

> Payns him wolde slen,
> Other al quic flen:

---

[4] 'Suddenne' and 'Westernesse' may have had only a vague directional sense, or they may have had a more specific meaning for their contemporary readers, one which is lost to us today.

[5] Diane Speed, 'The Saracens of *King Horn*', *Speculum* 65 (1990), 564–95 (565).

[6] Sidney, *Defence*, ed. Dorsten, 36.19.

[7] Henry James, *The Art of the Novel*, intr. Richard P. Blackmur (New York and London, 1934), 32; my emphasis.

Yef his fairnesse nere,
The children alle aslaghe were.
(85–98)[8]

(The pagans wanted to slay him or flay him alive. If it were not for his beauty, all the children would have been killed.)

The saints' lives which feature in certain manuscripts also containing *Horn* offer the same perspective of 'historical' characters who live in a fallen world of persecution and suffering, and yet whose careers also demonstrate the interactive assistance of God within that world. Considering further the story of *Horn* will illustrate how the real or historical world is there drawn into a romance mode which derives its credibility from providence. This perspective will remain important to the native romances which follow as well as to *The Faerie Queene*.

The story of Horn is the key story for male heroes in the native romance tradition: a youth who seeks to regain his patrimony from which he has been unjustly displaced. Horn's father is killed by pagan pirates, and Horn and some Christian companions are set adrift in a boat; they come ashore in Westernesse and are taken in by King Aylmar. The king's daughter, Rymenhild, falls in love with Horn, who fears that because he is a foundling his social position is too low for such a match. The condition of the displaced youth as a foundling is an important feature not only in this story but in numerous other Middle English romances. The emphasis on the restrictions enforced by social hierarchy is another realistic feature of *Horn* which would relate the work to the actual world of its contemporary readers. What it highlights is that the hero's recovery of his patrimony really involves a recovery of his proper identity, conceived of here in terms of social status. Horn realizes, in a negative way, who he is and the restrictions placed upon him when Rymenhild declares her love:

'Ihc am ibore to lowe
Such wimman to knowe:
Ihc am icome of thralle,
And fundling bifalle.

[8] Susan Dannenbaum, '"Fairer bi one ribbe / Þan eni man þat libbe" (*King Horn*, C 315–16)', *NQ* 28 (1981), 116–17 interprets the couplet in her title as an association between Horn and the physical perfection of Adam and Christ. Cf. the commentary to this line in Fellows (ed.), *Of Love and Chivalry*.

Ne feolle hit the of cunde
To spuse beo me bunde:
Hit nere ne fair wedding,
Bitwexe a thral and a king'.
(417–24)

('I am too low-born to know such a woman. I descend from a slave and have become a foundling. It would not be natural for you to be bound to me as a spouse; it would not be a fair match, between a slave and a king!')

Horn is in fact aware of his true royal identity (143–6), but he needs to grow into that identity before he can assume its privileges: that is his quest. Later Horn repeats this theme when he prepares to regain the kingdom of Suddenne:

'Thu kep hure [i.e. Rymenhild] a stunde,
The while that I funde
Into min heritage,
And to mi baronage.
That lond I schal ofreche,
And do mi fader wreche.
I schal beo king of tune,
And bere kinges crune.
Thanne schal Rymenhilde
Ligge bi the kinge!'
(1281–90)

('Take care of her for a time, whilst I fight to gain my birthright. I shall obtain that land and avenge my father. I shall be king in the city and bear the king's crown. Then Rymenhild will lie by the king!')

The theme of identity is crucial in the romances of dispossessed or displaced youths as well as in Book I of *The Faerie Queene*. There is a double, seemingly contradictory emphasis on the importance of nobility bestowed on the hero through high birth, something which is innate and unobtainable to those born in lower stations, as well as a strong interest in the hero's struggle out of exile during which he demonstrates that he is worthy of his nobility. In some cases the hero needs to excise from his own character negative qualities which are the result of his displacement, and in those instances the hero paradoxically seems to earn what he was in fact given at birth—nobility and his identity as his father's son. The emphasis on 'achieving' legitimacy—a concern, we noted, in

The Shepheardes Calender—is clear when Horn avenges his father's death. Horn's opponents in battle, unaware of his identity, coincidentally remark that his sword-strokes are as powerful as those of King Mury, Horn's father:

> He sede hi nevre nadde
> Of knighte dentes so harde,
> [Bute of the King Mory,
> That was so swythe stordy:]
> He was of Hornes kunne,
> Iborn in Suddenne.
> (863–8)

(They said that they had never received such hard blows from a knight, except from King Mury, who was exceptionally strong. He was kin to Horn, born in Suddenne.)

Horn recovers his patrimony not only in a legal sense but also at a deeply personal level. And his personal recovery, enabled by providence, is part of God's plan for the society as a whole. As Horn prepares to invade his rightful kingdom, now possessed by pagans, he encounters a Christian knight who was forced to serve under the pagans but is now eager to aid him in God's cause:

> He sede, 'Ihc have, ayenes my wille,
> Payns ful ylle!
> Ihc was Cristene a while;
> Tho icom to this ille
> Sarazins blake,
> That dude me forsake;
> On Crist ich wolde bileve.'
> (1317–23)

(He said, 'I have suffered from pagans against my will. I was once a Christian. Then black Saracens came to this island and forced me to forsake my faith. I want to believe in Christ.')

Horn's recovery of his father's kingdom means the expulsion of paganism and a renewal of Christian worship:

> Horn let wurche
> Chapeles and chirche;
> He let belles ringe,
> And masses let singe.
> (1381–4)

(Horn caused chapels and churches to be made; he allowed bells to be rung and masses sung.)

Horn's recovery of his identity relies in this story on the assistance of providence, and providence works through Horn to its larger goal of the restoration of Christian faith. Thus Horn's achievements are partially offset by a sense of divine orchestration, reflecting St Augustine's emphasis on God's providential care.

The vigour and deftness with which *Horn* handles its themes make it an outstanding work. Almost a century later, this story was given a new version, *Horn Childe* (*c.* 1320), which amplifies the sense of realism and historicity in the story.[9] That development is especially significant because it reflects a general tendency of Middle English romance writers, including Malory, to connect the narrative world to their known world. When the Yorkshire redactor of *Horn Childe* notes that 'On Alerton More al þai mett... / Seþþen to Clifland þai rade' (67–70),[10] he locates the story in a setting which would be familiar to his audience or readers. Such details add force to the narrator's insistence that the work is a true account of the audience's ancestors:

> Stories ȝe may lere
> Of our elders þat wer
> Whilom in þis lond.
> (4–6)

(You can learn stories concerning our ancestors who were once in this land.)

When the Danish army invades England, the use of precise place-names invokes the historical mode as well as inciting in the readers a sense of territorial, even national, identity:

> Out of Danmark come an here
> Opon Inglond forto were,
> Wiþ stout ost & vnride;

[9] The edition cited is *Horn Childe and Maiden Rimnild*, ed. Maldwyn Mills (Heidelberg, 1988). *Horn Childe* and *King Horn* appear to be separate, collateral descendants of the same source, the Anglo-Norman *Romance of Horn*; see ibid., 44–6, 49. Moreover, *Horn Childe* draws upon other Middle English romances, such as *Sir Tristrem* and *Amis and Amiloun* (ibid., 55–6, 69–73)—an indication of literary tradition. *Horn Childe* survives in a unique witness, the Auchinleck MS, which also contains most of the other romances which are a concern in this chapter.

[10] 'They all met on Allerton Moor... After, they rode to Cleveland.'

Wiþ yren hattes, scheld & spere:
Alle her pray to schip þai bere,
In Clifland bi Teseside.

(49–54)

(An army came from Denmark to attack England with a strong and cruel host—with iron helmets, shield, and spear. They bore all their booty into a ship in Cleveland by Tees-side.)

The narrator insists that these events have left imprints which are still there for people to see, evidence that these events did indeed happen:

Whoso goþ or rideþ þerbi,
ʒet may men see þer bones ly,
Bi Seyn Sibiles Kirke.

(79–84)

(Whoever goes or rides by there may see still see their bones lying by St Sybil's church.)

The item which precedes *Horn Childe* in the Auchinleck MS, the *Liber regum Anglie* or *Anonymous Short English Metrical Chronicle*, indicates the favourable sense of national identity which was emergent in the early fourteenth century.[11] Like *Horn Childe*, it shapes the historical events and characters pertaining to England into patterns which will educate and satisfy:

Here may men rede who so can
Hou Jnglond first bigan
Men mow it finde jn Englische
As þe Brout it telleþ ywis.[12]

Like *Horn Childe*, the *Short Metrical Chronicle* indicates the origins of features which its readers would have known. For example, Julius Caesar captures the city of Hengisthom and renames it London: 'so it schal be cleped ay / Til þat it be domesday' (A-text, p. 66). *Horn Childe* combines this historical and topographical specificity with the same emphasis, seen in the earlier *Horn*, on the role of providence in the hero's moral

---

[11] Turville-Petre, *England the Nation*.
[12] *An Anonymous Short English Metrical Chronicle*, ed. Ewald Zettl, EETS 196 (London, 1935), note to 1, giving the variant opening of the Auchinleck MS. On the relationship of the *Chronicle* to the other items in the Auchinleck MS, see further Turville-Petre, *England the Nation*, 112.

victories. In this way, *Horn Childe* requires a more complex response from its readers than the *Metrical Chronicle*, which does not emphasize the providential momentum of native history and its concomitant narrative closure to the same degree. Reading *Horn Childe*, we are asked to believe that the events are true, or 'matter of iust memory', rather than a 'leysynge'.[13] At the same time, however, we are asked to believe that providence interacted with history in an extraordinary way. For a medieval audience, deeply familiar with the narrative events of the Bible and related apocryphal legends through texts such as *Cursor Mundi*, that providential synthesis of history and romance would have been quite comfortable.

Havelok (*c*. 1280–1300) offers a narrative closely similar to that of *Horn* and *Horn Childe*—another tale of exile and return— but with an even greater sense of historicity.[14] *Havelok* abounds in accurate geographical references and allusions to things 'still there', relating the actions of the romance to the real world known to its readers. For example, Grimsby derives its name from the landing at this spot of Grim, Havelok's guardian:

> And for þat Grim þat place aute
> Þe stede of Grim þe name laute,
> So þat Grimesbi it calle
> Þat þer-offe speken alle;
> And so shulen men callen it ay
> Bituene þis and Domesday.
>
> (744–9)

(Because Grim possessed that place, the location received its name from Grim, so that people who speak of it call it Grimsby; and people shall call it that always, from now to Domesday.)

By a false logic, the fact that Grimsby is 'still there' proves that the eponymous landing of Grim and Havelok really occurred. Another example is the foundation of Grimsby's Benedictine Priory:

---

[13] *Lesynge*, meaning 'lie' or 'deception', is the description given to romance in *The South English Legendary*, ed. Charlotte D'Evelyn and Anna J. Mill, EETS 235, 236, 244 (London, 1956, 1959), 3.60. The Caius MS of *Guy of Warwick* begins with the narrator's promise that this is a true story 'withoute lesynge' (23).

[14] The edition cited is *Havelok*, ed. Smithers. *Havelok* survives in two manuscripts, one of which is fragmentary.

Þo swor Hauelok he sholde make,
Al for Grim, of monekes blake
A priorie to seruen inne ay
Jesu Crist til Domesday...
And þer-of held he wel his oth,
For he it made, God it woth,
Jn þe tun þer Grim was grauen,
Þat of Grim yet haues þe naue[n].
(2521–30)[15]

(Then Havelok pledged that he would have built, for Grim's sake, a priory for Benedictine monks always to serve Jesus Christ until Domesday. Thereof he kept his word; for he founded it, God knows, in the town where Grim was buried [and] which still takes its name from Grim.)

The *Havelok*-poet insistently draws attention to the shared experience of Havelok's world and the readers' world: the execution of Godrich, who usurped the English throne, occurred in Lincoln on a green 'Þat þare is yet, als Y wene' (2830). Contemporary readers were clearly eager to see the story as an account of their own origins, the 'matter of iust memory'. The *Havelok*-story is intercalated into Robert Mannyng's *Chronicle of England* in Lambeth Palace MS 131. Furthermore, a version of *Havelok* appears in the Anglo-Norman *L'Estoire des Engleis* of Geoffrey Gaimar, in some versions of the *Anonymous Short English Metrical Chronicle*, and in the prose *Brut*.[16] In addition to textual

---

[15] In fact, no record of a Benedictine Priory exists for Grimsby, but the rhetorical effect of the passage is the same. Furthermore, like Horn's restoration of Christianity, this passage emphasizes that Havelok's personal recovery is part of God's providential plan. The passage does not appear in the Anglo-Norman version of the romance and appears to be the work of an English redactor; see *Havelok*, ed. Smithers, 144.

[16] The text of the *Havelok*-section in Mannyng is reproduced in *Havelok*, ed. Smithers, pp. xxii–xxiv, and a summary of the story in Gaimar's *L'Estoire* is also there, pp. xvii–xix. In the second half of Mannyng's work, following Peter Langtoft's *Chronicle*, he describes his failure to find authenticating proof of Havelok's 'historical' achievements; *Peter Langtoft's Chronicle*, ed. Thomas Hearne, 2 vols. (London, 1810). The only evidence for historicity unearthed by Mannyng are things 'still there':

> Men sais in Lyncoln castelle ligges ჳit a stone
> Þat Hauelok kast wele forbi euerilkone;
> And ჳit þe chapelle standes þer he weddid his wife. (II, 26)

But Mannyng can 'fynd no man / Þat has writen in story how Hauelok þis lond wan'. The arguments against historicity, though far fewer in number for this period, are as significant as those for; they attest to the widely perceived historicity of the hero and the desire or need to authenticate that popular image through authority. For an

witnesses, the medieval Seal of Grimsby, which contains representations of Havelok, Grim, and Goldeborw, is a surviving object which encourages belief in the historicity of the romance.[17] While such local references indicate the poem's ability to be accessible to its north-eastern audience, the frequent invocations of England also suggest an interest in self-understanding at the national level.[18]

To an even greater extent than the two versions of *Horn*, *Havelok* illustrates the providential treatment of history which here defines the romance mode. *Havelok* is a more dynamic text because it stretches to greater separation the sense of realism and the sense of romance, located in the shaped narrative and the manifestations of divine grace through supernatural means. The realism of the tale makes 'our' entry into it easier,[19] but it potentially militates against an acceptance of the paradoxically idealizing tendencies of its narrative. Reconciling these two extremes involves the reader's cooperating belief in the effective reality of divine providence, in relation to both individual human lives and the entire English nation. The realism in *Havelok* emerges not only in references to English geography, but in the treatment of its theme, also seen in *Horn*, concerned with the displacement of a noble youth and his struggle to regain his patrimony. *Havelok*

---

historian of Mannyng's calibre, that means reliable documents, but for others belief can be sustained by the tactile things 'still there'. For Havelok's presence in the prose *Brut*, see: *The Brut*, ed. Friedrich W. D. Brie, EETS 131, 136 (London, 1906, 1908), 92 (Havelok is here named Curan and identified as 'Hauelockes sone'). See further: Robert Huntingdon Fletcher, *The Arthurian Materials in the Chronicles*, 2nd edn. (New York, 1966), 126–7; Turville-Petre, *England the Nation*, 143–75.

[17] On the Grimsby Seal, see *Havelok*, ed. Smithers, fig.1 and app. B.

[18] Thorlac Turville-Petre, '*Havelok* and the History of the Nation', in Meale (ed.), *Readings in Medieval English Romance*, 121–34 locates *Havelok* in the context of the late thirteenth- and early fourteenth-century concern with nationhood. Diane Speed, 'The Construction of the Nation in Medieval English Romance', in ibid., 135–57 (149–50) notes that England is mentioned by name in *Havelok* thirty-nine times and the adjective/noun 'English' occurs six times; furthermore, whereas Gaimar's *L'Estoire des Engleis* and the Anglo-Norman *Lai d'Haveloc* represent England as a collection of petty kingdoms, the Middle English *Havelok* portrays England as a unified kingdom.

[19] In *Havelok*, ed. Smithers, p. lxii, the editor notes that the 'extent to which he [the *Havelok*-poet] has filled his story with facts, events, and instructions of the real life of his own time goes far beyond what is normally found in medieval romances'. See further pp. lxiii–lxiv for details unique to the Middle English version which, in comparison with the *Lai d'Haveloc*, increase the realistic and historical impression of the work.

offers realistic touches, such the hero's need to do manual labour (791–824) or the threats of poverty and hunger (825–57), which were less prominent in *Horn*. Because of the poverty of his guardian Grim, the exiled heir to the Danish throne must seek his fortunes in Lincoln, provided with the crudest of garments by Grim:

> He tok þe sh[e]res of þe nayl
> And made him a couel of þe sayl,
> And Hauelok dide it sone on.
> Hauede neyþer hosen ne shon,
> Ne none kines oþe[r] wede:
> To Lincolne barfot he yede.
>
> (858–63)

(He took the scissors off the nail and made from a sail a garment for Havelok; he immediately tried it on. Havelok did not have stockings, shoes, or any other kind of clothing. He went to Lincoln barefoot.)

Havelok eventually finds employment as a cook's assistant—as the prose *Brut* puts it, 'a knaf of ... [the] kechyne' (92).

Rather than displaying an aristocratic aversion to his unnatural condition of poverty—a reaction which we will see in other displaced heroes—Havelok is reconciled to his duties:

> 'Fir and water Y wile you fete,
> Þe fir blowe an ful wel maken.
> Stickes kan Ich breken and kraken,
> And kindlen ful wel a fyr,
> And maken it to brennen shir.
> Ful wel kan Ich cleuen shides,
> Eles to-turuen of here hides;
> Ful wel kan Ich dishes swilen,
> And don al þat ye euere wilen.'
>
> (913–21)

('I will fetch fire and water for you; I will blow and make the fire very well. I can break sticks and kindle a fire very well and make it burn brightly. I can split pieces of wood very well, or else strip hides clean. I can wash dishes very well and do everything that you want.')

Havelok's willingness to serve both suggests a notion of kingship which prizes humility before tyranny[20] and coincidentally serves

---

[20] See further: David Staines, '*Havelok the Dane*: A Thirteenth-Century Handbook for Princes', *Speculum* 51 (1976), 602–23. Significantly, when Havelok does achieve

as a realistic explanation of one of the crucial stages by which this hero regains his rightful kingdom. The reputation which he gains, while a cook's assistant, for strength, beauty, and character (1061–7) leads Godrich, with malicious intent, to marry him to Goldeborw in the hope of preventing her accession to the English throne—'For he wende þat Hauelok wore / Sum cherles sone and no more' (1092–3). That act ironically unites the two deposed heirs and leads to their eventual victory.

The fact that Godrich's plans backfire suggests divine providence working through and despite the intentions of those who would oppose it. This particular manifestation of God's shaping of events has been veiled; the divine orchestration is invisible and the outcome of events, though remarkably coincidental, is not incredible. Elsewhere in *Havelok*, however, God's will is manifested through frankly supernatural means, and here the contemporary reader must be prepared to accept the historical reality of a previous age of miracles. For example, the heavenly light which shines from Havelok's mouth 'Als it were a sunne-bem' (593)[21] is a divine token of his regality, comparable to God's recognition of Christ as his son following his baptism (Matt. 3:16–17). The Christological analogy is also suggested when Ubbe sees the other sign of Havelok's regality, the birthmark cross on his shoulder. Ubbe's response resonates with the *Nunc dimittis*, Simeon's recognition of and praise for the coming of the Messiah (Luke 2:25–33):

> Quoth Ubbe, 'Louerd, ne dred þe nowth!
> Me þinkes þat J se þi þouth.
> Dere sone, wel is me
> Þat Y þe with eyn se!
> Manred, louerd, bed Y þe—
> Þi man auht I ful wel to be,
> For þu art comen of Birkabeyn,
> Þat hauede mani knith and sweyn.
> And so shalt þou, louerd, haue:
> Þou þu be yet a ful yung knaue
> Þou shalt be king of al Denemark.'
>
> (2169–79)

his proper identity, he remembers to reward the cook, a kind employer, with the earldom of Cornwall (2897–928).

[21] 'As if it were a sunbeam'. See also 1248–58 and 2107–14.

(Ubbe said, 'Lord, do not be afraid! It seems to me that I see your thought. Dear son, it is good for me that I see you with my eyes. I offer you fealty, lord. I should be your retainer, since you are descended from Birkabeyn, who had many knights and attendants; and so you shall have, lord. Although you are still a very young man, you shall be king of all Denmark.')

As with Christ, so with Havelok the crucial condition for the recovery or recognition of his correct identity and patrimony is his 'parentage', or birthright; Christ is the son of God, and Havelok is the son of a king. In this kind of story, there are no self-made men. Havelok is aware that his efforts towards recovery are not independent, personally determined victories but rather are contained within a divine will and the fact of his birth. Accordingly, he prays before attempting to regain Denmark:

> '... Louerd, þat al weldes—
> Wind and water, wodes and feldes—
> For þe holi milce of you
> Haue merci of me, Louerd, nou!
> And wreke me yet on mi fo ...'
>
> (1360–4)

('Lord, who rules over all, wind and water, woods and fields, have mercy on me now lord, out of your holy mercy, and let me have revenge against my enemies')

The visitation of an angel to Goldeborw to confirm Havelok's royal identity (1248–82)—like the Annunciation to Mary—adds to the impression that this narrative world, however realistic and comparable to our own location, is fully shaped according to the ideal patterns of providence. Another romance in the Auchinleck MS, *Amis and Amiloun* (late thirteenth-century) is a semi-hagiographical work which incidentally increases understanding of the romance mode seen from a Christian perspective.[22] Here two heavenly voices and miracles add an even stronger sense of God's intervention in human affairs.[23] The Christian paradigm

---

[22] *Amis and Amiloun*, ed. MacEdward Leach, EETS 203 (London, 1937); it survives in four manuscripts. On the hagiographical character of the work and the differing versions, see: ibid., pp. ix–xxxii; Kratins, 'Middle English *Amis and Amiloun*'; Hume, 'Structure and Perspective'.

[23] Leprosy is cured by washing in the blood of two sacrificed children on Christmas day, but the children are afterwards miraculously restored.

allows the human achievement of the romance world, even
though *Amis and Amiloun* does not present an historical aspect
which connects that romance world strongly to a specifically
English or contemporary experience. The collection of both
works in the same manuscript, however, does provide the means
for mutual enhancement.

The emphasis on local and national history, geography, and
society in *Havelok* means that the providential character of its
world supports a strongly patriotic viewpoint. *Havelok* forces the
conclusion that God has offered in the past a special protection to
the English nation—a conclusion which becomes the basis for a
flattering sense of present identity. Even if those events and characters are not recoverable in time, their physical vestiges, we are
constantly reminded, may still be located. The romance treatment
of history as providential encourages contemporary readers to see
themselves as a chosen people, a nation which is favoured in
God's eyes. Because the idealization of historical experience
derives from God's providential care, which is a 'truth' apparently
beyond the text's construction, it can be taken as genuine. *Havelok*, in other words, is 'matter of iust memory', where 'iust' allows
both senses of 'righteous' and 'only'—only what really happened,
the prerequisite to something being truthfully remembered.

(II) *OF ARTHOUR AND OF MERLIN* AND *RICHARD COEUR
DE LION*

Of Arthour and of Merlin (*c.* 1250–1300) and *Richard Coeur de
Lion* (*c.* 1300), both appearing in the Auchinleck MS, are notable
for their representation of native historical material in accordance with the idealizing tendencies of the romance mode, in
particular the sense that the shaped narrative of national experience really derives from God's will.[24] The narrator of *Arthour
and Merlin* impresses on his audience that the work deals with

---

[24] *Of Arthour and of Merlin*, ed. Macrae-Gibson. *Arthour and Merlin* exists in two
versions; the larger version is in the Auchinleck MS and a shorter version is found in
two fifteenth-century manuscripts. British Library MS Harley 6223 is a late sixteenth-
century transcript by John Stowe of the poem's first sixty-two lines; a Renaissance
manuscript copy also exists in the Percy Folio. Wynkyn de Worde printed the work
three times, in 1500, 1510, and 1529. The edition of *Richard Coeur de Lion* is *Richard
Löwenherz*, ed. Brunner. *Richard* survives in seven manuscripts and two early prints.

their roots and consequently bears on their self-understanding. In the text preserved in Lincoln's Inn MS Hale 150, the narrator promises to tell of events that 'Sum whyle byfeol in Engelonde' (9). The intended relevance of this history to its audience emerges in the presentation of Arthur as an English hero, despite the fact that Geoffrey of Monmouth's *Historia regum Britanniae* defined Arthur as a British Celt fighting the Anglo-Saxon, or English, ancestors of the poet and his readers. The narrator apparently understands the British-English distinction: 'Ac Inglond was yhoten þo / Michel Bretyne wiþouten no' (117–18).[25] Nevertheless, this distinction is ignored in the interest of a patriotic empathy with the events. The British become 'our men' (139) and the rulers of 'Inglond' (33), while the Saxons conveniently become Saracens, intensifying the Christian orientation of the work; God's protection of the British/English cause is more credible given the religious nature of the conflict. During the course of a battle, for example, Christ intervenes to give victory to the Christian Britons over the pagan Anglo-Saxons:

> Ac Ihesu Crist on hem þouȝt
> For he ȝaue hem strengþe and miȝt
> Oȝaine þo deuelen forto fiȝt.
>   (7876–8)[26]

(But Jesus Christ thought about them, for he gave them strength and power to fight against those devils.)

Concerning *Arthour and Merlin*, Elizabeth S. Sklar writes:

Comparison of the English romance with its French source reveals that the writer was Englishing by adaptation rather than by translation, an adaptation characterised by a strong nationalistic bias not present in the source, clearly speaking to the interests of the specifically English audience for whom *Arthour and Merlin* was intended.[27]

History, politics, and religion are densely interwoven in a text which is representative of the character of not only the Auchinleck volume but also of much native romance.

---

[25] 'But England was then called Great Britain, to tell the truth'. Citations are to the text of the Auchinleck MS.

[26] On the Norman and English adaptations of the British history for their own causes, see Turville-Petre, *England the Nation*, 81–5, 125–7.

[27] Elizabeth S. Sklar, '*Arthour and Merlin*: The Englishing of Arthur', *Michigan Academician* 8 (1975), 49–57 (49–50).

The challenge which faced the author of *Arthour and Merlin* was not in securing acceptance of the work's historicity, at least broadly conceived; despite the objections raised by Henry of Huntingdon and William of Newburgh, the Arthurian world was regarded in thirteenth-century England as an historical occurrence. The difficulty lay in making this troubled and tumultuous history into a flattering mirror for its English readers. The fact that the writer has to recreate his audience as 'Britons' is an aberration from memory which the audience might submit to in order to derive a favourable sense of national identity; but it is a manipulation which is required to make the history seem providential in relation to its contemporary readers. The conflation of Saxon and Saracens is an ingenious solution since it shows, as in *Horn Childe* or *Richard*, God interacting for the benefit of Christianity. However, the author should be aware that his assertion— that 'Þe Bretouns . . . beþ Inglisse nov' (119)—is a false link in this providential history. The prose *Brut* highlights this fallacy in national genealogy; there, 'fram þe tyme þat Brut come ferst into Engeland, þis land was callede Britaigne, & þe folc Britons, til þe tyme þat þis Gurmond eftesones conquerede hit & gaf it vnto Saxonus, and þai anone riȝt chaunged þe name' (95). The prose *Brut* identifies a change of people in 'þis land', but *Arthour and Merlin* maintains a change of name only in relation to a constant people. The readership of the latter work can identify themselves with the Britons in the text through their shared Christian identity, however that empathy must be at odds with the understanding which writers such as Geoffrey of Monmouth, Bede, and derived vernacular texts gave of English origins. Later in this chapter, and in discussion of Malory and Spenser, Arthurian subject-matter will be considered in more detail from this perspective: although appearing to offer the greatest potential for a history-becoming-romance, it also presents severe difficulties which impede that transformation.

Richard Coeur de Lion is a less problematic adaptation of history to the romance mode. The subject is historical—Richard I and the Third Crusade—and the narrator emphasizes the relevance of his subject-matter, 'Off douȝty knyȝtes off Yngelonde' (28), for 'Lewede men [who] cune Ffrensch non' (23). Historical figures such as William Longespee, earl of Salisbury, Thomas de Multon, and Fulke Doilly appear in the text, and the narrator

comments that it is pleasing 'to han in memorie' the life of
Richard, who is catalogued with the chief heroes of romance.[28]
Because the saracens really are pagan and foreign, contemporary
readers could have accepted easily the vision of providence interacting to control the events of the crusade. Despite the work's
crude definition of Christian values (Richard acquires a taste for
cooked Saracen, a sustenance more man than manna), *Richard*
delivers an objectively derived sense of England as a favoured
nation, similar to *Horn Childe*. For example, St George, England's saint,[29] appears in response to Richard's prayer to aid the
Christians in their battle against the pagans:

> Kyng Richard was almoost ateynt,[a]
> And *i*n þe pouder[b] ny3 adreynt.[c]
> On hys knees he gan dou*n* ffalle,
> Help! to J*hes*u he gan calle,
> Ffor loue off his modyr Mary;
> And as j ffynde i*n* his story,
> He sey3[d] come Seynt George þe kny3t,
> Vpon a stede *good* and ly3t,
> In armes whyte as þe fflour
> Wiþ a croys off red colour.
> Al þat he mette i*n* þat stou*n*de,
> Hors and man he felde to grounde.
>
>   (4883–94)[30]

    [a] 'exhausted';   [b] 'dust';   [c] 'drowned';   [d] 'saw'.

(III) SIR BEVIS OF HAMPTON AND GUY OF WARWICK

Two main themes have emerged thus far, and in some works they
are tightly connected. One is the self-understanding at a societal

[28] From the text of the Auchinleck MS (designated L in Brunner's sigla), printed in
the note to 1 of the main text.

[29] St George's position as patron saint was not officially endorsed until later,
probably at the time of Edward III's foundation of the Order of the Garter (*c*. 1347).
However, St George may have had a particularly English or national association
before that date, as this and other uses suggest.

[30] Richard is also associated with St George by his destruction of pagan idols
(6259–90). For St George as an iconoclast, see his legend in Jacobus de Voragine,
Legenda aurea, ed. T. Graesse, 2nd edn. (Leipzig, 1850), 263. Bevis of Hampton, who
invokes St George during a dragon-fight in the text of the Auchinleck MS (A-text,
2817) also casts down pagan idols (A-text, 1353–6, and augmented in later versions,
V-text, 1161–70 and CUL MS Ff.2.38, note to A- text, 1353).

level which derives from providential historiography and narrative. The other is the identity which a displaced hero acquires as
he regains his patrimony; the sense that he earns that reward
is offset both by the importance of his birth and by providence's
assisting the hero in order to achieve its larger aims in relation to
the whole society. These themes are prominent in the two
romances which are the centre pieces of the Auchinleck MS
collection and central to the native romance tradition as a
whole, *Bevis of Hampton* and *Guy of Warwick* (both *c.* 1300).[31]
These romances are not only the 'matter of iust memory' in terms
of their intertextual relationships to other native romances and to
each other; they are also memorial through their shared pretension to historicity. Both Bevis and Guy were regarded as historical
figures in the Middle Ages, and there was an abundance of
monuments, or things 'still there', which attested to the reality
of their lives. Bevis' associations were with Southampton and
Arundel Castle, reputedly built by him and named to commemorate his eponymous horse.[32] The adoption of Guy as their
legendary ancestor by the Beauchamp family, holders of the earldom of Warwick, led to the creation of relics and sites which
associated Guy's 'descendants' with the romanticized world of
Guy himself.[33] In the 1270s, William Beauchamp, earl of

[31] Derek Pearsall suggests that *Guy of Warwick* may have been intended as the item
of focal interest in the Auchinleck MS; *Auchinleck MS*, intr. Pearsall and Cunningham,
pp. vii–xi. Other items in the manuscript, such as *Amis and Amiloun, Bevis*, the
Chronicle (item 40), and the *Speculum Gy de Warewyke* all relate to *Guy* in various
ways and suggest a degree of organization to produce a collection of texts with a
principal, though not exclusive, interest in the figure of Guy of Warwick.
[32] A figure of Bevis used to exist on the Bar Gate at Southampton: Jennifer Fellows,
'Sir Bevis of Hampton in Popular Tradition', *PHFCAS* 42 (1986), 139–45; Adrian B.
Rance, 'The Bevis and Ascupart Panels, Bargate Museum, Southampton', *PHFCAS* 42
(1986), 147–53.
[33] On the Beauchamps' extensive use of Guy of Warwick as a dynastic history, see
William Dugdale, *Antiquities of Warwickshire* (London, 1656), 297–339 (esp. 314);
*Pageant of the Birth, Life, and Death of Richard Beauchamp Earl of Warwick K. G.
1389–1439*, ed. Viscount Dillon and W. H. St John Hope (London, 1914), 36; *The
Beauchamp Cartulary*, ed. Emma Mason (Lincoln, 1980), esp. p. xxiv; John Rous, *The
Rous Roll*, ed. Charles Ross (Gloucester, 1980), item 21. See further: Ronald S. Crane,
'The Vogue of *Guy of Warwick* from the Close of the Middle Ages to the Romantic
Revival', *PMLA* 30 (1915), 125–94; Susan Crane, 'Anglo-Norman Romances of
English Heroes: Ancestral Romance', *Renaissance Papers* (1981–2), 601–8; Emma
Mason, 'Legends of the Beauchamps' Ancestors: The Use of Baronial Propaganda in
Medieval England', *JMH* 10 (1984), 25–40; S. Crane, *Sinful Knights*, 85, 197; Fewster,
Traditionality and Genre, 104–22; Richmond, *Legend of Guy of Warwick*, 107–62.

Warwick, named his son and heir Guy.[34] Thomas, earl of Warwick from 1369–1401, built a structure called 'Guy's Tower' at Warwick Castle. A chapel, furthermore, founded at 'Guy's Cliffe' contains an eight foot statue of the legendary ancestor,[35] and Guy's armour is still on display in Warwick Castle. The romances considered thus far are important for establishing the concerns of the tradition, but *Bevis* and *Guy* are especially important because they are two romances which Spenser knew and drew upon, the most popular of the native verse romances in the later sixteenth century.

The story of *Bevis* recalls *Horn* and *Havelok*.[36] Bevis' father, earl of Southampton, is murdered by Bevis' mother and her lover, and the seven-year old Bevis is driven into exile. In Armenia, Josian, the daughter of a pagan king, falls in love with Bevis. He agrees to marry her if she will become Christian, which she promises to do, and they plight themselves to each other. Bevis is imprisoned, however, when a jealous courtier, reminiscent of Fikenhild in *Horn*, slanders him, and Josian is forced to marry a pagan king. Bevis eventually escapes from prison and rescues Josian (she has preserved her virginity in marriage through magic). Josian is baptized, and Bevis accomplishes numerous heroic and chivalric deeds, such as slaying a dragon and fighting pagans. He and Josian return to England together, and, interwoven with more adventures including the separation and reunion of Bevis and Josian again, Bevis avenges his father and regains, with Josian, his patrimony. They end their lives as King and Queen of Mombraunt in the Middle East.

Like *Horn* or *Havelok, Bevis* represents the hero's overcoming of exile as a providentially guided achievement which benefits both the individual, who must regain his 'eritage' (A-text, 3502;

---

[34] Fewster, *Traditionality and Genre*, 107.
[35] For a picture of the statue and chapel, see Nikolaus Pevsner and Alexandra Wedgwood, *The Buildings of England: Warwickshire* (Harmondsworth, 1966), pl. 11a.
[36] The edition cited is *Bevis*, ed. Kölbing. Unless otherwise specified, citations will be from Kölbing's A-text, the upper of the two texts in his parallel edition, based on the Auchinleck MS. This early text is the basis of the present discussion in order to focus interest on the development of the tradition as well as the intertextuality of the romances in the Auchinleck MS. *Bevis* survives in seven manuscripts, and it was printed at least seven times in the sixteenth century, with continued printing in the seventeenth century.

cf. 2940, 3001–2), and a larger community, who are the unfortunate subjects of an illegitimate rule. But in comparison to *Guy of
Warwick*, the main emphasis in *Bevis* is on the first of these
outcomes, and *Bevis* explores in engaging detail the effect
which exile has on the hero and the sources of his recovery.
Havelok placed greater emphasis than *Horn* on the displacement
of the hero in exile, in particular his need to do manual labour.
Bevis is even further removed from his proper station; he stays
within the social environment of a court, but his service is to a
pagan king. The tension resides in the interplay between the
innate nobility and Christianity of the hero, conferred by birth
and baptism and represented as indelibly in his blood, and the
detrimental effects of exile in relation to his development. There
is, furthermore, an intriguing tension in relation to the causes of
Bevis' eventual recovery: his martial and heroic feats need to be
set against an awareness of what birth has given him and how too
providence supports and enables 'his' victories. Bevis' regaining
of his patrimony must begin with his recognition of the most
important aspect of his identity—his Christianity. When King
Ermin offers Bevis his kingdom and daughter if he will convert
to Islam, Bevis replies:

> 'For gode!' queþ Beues, 'þat i nolde
> For al þe seluer ne al þe golde,
> Þat is vnder heuene liȝt,
> Ne for þe douȝter, þat is so briȝt:
> I nolde for-sake in none manere
> Iesu, þat bouȝte me so dere:
> Al mote þai be doum and deue,
> Þat on þe false godes be-leue!'
>   (A-text, 561–8)

('For God,' said Bevis, 'I will not do that for all the gold and silver that is
under the light of heaven, nor for your daughter, who is so radiant. I will
not forsake in any way Jesus, who ransomed me so dearly. All those who
believe in false gods ought to be cursed!')

More so than *Horn* and *Havelok*, *Bevis* emphasizes that exile has
left the hero ignorant of the basic knowledge which he would
possess had he received his intended upbringing. On Christmas
day in Armenia, some pagan knights ask the fifteen-year old Bevis
if he understands the significance of the day:

Beues seide: 'For soþ y-wis,
I no*t* neuer, what dai it is,
For i nas boute seue winter old,
Fro Cristendome ich was i-sold;
Þar fore i ne can telle nouȝt þe,
What dai þat hit miȝte be.'

(A-text, 593–8)

(Bevis said, 'Truly, I do not know what day it is. I was only seven years old when I was sold out of Christendom; therefore I cannot tell you what day it might be.')

Overcoming exile will require an act of memory: Bevis must recollect, in all possible senses of the word, his social and personal identity. Innate tendencies have been weakened by ignorance, and nature and nurture are at odds.

Bevis requires divine assistance if he is to remember or recover his 'eritage' and rightful place. In fact, what he needs to remember, or develop, is his inkling sense of the significance of the Christian faith and his dependence upon God. That pious theme is evident, for example, when Bevis is imprisoned in Damascus during the time of Josian's enforced marriage. The elapsement of time is the potential pinprick of the romance mode, but providence is a force which, by its nature, foresees and orders the occurrence of events into a just sequence. Bevis' prayer to the 'Schepere of erþe & alle þing' (A-text, 1580) for deliverance from prison is answered by a miracle:

So ȝerne he gan to Iesu speke,
Þat his vetres gonne breke
And of is medel þe grete ston.
Iesu Crist he þankede anon;
A wente quik out of prisoun.

(A-text, 1647–51)

(He spoke to Jesus so earnestly that his fetters broke and the great stone fell from his waist. At once he thanked Jesus Christ and went lively from the prison.)

As in *Havelok*, the miraculous exists in the context of the familiar. In a scene which appears to be the work of the English redactor, a fight between Bevis and his enemies in London is described with accurate topography: Putney (4290), Westminster (4295), the

City of London (4317), Cheapside (4328), God's Lane (4397), and Ludgate (4492).[37] The appeal of the work resides precisely in its location of the heroic and even the providential within the grasp of its readers. In *Guy of Warwick*, the sense of God's providential care for England is even stronger.

Guy of Warwick is bipartite in structure, and although the two parts might be characterized in loose terms as chivalric and hagiographical respectively, they are in fact strongly connected, like two panels of a diptych which only achieve their full significance through their juxtaposition.[38] In the first part of the romance, Guy, who is the son of a steward, loves Felice, the daughter of the earl of Warwick, but she initially rejects him because of his social inferiority. Consequently Guy journeys abroad in order to earn his knighthood through brave deeds and thereby win Felice. After proving his chivalric worth in many adventures, he returns to England and marries Felice. In the second part of the romance, Guy realizes that his blinkered pursuit of Felice's love has caused him to neglect the debt of love which he owes to God. He leaves his wife and sets out as a pilgrim. As before, he has adventures, but the emphasis is now on the Christian causes which underpin these battles.[39] Guy

[37] References are to the A-text. The three major passages in *Bevis* which are not found in the Anglo-Norman *Boeve de Haumtone*—the boar-fight, the dragon-fight, and the battle in the streets of London—are examined in Judith Weiss, 'The Major Interpolations in *Sir Beues of Hamtoun*', *MÆ* 48 (1979), 71–6.

[38] The main editions are *The Romance of Guy of Warwick*, ed. Julius Zupitza, EETS ES 42, 49, 59 (London, 1883, 1887, 1891), a parallel edition of the texts of the Auchinleck and the Caius MSS; and *Guy: The Second or 15th- Century Version*, ed. Zupitza. The Middle English *Guy* exists in three versions. The Auchinleck MS represents a distinct version, with its unique treatment of the material relating to Reinbroun, Guy's son, and its stanzaic form for the second half. An early couplet version is preserved in two manuscripts, and this second version of the poem is represented by the text based on the Caius MS in *Guy*, ed. Zupitza (1883, 1887, 1891). A third version of *Guy* is a late medieval couplet-version, surviving in one manuscript and one fragment; this is the text of *Guy: The 15–Century Version*, ed. Zupitza. The printed editions of *Guy*, based on the latter textual tradition, involve a history of continuous small-scale revision and adjustment. For the same reasons given above in relation to *Bevis*, at this stage I am quoting from the text based on the Auchinleck MS.

[39] The text of *Guy* in the Auchinleck presents a heightened sense of God's providence acting to support the lives of Guy and the English nation. For example, when Berard treacherously has Guy cast to sea in his bed (!), Guy prays to Jesus for deliverance (st. 197). The redactor of the Auchinleck MS specifies that Jesus sends the fisherman who saves Guy (st. 198). In the Anglo-Norman *Gui de Warwic* (*Gui de Warewic*, ed. Alfred Ewert (Paris, 1932, 1933), 10255–7), the Middle English text of

finally returns to England, disguised as a palmer, and saves England from an invading Danish army by defeating its champion. On his deathbed, Guy sends for Felice. After a brief reunion, he dies, and his soul is carried aloft by angels.[40]

Guy of Warwick offers two kinds of romance: one (the first of its kind in this study) in which the heroic idealization of experience is pure fantasy, and another, in the second part, in which the knight's extraordinary abilities derive from providence, a support which the knight earns through his extreme piety. Unlike the orphans Horn, Havelok, and Bevis, Guy in the first part is a self-made man. But significantly, he rejects his own achievements as vainglorious at the start of the romance's second part. The dramatic force of his almost Pauline conversion means that Guy's experiences represent, more intensely than the other texts considered thus far, an Augustinian belief in the effectiveness of providence. The 'prologue' to *The South English Legendary*, a thirteenth-century hagiographical compilation, indirectly summarizes the shift in *Guy* from romance as secular wish-fulfilment to romance as pious and didactic narrative:

> Men wilneþ muche to hure telle · of bataille of kynge
> And of kniʒtes þat hardy were · þat muchedel is lesynge
> Wo so wilneþ muche to hure · tales of suche þinge
> Hardi batailles he may hure · here þat nis no lesinge
> Of apostles & martirs · þat hardy kniʒtes were
> Þat studeuast were in bataille · & ne fleide noʒt for fere.
> (3.59–64)

(People wish very much to hear of the battles of kings and of knights who were brave—that is all lies. Whoever wants greatly to hear tales of such things, he may hear of brave battles that are not lies—of apostles and martyrs who were brave knights, steadfast in battle, and who did not flee for fear.)

Caius MS 107 (9806–8), and the text of CUL ff.2.38 (9495–6; fifteenth-century version), the fisherman appears by chance, without divine instigation.

[40] A subplot in *Guy* is the Telemachus-like wanderings of Guy's son, Reinbroun, after Guy has set out on his pilgrimage. In the Auchinleck MS, the layout and colophons clearly define the story of Reinbroun as a separate romance. *Guy* ends with the colophon 'Explicit' (f. 167.r) and a title, 'Reinbrun. gij sone of Warwike', announces a new text. The layout of the manuscript, with a *littera notabilior* of 6–lines in height, spacing, and a miniature all between the end of *Guy* and the start of 'Reinbrun', also enforces the sense of two separate items in the manuscript. *Auchinleck*, intro. Pearsall and Cunningham . In Caius College MS 107, the Reinbroun-episode is interlaced with the main story.

The hagiographer's description of saints in chivalric terms is matched by the second part of *Guy*, where Guy is both a knight and a quasi-saint. Just as the author of the *Legendary* here transfers the accoutrements of chivalry to the saints, so the *Guy*-poet uses the same linguistic palette in the first and second parts, allowing the different contexts to signal a series of radical semantic shifts. In the first part, for example, Guy says to Felice:

> 'Wiþouten þe haue y no blis;
> Y loue þe and tow nouȝt me,
> Y dye for loue of þe.
> Bot þou haue merci on me,
> For sorwe ichil me self sle.'
> (366–70)

('I have no happiness without you. I love you, and you do not love me. I die for love of you. Unless you have mercy upon me, I will kill myself for sorrow.')

The context is secular, though the lover has daringly appropriated the language of religious love: unless Felice extends her 'grace', Guy cannot be 'saved'. In the second part of *Guy*, however, human love is an impediment to divine love; or, at best, secular love is a transitory stage through which one passes on to divine love. As Guy prepares to leave Felice, he tells her how God's grace will save the faithful lover:

> ¶ 'Bot god is curteys & hende,
> & so dere he haþ bouȝt mankende,
> For noþing wil hem lete.
> For his loue ichil now wende
> Barfot to mi liues ende,
> Mine sinnes for to bete.'
> (st. 26.1–6)

('But God is courteous and graceful. So dearly has he ransomed mankind that nothing will hinder him. I will now travel barefoot for his love until the end of life, to remedy my sins.')

'Curteys' and 'hende' are more typically found in secular contexts; their placement here, describing the nature of God's love, enforces both the connections and the fundamental differences between mundane and spiritual values. *Guy of Warwick* reflects the Boethian doctrine that secular values and patterns of behaviour, such as love, can only be an imperfect imitation of their true, divine originals. Another scene which exploits the ambiguity of language to indicate the need for a redefinition of secular values, such as chivalry and feudalism, in terms of their spiritual archetypes occurs when Guy undertakes to fight a giant for King Triamour.[41] Triamour assumes from Guy's ragged clothes that either he serves an impecunious lord or else he has fallen out of favour. Guy responds:

> ¶ 'Nay, sir, for god, . . .
> A wel gode lord [ar] þan serue[d] y:
>   Wiþ him was no blame.
> Wel michel honour he me dede,
> & gret worþschipe in eueri stede,
> & sore ich haue him grame[d],
> & þer-fore icham þus y-diȝt,
> To cri him merci day & niȝt,
>   Til we ben frendes same.'
>   (st. 85.1–9)

('No sir, for God . . . I served a very good lord then; there was nothing wrong with him. He did me great honour and worship in every place. I have sorely angered him. For that reason, I am dressed thus, in order to beg his mercy day and night until we be friends.')

Of course the 'lord' whom Guy intends is God, though Triamour does not grasp his meaning. The danger of language being misunderstood is a repercussion of the Fall, and in this scene Guy attempts to restore language to its true meaning from a Christian perspective. Taken out of context, E. K.'s words could be applied here to Guy's spiritualization of language in the second part: 'he hath laboured to restore, as to theyr rightfull heritage such good and naturall English words, as have ben long time out of use and almost cleare disherited'. Comparable to the opening lines of the *Legendary* and the second part of *Guy*, Book I of *The Faerie Queene* will involve the redefinition of romance language and narrative structures according to a Christian, though specifically Protestant, perspective.

One other aspect of the tremendously influential and popular *Guy of Warwick* requires consideration, and it connects the work

---

[41] This episode is prior to the similar, climatic scene, discussed below, in which Guy is the champion of the English king against a giant from the invading Danish army.

strongly to others already examined. As said, *Guy* examines a
crossing over from secular to divine values, and the place where
this crossing over most effectively occurs in the narrative is in
England. The spirituality of *Guy* does not involve a total sense of
contemptus mundi—or at least not *contemptus Britanniae*. The
climactic scene of the romance is Guy's battle against the pagan
giant Colbrond, champion of the invading Danish army, outside
Winchester, and in that battle God intervenes extraordinarily to
support the Christian and English cause. Through 'grace of godes
sond', an angel is sent to the English 'king Aþel-ston' by 'king
Iesu' (st. 243.3–6); the direct repetition here of 'king' suggests,
like Guy's earlier use of language, a hierarchical relationship
between the secular and the divine. The angel directs Athelston
to enlist Guy as his champion, and Athelston consequently
appeals to Guy on the basis of both religion and 'þe riȝt of
Inglond' (st. 246.11). Guy echoes Athelston when he connects
God's purpose with the welfare of England:

> ¶ Sir Gij tok vp þe king anon,
> & bad þe lordinges euerichon
> Þat þai schuld vp stond,
> & seyd, 'for god in trinite
> & for to make Inglond fre,
> Þe batayle y nim on hond.'
> (st. 248.1–6)

(Sir Guy answered the king at once and asked the lords that they should
stand; he said, 'For God in Trinity and in order to make England free, I
undertake the battle.')

Before the battle, Guy prays to the Virgin Mary to 'saue Inglondes
riȝt' (st. 252.11). And when after defeating Colbrond Guy dies, a
field somewhere outside Winchester becomes momentarily an
epiphanic passage to the divine:

> His soule fram þe bodi gan fare.
> A þousand angels & seuen
> Vnder-fenge þe soule of Gij,
> & bar it wiþ gret molodi
> Into þe blis of heuen.
> (st. 293.8–12)[42]

[42] A direct ascension to heaven is a feature of hagiography which indicates that the
virtuous soul has been dispensed from purgatory. See 'St Quentin', in *South English*

(His soul went from his body. A thousand and seven angels took the soul of Guy and bore it with great music into the joy of heaven.)

The Christian bias of Guy's victory does not exclude the importance of 'England the nation', in Turville-Petre's phrase—just as God's providence acts in the Old Testament in favour of Israel. When Guy is fighting a different pagan giant in an earlier scene, he identifies himself initially with the stark phrase—'Cristen icham'—and then adds 'Of Inglond born' (st. 110.5–6).[43] Like Israel, England is constructed in this romance as a nation uniquely favoured by God, and the location of its narrative in a recognizable and accessible landscape urges contemporary readers to sense their own proximity, as English Christians, to the divine. John Hardyng's incorporation of Guy's fight against Colbrond into his *Chronicle* reflects the historical credit given to a story in which providence and Englishness are interwoven.[44]

(IV) HISTORY, ROMANCE, AND NATIONAL IDENTITY: ARTHUR

When the composers of Middle English romances indicate, either demonstratively or allusively, things or places which feature in the narrative world of the text and which 'may yet be seen', they reveal the generic shading of romance into historical writings and hagiography. Geoffrey of Monmouth's *Historia regum Britanniae* (c. 1135), replete with eponyms and accounts of origins, exercised a profound influence on the development of this concern in the romances. Saints' lives too are deeply concerned with

---

Legendary, 460.121–7. Guy's death is also saintly in the detail of his corpse giving forth a sweet smell (st. 294.8–12). In the version of Caius MS 107 (10960–7) and the fifteenth-century version (10684–96), the sweet smell cures the sick—a token of special sanctity. For 'All Souls', the author of *The South English Legendary* says that there are three categories of souls which go directly to heaven: infants who die straight after baptism, martyrs who die for the love of God, and 'clene men · þat er hi hunne wende / Alle here sinnes beteþ her' (472.268–73). Guy belongs in the third category. The relationship of Guy to a specific saint, St Alexius, is explored in Klausner 'Didacticism and Drama in *Guy*'.

[43] Cf. 'St George' in *South English Legendary*, 156.23: 'Gorge ich hatte quaþ þis oþer · Cristen man ich am.'

[44] Hardyng even echoes the patriotic motives of the romance—Guy 'The battaill toke on hym for Englandis right'; *The Chronicle of John Hardyng*, ed. Henry Ellis (London, 1812), 211.

the vestiges left by their events; satisfying more than just historical interest, the things which are 'still there' in hagiography are frequently relics or at least a witness to God's grace manifested on earth. The emphasis of *The South English Legendary* on English saints makes its relevance to the 'historical' romances strong.[45] Just as in *Horn Childe* the carnage of battle may still be seen, so too the life of St Oswald has left tangible monuments in Winchester:

> ¶ Angles bere is soule forþ · to þe ioie of heuene heiȝe
> Louerd wat deol þe monekes made · þo hi þen deþ seie
> Hy nome & burede him at Wircetre · heilich atte fine
> Þer is bones liggeþ ȝut · noblich in fair ssryne.
> (78.217–21)

(Angels bore his soul forth to the joy of high heaven. Lord, what grief the monks showed when they saw his death. They buried him at Winchester, high up at the end. His bones lie there still, nobly in a beautiful shrine.)

Another example, from the life of St Edmund the King, describes his burial at Bury St Edmunds:

> Hi ladde him to seint Edmundesbury · as me clepeþ þane toun
> Þis holi man al isound · & leide him þeradoun
> In noble schryne hi him brouȝte · as riȝt was to do
> Þer he lyþ al hol & sound · as hi seoþ þat comeþ him to.
> (514.89–92)[46]

(They led him to Bury St Edmunds, as people call that town. They laid this holy man down there. They put him in a noble grave, as was fitting. He lies there all whole and sound, as the people who come to him see.)

Eamon Duffy's interpretation of the medieval experience of pilgrimage is not dissimilar to the rhetorical effect aimed at in romances, when these texts indicate surviving vestiges:

---

[45] It is interesting to note a piece of manuscript-evidence suggesting the compatibility of *The South English Legendary* with two romances treating 'historical' English heroes, *Horn* and *Havelok*. Bodleian Library MS Laud Misc. 108 is a compilation of two originally separate parts bound together in the fifteenth century. Part I (late thirteenth- or early fourteenth-century) is chiefly a text of the *Legendary*. Part II contains texts of *Havelok* and *Horn* (late thirteenth- or early-fourteenth century) followed by more saints' lives added in the fifteenth century, at the time of compilation. For a description of the manuscript see Guddat-Figge, *Catalogue*.

[46] Other instances in the *Legendary* of this topos, where something is produced which is 'still there' or 'yet may be seen', are: 112.79–80; 114.143–4; 116.204; 118.249–50; 279.5; 289.293–8; 290.331–2; 291.359–60; 358.40; 497.137–44; 610.519–20.

The primary purpose of pilgrimage had always been to seek the holy, concretely embodied in a sacred place, a relic, or a specially privileged image...the practice of pilgrimage, travel to seek the sacred outside one's immediate locality, had important symbolic and integrative functions, helping the believer to place the religious routine of the closed and concentric worlds of household, parish, or gild in a broader and more complex perception of the sacred, which transcended while affirming local allegiances.[47]

The *Havelok*-poet's description of Lincoln did not offer contemporary readers 'the holy, concretely embodied in a sacred place', but it did offer them the basis for understanding and believing in a heroic story in which providence was openly manifested through miracles. It also, presumably, presented (Lincolnshire) readers with a new way of thinking about their own world—as Duffy writes, 'affirming local allegiances'. As a relatively modern analogy, Baker Street in London has never been the same since Conan Doyle created Sherlock Holmes—at least not to those who have read the stories. A similar enrichment of place appears to be happening in most of the native romances we have discussed so far. *Athelstan* (*c.* 1355–80), a work which straddles romance, history, and hagiography, also illustrates this point. The poem's account of the miraculous and providential birth of St Edmund occurs among highly detailed and accurate topographical references, relating to London and the pilgrimage route from London to Canterbury.[48] The treatment of romance as localized, providential history, in which references to 'relics' and signs create an identity for a region or the nation, occurs most notably in the figure of Arthur and through his association with Glastonbury.

Glastonbury was identified with Avalon, the place where Arthur was taken to be healed, when or possibly just before the Glastonbury monks exhumed the bones of Arthur and Guinevere in the abbey grounds in 1191.[49] Glastonbury Abbey had suffered

---

[47] Eamon Duffy, *The Stripping of the Altars* (New Haven and London, 1992), 191.

[48] *Athelstan*, ed. A. McI. Trounce, EETS 224 (London, 1951), 335–56.

[49] On the Glastonbury legends, a selective bibliography is: J. Armitage Robinson, *Two Glastonbury Legends* (Cambridge, 1926); Reginald F. Treharne, *The Glastonbury Legends* (London, 1967); Antonia Gransden, 'The Growth of the Glastonbury Traditions and Legends in the Twelfth Century', *Journal of Ecclesiastical History* 27 (1976), 337–58; Lesley Abrams and James P. Carley (eds), *The Archaeology and History of Glastonbury Abbey* (Woodbridge, 1991). The primary documents for a study of the history of Glastonbury abbey and the growth of its legends are: William of

a disastrous fire in 1184, and the timely location of the Arthurian remains was (to a modern perspective) part of a well conceived promotional scheme which gave the abbey renewed status and revenue from pilgrimage.[50] The fame of Arthur's tomb in the abbey quickly spread, and as a result several Middle English Arthurian texts treating the king's ending identify Avalon as Glastonbury and indicate that Arthur's tomb is 'still there' for us to see. In contrast to the instances of the topos already discussed, the abiding evidence of Arthur's tomb raises conceptual difficulties appropriate to the complexity of Arthur himself. The tomb may indeed prove the historicity of Arthur, but in doing so it is a monument to his tragic death and the destruction of his kingdom through internecine strife. In other words, Arthur's tomb can only with severe difficulty be seen as a 'way in' to a providential sense of nationhood. Arthur can, on the other hand, be understood as a providential figure if Avalon is the Celtic 'fortunate isle' where he will be healed and whence he will return to free the Britons from Anglo-Saxon rule.[51] But in that tradition,

---

Malmesbury, *The Early History of Glastonbury*, ed. and trans. John Scott (Woodbridge, 1981); Adam of Domerham, *Historia de rebus gestis Glastoniensibus*, ed. T. Hearne, 2 vols. (Oxford, 1727); John of Glastonbury, *The Chronicle of Glastonbury Abbey*, ed. James P. Carley and tr. David Townsend (Woodbridge, 1985); Caradoc of Llancarvan, *Life of Gildas*, ed. Hugh Williams, 2 vols. (London, 1899–1901), II.395–413; [Gerald of Wales], *Giraldi Cambrensis Opera*, ed. J. S. Brewer, J. F. Dimock, and George F. Warner, RS 21, 8 vols. (London, 1861–91). Geoffrey of Monmouth, who does not identify Avalon with Glastonbury, writes that Arthur was 'mortally' (letaliter) wounded and 'carried to the Isle of Avalon so that his wound might be healed' (ad sananda uulnera sua in insulam Auallonis euectus [est]); *The Historia regum Britannie of Geoffrey of Monmouth*, ed. Neil Wright (Cambridge, 1985), 132.

[50] R. W. Southern, 'Aspects of the European Tradition of Historical Writing: 4, The Sense of the Past', *TRHS* 5th ser. 23 (1973), 243–63; Antonia Gransden, 'Propaganda and English Medieval Historiography', *JMH* 1 (1975), 363–82. The earliest record of the identification of Glastonbury with Avalon is Gerald of Wales' *De principis instructione* (*Opera*, VIII.128). The association was strengthened by a thirteenth-century interpolation in William of Malmesbury's *De antiquitate ecclesie Glastonie*, ch. 4. Gerald of Wales also gives accounts of the exhumation of Arthur and Guinevere in the *Speculum ecclesiae* (*Opera*, IV.47–51) and *De principis instructione* (*Opera*, VIII.127–9). That the exhumation became quickly and widely famous is suggested by the evidence of the Old French prose romance *Perlesvaus* (early thirteenth-century) where the description of Avalon corresponds in close detail to the actual topography of Glastonbury, in particular the famous Tor; see further W. A. Nitze, 'The Exhumation of King Arthur at Glastonbury', *Speculum* 9 (1934), 355–61.

[51] In his *Vita Merlini*, Geoffrey describes Avalon as a golden world; Geoffrey of Monmouth, *Life of Merlin*, ed. and tr. Basil Clarke (Cardiff, 1973), 908–40. Wace's *Roman de Brut* (c. 1155) makes cautious mention of 'Bretun' belief in Arthur's

which Gerald of Wales attributes to 'myth-making' (fabulosi) Britons who expect his second coming 'like the Messiah of the Jews' (sicut judaei Messiam),[52] Avalon cannot be Glastonbury, and the tomb must be empty—so we have lost our evidence for the historical reality of Arthur. Henry II understood this dilemma and sought to use it to his political advantage; Gerald of Wales notes that the king instigated the search for Arthur's tomb in order to silence Celtic expectation of his return.[53] Arthur's historical identity resides in his death, and his romance identity resides in his disappearance and the promise of his return. In the first, he submits to the process of time, and in the second he is able to defeat that process. Arthur is *rex quondam rexque futurus*, where *quondam* reflects the mode of history and *futurus* of romance. What is difficult here is the -*que*; a reconciliation of Arthur's historicity and his coming again seems impossible. Rather than offering a way back through time, here the thing which is 'still there'—Arthur's corrupted body—records the victory of time itself. Examining the treatment of Arthur's ending in some key Middle English texts will help to build a set of concerns which is central not only to these texts but also relevant to Malory's and Spenser's reception of the Arthurian tradition.

In *Arthur* (*c.* 1350–1400) and the alliterative *Morte Arthure* (*c.* 1400), the localization of the events in familiar Glastonbury allows for Arthur's historicity, even as it removes the hope for his Messianic return.[54] In *Arthur*, the narrator informs that:

> At Glastyngbury on þe qweer
> Þey made Artourez toumbe þere,

survival in Avalon and the anticipation of his return; Wace, *Le Roman de Brut*, ed. Ivor Arnold, SATF, 2 vols. (Paris, 1938, 1940), 13275–98. Laȝamon's *Brut* (*c.* 1200) amplifies Wace's account, giving it rhetorical force through the insertion of Arthur's final speech (Caligula MS, 14266–87, 14290–7). See further: Roger Sherman Loomis, 'The Legend of Arthur's Survival', in *Arthurian Literature in the Middle Ages*, ed. Roger Sherman Loomis (Oxford, 1959), pp. 64–71; Constance Bullock-Davies, '"*Exspectare Arturum*": Arthur and the Messianic Hope', *Bulletin of the Board of Celtic Studies* 29 (1982), 432–40.

[52] *Opera*, IV.49.

[53] *Opera*, VIII.128. This incident also enforces what *should* be the difficulty of Arthur as a national hero for English readers.

[54] *Arthur*, ed. Frederick J. Furnivall, EETS 2 (London, 1864); *Morte Arthure*, ed. Edmund Brock, EETS 8 (London, 1871). Both works survive in single manuscripts.

And wrote wyth latyn vers þus,
Hic iacet Arthurus rex quonda*m* rex que futur*us*.

(621–4)

(They made Arthur's tomb at Glastonbury in the quire, and they wrote thereon with Latin verse thus: 'Here lies Arthur, the once and future king'.)

Although the 'Bretou*n*s & Cornysch' are said to believe that Arthur will return (618–20), the narrator does not endorse the view. The alliterative *Morte Arthure* gives an even stronger sense of the finality of Arthur's death at Glastonbury, dwelling with fatal detail on the nature of the king's wounds:

A surgyne of Salerne enserches his wondes,
The kyng sees be asaye *th*at sownde bese he neu*er*...
He saide *In manus* with mayne one molde whare he ligges,
And thus passes his speryt, and spekes he no more!
The baronage of Bretayne thane, bechopes and othire,
Graythes theme to Glaschenbery w*ith* gloppynnande hertes,
To bery thare the bolde kynge, and bryn*g*e to *th*e erthe,
With all*e* wirchipe and welthe *th*at any wy scholde.

(4324–31)

(A surgeon from Salerno examined his wounds. The king realised from this examination that he would never be sound. He said, 'Into [your] hands', with power on earth, where he lay; thus his spirit fled, and he spoke no more. Then the barony, bishops, and others of Britain hastened to Glastonbury with terrified hearts, to bury the bold king there, to put him in the earth with all the honour and expense that was possible.)

The monks of Glastonbury were able to present history as providential in relation to Joseph of Arimathea, the legendary founder of the abbey. *The Lyfe of Ioseph of Armathia* (pr. 1520) says that an image of the Virgin Mary made by Joseph 'is yet at Glastenbury, / In the same churche; there ye may it se'.[55] This writer asserts that 'Sothely Glaste*n*bury is *th*e holyest erth on england'

---

[55] The text is edited in an appendix to *Joseph of Arimathie*, ed. Walter W. Skeat, EETS 44 (London, 1871), pp. 37–49 (212–13). On Joseph of Arimathea and Glastonbury, see further: Valerie M. Lagorio, 'The Evolving Legend of St Joseph of Glastonbury', *Speculum* 46 (1971), 209–31; Valerie M. Lagorio, 'The *Joseph of Arimathie*: English Hagiography in Transition', *MH* n.s. 6 (1975), 91–101; Felicity Riddy, 'Glastonbury, Joseph of Arimathea, and Grail in John Hardyng's *Chronicle*', in Abrams and Carley (eds), *Archaeology and History of Glastonbury*, 317–31.

(369). In contrast, Arthur's death cannot work in the same way because his tomb directly opposes the promised return which is the basis for understanding his life as providentially supported. Romance heroes such as Guy and Bevis certainly die at the end of their texts, but crucially they do not die before saving or regaining their kingdoms and righting all wrongs. For Arthur alone time apparently runs out, so the possibility of his eventual return is needed to relocate him as a romance hero, as one who is providentially or magically able to defeat his enemies.

The stanzaic *Morte Arthur* (*c.* 1400) does present the king in the romance mode through a handling of his ending radically different from that of the alliterative poem.[56] Unlike the geographically specific alliterative *Morte*, the stanzaic poem offers no real sense of where Avalon is. The most which we can gather from Arthur's carefully vague description is that Avalon is a beginning or a continuation rather than an ending:

> 'I wylle wende a lytell stownde
> In-to the vale of Avelovne,
>   A whyle to hele me of my wounde.'
>   (3515–17)

('I will go for a little time into the vale of Avalon to be healed of my wounds.')[57]

A faerie-type ship bears Arthur away. Later, Bedivere comes across a chapel with a new tomb and asks an attendant hermit if he knows who is buried there:

> The ermyte Answeryd swythe yare:
>   'There-of can I tell no more.
> A-bowte mydnyght were ladyes here,
>   In world ne wyste I what they were;
> Thys body they broght uppon a bere
>   And beryed it *with* woundys sore.'
>   (3536–41)

(The hermit quickly answered, 'I cannot tell you any more. About midnight, there were three ladies—I do not know what in the world

---

[56] *Le Morte Arthur*, ed. J. Douglas Bruce, EETS ES 88 (London, 1903). The poem survives in one manuscript.

[57] Almost 400 lines later, we are told that a tomb (which may or may not be Arthur's) is at Glastonbury. But we have no justification on the basis of the poem for believing that this is the same place as the Avalon which Arthur mentions.

they were. They brought this sorely wounded body upon a bier and buried it.')

The sense of absolute finality witnessed in the alliterative poem is here missing. In the stanzaic *Morte Arthur* we do not *see* Arthur die; the hermit cannot tell us that Arthur is in the tomb; though Bedivere gathers from the inscription that it is Arthur's tomb, we are not given the text of the inscription to judge for ourselves. Furthermore, the ladies who stage-manage all this are mysterious figures—'In world ne wyste I what they were'—such as might effect a supernatural outcome. By contrast, in the final part of the thirteenth-century French Vulgate Cycle of Arthurian romance, *La mort le roi Artu*, Girflet discovers a tomb whose inscription— 'Ci gist li rois Artus qui par sa valeur mist en sa subjection .xii. roiaumes'[58]—is both given and unambiguous. Furthermore, the hermit at the tomb explicitly confirms that Arthur lies therein: 'Girflet li demande meintenant: «Sire, est il voirs que ci gist li rois Artus?—Oïl, biax amis, il i gist voirement»' (p. 251.30–2).[59] The stanzaic *Morte Arthur*, however, contains loopholes which could be easily exploited in order to write a sequel in which Arthur did not really die. The stanzaic poem is full of prevarications and deliberate ambiguity, in contrast to the insistent appeals of the historical mode to see with our own eyes what is 'still there'.

Arthur's exhumation at Glastonbury and the interest which writers show in the vestiges of his historicity raise a dilemma for those who seek to use Arthurian materials as providential history and the basis for national identity. Gerald of Wales' account of the discovery of Arthur and Guinevere contains a vivid narrative of a monk eagerly snatching at Guinevere's hair, preserved on her skull, only to have it turn to dust in his hands. Gerald adds that there were 'ten or more' wounds on Arthur's skull.[60] The things which are 'still there' point only to death, decay, and the ruin of time. Drayton's post-Reformation description of the ruins of Glastonbury Abbey emphasizes the reality of a world where, in contrast to its representation in *Havelok*, *Bevis*, *Guy*, and others,

---

[58] *La mort le roi Artu*, edn. Jean Frappier, TLF 58, 3rd edn. (Geneva and Paris, 1964), 251.23–5. ('Here lies King Arthur who, through his worthiness, conquered twelve realms.')

[59] 'Girflet then asked, 'Sir, is it true that King Arthur lies there?' 'Yes, dear friend, he truly lies there.'

[60] *Opera*, VIII.127, 129.

providence does not invariably intervene on the side of the righteous before their time runs out:

> Is there a power in Fate, or doth it yeeld to Time?
> Or was their error, such that thou could'st not protect
> Those buildings which thy hand did with their zeale erect?
> To whom didst thou commit that monument, to keepe,
> That suffreth with the dead their memory to sleepe?
> §. When not great *Arthurs* Tombe, nor holy *Josephs* Grave,
> From sacriledge had power their sacred bones to saue . . .
> (*Poly-Olbion*, III.302–7)

Spenser, translating Joachim du Bellay's *Les Antiquitez de Rome*,
expresses how monuments underscore our temporal separation
from the past rather than offer a chance to sublimate time and
enter a past age. The speaker addresses the 'sacred ruines', 'Olde
moniments', and 'Triumphant Arcks' of Rome:

> And though your frames do for a time make warre
> Gainst time, yet time in time shall ruinate
> Your workes and names, and your last relique marre.
> (*Ruines of Rome* 93–5)

The topos of things 'still there', which needs to be picked up in
relation to Malory and Spenser, is a significant and complex
feature of Middle English romance as a tradition. The vestigial
object may be likened to a memory of the earlier narrative world.
But to say that the greensward at Lincoln is a memory which
exists because Havelok lived requires a willing credulity rather
than a severe logic. Arthur is even more problematic, however,
because the memories which survive concerning him are only
convincing—Arthur's skull, if authentic, really does prove that
he lived—at the cost of belonging to a unprovidential world, a
world in which that kingly skull can receive 'ten or more'
wounds. But before developing this tradition in relation to Malory and Spenser, we need to consider another important group of
Middle English romances, not concerned with a sense of history
but rather highly intertextual in their exploration of a few didactic narrative-patterns and character-types. These popular
romances are also a vital part of the history of native romance
as it extends from the middle ages into the Renaissance.

4

Displaced Youths and Slandered Ladies in Middle English Romance

(1) EUSTACE–CONSTANCE–FLORENCE–GRISELDA LEGENDS

A number of Middle English verse romances—*Sir Isumbras, The King of Tars, Sir Eglamour of Artois, Octavian, Le Bone Florence of Rome, Sir Triamour,* and *Sir Torent of Portyngale*—have been designated as the 'Eustace–Constance–Florence–Griselda Legends'.[1] This classification properly signals the fact that these romances relate to various didactic and hagiographical traditions, such as the story of St Eustace whose faith is tested when, like Job, he loses all his wealth, or female figures such as Constance, Florence, and Griselda, virtuous women who are slandered or unfairly treated.[2] But it would be misleading to isolate these romances from the other texts in the native tradition; their key narrative elements resonate with the stories of earlier romances, and their influence extends into other romances to create mixed forms. In particular, the theme of the displaced or dispossessed youth who struggles to gain his proper identity and patrimony, which featured in several of the 'historical' romances considered in the last chapter, is also prominent in the texts studied here. The lack of a sense of historicity in the treatment of this theme in the following romances means that the interest is typically on the effect of providence on individual lives and also

---

[1] Hornstein, in Severs (gen. ed.), *Manual*, 120–32.

[2] On sources and analogues, see further: Gordon Hall Gerould, 'Forerunners, Congeners, and Derivatives of the Eustace Legend', *PMLA* 19 (1904), 355–448; Margaret Schlauch, *Chaucer's Constance and Accused Queens* (New York, 1927); Wirt Armistead Cate, 'The Problem of the Origin of the Griselda Story', *SP* 29 (1932), 389–405; Neil D. Isaacs, 'Constance in Fourteenth-Century England', *NM* 59 (1958), 260–77; Laurel Braswell, '*Sir Isumbras* and the Legend of Saint Eustace', *Mediaeval Studies* 27 (1965), 128–51; Hopkins, *Sinful Knights*. The story of St Eustace, or Placidas, is in Voragine, *Legenda aurea*, 714 ff.

on social hierarchy and the origins of personal nobility. At the same time, the characters are intended to be seen as credible in order that they, like saints, might be worthy of emulation. One of the romances under consideration, *Octavian*, introduces its subject-matter:

> Sothe sawys Y wyll yow mynge
> Of whom the worde wyde can sprynge,
> Yf ye wyll lystyn and lythe;
> Yn bokys of ryme hyt ys tolde
> How hyt befelle owre eldurs olde,
> Well oftyn sythe.[3]

(I will tell you true stories concerning people who are widely known, if you will listen and hear. Books of rhyme tell us what happened to our elders very many times.)

Moral truthfulness, at least, is insisted upon, even if these texts do not indicate the topographical details or vestigial remnants which would argue that their events actually happened. Their relevance to a contemporary readership would lie most of all in their lively didactic qualities, and their demonstration of the workings of God's grace in human lives was, from a contemporary perspective, a subject for belief rather than the product of fantasy. The great precedent for such providential narrative was the Bible, and its 'Sothe sawys' (as well as accreted narratives which would have been accepted as true) were well known through vernacular texts such as *Cursor Mundi* and sermon literature. The appeal of some of the following romances presumably lay in their sublimated resemblance to the great narratives of Christian experience—a judgement which needs further testing.

Sir Isumbras, a highly popular work, is related to the legend of St Eustace, with the important distinction that Isumbras does not suffer martyrdom.[4] This difference, put in the context of the work's story, means that *Isumbras* is concerned with the fulfilment of life, through God's grace, on earth—the same theme

---

[3] *Octavian*, 7–12, in *Six Middle English Romances*, ed. Maldwyn Mills (London and Melbourne, 1973).

[4] Citations are to the text in *Six Middle English Romances*, ed. Mills. The popularity of *Sir Isumbras* is attested by its survival in eight medieval manuscripts, one Elizabethan manuscript, and five sixteenth-century printed editions. There are also numerous allusions to it in medieval and Renaissance texts; see further Severs (gen. ed.), *Manual*, 122–3.

found in the 'historical' romances though without their political
dimension. Isumbras is content with the world—with his wealth,
his wife, and his three sons. In this state of complacency, he
forgets his debt to God:

> Into his herte a pryde was browghte
> That of God yafe he ryghte nowghte,
>   His mercy ones to nevenne;[a]
> So longe he regned in that pryde
> That Jesu wolde no lengur abyde:
>   To hym he sente a stevenne.[b]
>
>   (37–42)

[a] 'praise';   [b] 'voice, message'.

God decides to chastise and instruct Isumbras; he is given the
choice of suffering at once or in his old age, and he chooses the
former. Misfortune comes in the first instance with the loss of his
material possessions. Like Horn, Havelok, and Bevis, Isumbras
suddenly loses his social position and wealth, the things which
gave him a superficial sense of identity. Isumbras differs from
these other heroes in the fact that God has explicitly decreed this
punishment, but all these heroes are alike in their quest for a
retrieval or recollection of personal identity. In Isumbras' case,
the loss of wealth enforces a deeper self-knowledge. Consequently, when he learns that, despite his material losses, his
family are still alive, he realizes that the value which he places
upon his family is a basis for understanding his own nature:

> He seyde, 'If they on lyve be,
> My wyfe and my children thre,
>   Yet were I nevur so fayne.'[a]
>   (88–90)

[a] 'glad'.

When, as the second stage of his punishment, he is separated from
his wife and children, Isumbras must recognize his nature at its
deepest level, as a Christian. With that insight, he perceives his
existence and all worldly blessings as gifts rather than as things
earned. He is made to learn what Guy of Warwick perceived for
himself: that worldly advancement should not prevent a proper
sense of one's indebtedness to God. In his suffering, Isumbras
becomes a pilgrim-knight who is reminiscent of Guy. He begins
his penance:

> With his knyfe he share
> A crosse on his sholder bare,
>> In storye as clerkes seye.
> They that wer here frendes byfore
> They wepte and syked sore:
>> Her songe was 'wellawaye.'ᵃ
>>> (139–44)
>> ᵃ 'alas'.

This passage might incite recollection of Guy's setting out on pilgrimage:

> Now is Gij fram Warwike fare,
> Vnto þe se he went ful ȝare,
>> & passed ouer þe flod.
> Þe leuedyᵃ bileft at hom *in* care
> Wiþ sorwe, & wo, & sikeingᵇ sare:
>> Wel dreryᶜ was hir mode.
> 'Allas, allas!' it was hir song.
>>> (st. 34.1–7)⁵
>> ᵃ 'lady';   ᵇ 'sighing';   ᶜ 'sad'.

Reading about Isumbras' exile would encourage memories of scenes from other romances. For instance, at one point during his exile a pagan king offers Isumbras wealth if he will forsake Christ. The loss of his wealth is precisely the penance which God has imposed upon Isumbras for his earlier lack of piety, and now he demonstrates his acceptance of that punishment in his reply to the king:

---

⁵ During his pilgrimage, Guy meets a pilgrim who is very comparable to Isumbras. This man describes his condition:

> 'A man y was of state sum stounde,
> & holden a lord of gret mounde,
>> & erl of al Durras.
> Fair sones ich hadde fiftene,
> & alle wer*e* kniȝtes stout & kene.
>> Men cleped me þerl Ionas.
> Y trowe in þis warld is man non,
> Y-wis, þat is so wo-bi-gon,
>> Seþþen þe world made was;
> For alle min sones ich haue forlorn:
> Better berns wer*e* non born.
>> Þerfore y sing, "allas!"'
>>> (st. 49.1–12)

> 'Syr,' he sey[de], 'nay.
> Schall I nevur more
> Ayeyns Cristen werre,
>   Nor forsake my laye.'ᵃ
>   (267–70)
>
>   ᵃ 'faith'.

Isumbras' reply recalls Bevis' response to an identical situation;[6] or Bevis' response recalls Isumbras', depending upon which is read first. The emphasis needs to be on the congruence of these stories, along with other forms of writing, in the reader's mind and the sense acquired of a tradition, derived from the memorial character of the texts.

With the loss of his wife and sons, Isumbras reaches his nadir, though crucially he never falls into despair. He simply submits himself to God's will and prays for guidance:

> He seyde, 'Dere Godde, wo is me,
> I have loste my wyfe and children thre,
>   And am myselfe alone.
> I am as kerefull a manne
> As any with tonge telle can,
>   To God I make my mone.
> God, as thou werest hevenn crowne,
> Wysseᵃ me the wey to som towne,
>   For all amysse have I gone.'
>
>   (376–84)
>
>   ᵃ 'guide'.

Providential guidance comes to Isumbras in response to his prayer; he is led to a smithy and finds employment there. Living on 'mannes hyre' (401), he makes a suit of armour for himself. The act of making the armour symbolizes the laborious process by which Isumbras will regain his status as a knight. But this is not a self-willed victory, for he was only led to the smithy after acknowledging his dependence on God. The armour which he now forges, in the full recollection of his debt to God, is the Pauline *arma Dei* rather than the trappings of a secular knight.[7]

---

⁶ The passage, A-text, 561–6, was quoted in the previous chapter.
⁷ Ephes. 6:11. The phrase 'mannes hyre' may also allude to the Gospel passage, 'dignus enim est operarius mercede sua' (Luke 10:7); *Biblia sacra iuxta vulgatam versionem*, ed. Robertus Weber, 3rd edn., amended Bonifatius Fischer (Stuttgart, 1983).

Accordingly Isumbras' sins are forgiven by God, and after contests, recognition-scenes, and battles he regains his wife, children, and wealth. Isumbras' experiences depict a process of memory towards a goal which is his pious recognition that humankind derives from God. The romance world here is not an idealization of Britain, but it does argue for God's immanence and intervention in human lives.

A large number of intertextually related native romances represent penitential and pious themes similar to *Sir Isumbras*, but with greater emphasis upon the female figures. Chaucer's *Man of Law's Tale*, Gower's tale of Constance in the *Confessio Amantis*, *Emaré*, *Octavian*, *Sir Eglamour of Artois*, *Le Bone Florence of Rome*, and *Sir Torent of Portyngale* all offer representations or variations of the Constance–Florence figure, a virtuous woman who is separated from her husband through calumny or else a woman who is separated from her lover when their love affair is treacherously revealed. The usual fate of these women is to be put to sea in a boat or to be lost in a pathless forest. If they are pregnant at the time of their abandonment, then the children born in exile are often abducted (but not harmed) by wild beasts.[8] Although these female figures may appear to be passive, they are in fact fairly active and determining characters; their unwavering faith, manifested both in their domestic relationships and their belief in God's providence, is the bedrock upon which a society broken by intrigue and jealousy can be rebuilt. In the romances of displaced male youths, we saw (and will continue to see) great value attached to aristocratic birth as the prerogative of chivalric nobility; even if the character's behaviour is boorish or incompetent because of his displaced upbringing, his birth ensures that he will eventually regain his correct position in society. In contrast, the female characters of the Constance–Florence type are judged not according to their birth but entirely by their deeds—or, more unfortunately, their alleged misdeeds. Although these women are usually of aristocratic birth, their social nobility is never seen by characters in the text as evidence that they are virtuous and chaste, or noble in a behavioural sense. Indeed, the related Griselda legend, as told by Chaucer's clerk, carefully demonstrates perfect chastity in a peasant girl.

---

[8] The wild beasts are an aspect of the Eustace-legend, but it works itself into romances of the 'Constance–Florence' type, as will be discussed below.

For the aristocratic female characters of the Constance–Florence type, deeds rather than birth are the priority, and their different treatment, in contrast to the male characters, possibly reflects social attitudes moulded by Christian beliefs. The distinctive birth of displaced male biblical heroes, such as Moses and Jesus, emerges in their eventual sense of their true identities, patrimony, and vocation, despite their upbringing; the representation of female characters such as Eve and the Virgin Mary, however, promotes an emphasis on women's behaviour with the sense that women's deeds can (from a masculine point of view) be crucially beneficial or harmful. Unlike the displaced youths, Constance–Florence figures are not allowed a 'trial and error' progress towards chastity, most obviously because of the strong logical connections between the two story-types: women must remain chaste in order to preserve the legitimacy of birth which is so crucial in the makeup of the male hero. Needless to say, the perspective of these stories is patriarchal. The Virgin Mary, who appears to Joseph to be unchaste when she conceives a child before they have carnal relations (Matt. 1:18–25), is the model for the following female characters whose chastity unfairly comes under question. In the *Cursor Mundi*, Joseph returns from three-months' absence to discover Mary pregnant. He

> ... fonde wiþouten more warn
> Þat his lady was wiþ barn
> whenne he knew hir in such state
> Was he neuer mon so mate
> So sory was he neuer his lif
> As to fynde wiþ childe his wif
> Þat he neuer touched tille
> he wex þouȝtful & loked ille.
> (Trinity, 11133–40)

Like Mary, whose virtue is proven to Joseph by the visitation of an angel, the Constance–Florence figures are frequently upheld in their travails by providence; though unlike Mary, their suffering through slander and banishment is protracted, and they only recover their former place through extraordinary faith and perserverance.[9] What their travails are meant to demonstrate—apart

---

[9] It is interesting that various non-Canonical Middle English versions of Mary's conception of Jesus place a stronger emphasis, compared to the Gospel account, on the

from providence's *eventual* correction of injustice—is difficult to understand, since the women are virtuous from the start and consequently are not engaged in a process of greater self-understanding and moral perfection. However, they do provide a narrative framework into which, in some texts, the kinds of male heroes we have seen are fitted: the child born to the slandered woman and then abducted by wild beasts is raised, in the same manner as Bevis or Havelok, practically ignorant of his aristocratic birth, and the husband who realizes that his wife has been unfairly slandered becomes a penitential figure reminiscent of Guy and Isumbras, albeit with different goals.

In *Octavian* (mid fourteenth-century) a jealous mother-in-law slanders Florence, the wife of her son the emperor Octavian, by engineering a deceit which portrays Florence as an adulteress.[10] Florence gives birth to twin sons and then is forced into exile. The children are abducted by wild beasts and raised in ignorance of their parentage. The mother waits in exile until her truthfulness is recognized; the Emperor Octavian, realizing the deceit of his mother, undergoes a penitential search for his wife. The children are eventually restored to their parents, after the children and Octavian have won a Christian victory over pagans in battle.

scandal and rumour which may surround Mary's conception of Jesus. For example, in *Cursor Mundi*:

> ... þe iewes ful of strif
> wolde haue stoned mary þat stounde
> If she wiþ childe had be founde
> And she no husbonde had I-had
> hir to haue gouerned & lad
> For lawe was þat tyme in londe
> wommon þat had no husbonde
> And she founde were wiþ childe
> Fro stonyng shulde noon hir shilde.
> (Trinity, 10800–8)

Furthermore, Joseph takes Mary to Bethlehem, not primarily for the census, but 'for wordis of þo iewes felle / For to fle her fals fame' (Trinity, 11179–84).

[10] The text cited is in *Six Middle English Romances*, ed. Mills. *Octavian* survives in three medieval manuscripts and one early sixteenth-century print. There are two, apparently independent, versions of the romance, designated Northern and Southern. (The edition by Mills is the Northern.) The Southern version may be the work of Thomas Chestre, the author of *Sir Launfal* and possibly also *Lybeaus Desconus*; see further Maldwyn Mills, 'The Composition and Style of the "Southern" *Octavian*, *Sir Launfal*, and *Libeaus Desconus*', *MÆ* 31 (1962), 88–109.

Florence is more significant in this story than the female figures in the other romances considered thus far. The need to recognize her innocence is the driving force of the tale and the projected point of narrative closure. Comparable to the Virgin Mary, her apparent passivity as a character must be offset with recognition of the force of her faith as well as providence's shaping of events around the fact of her innocence. The other character who enacts biblical (or really apocryphal) narratology is Florent, one of the two abducted sons, whose subsequent adventures concern the conflict between his innate nobility of behaviour as the son of an emperor and his displaced upbringing by a foster-parent who is a bourgeois Parisian merchant. Like Havelok and Bevis, Florent is a displaced youth who struggles to grow into the image of his father, responding to the call of a higher birth. Even more than Havelok and Bevis, Florent is quixotic in his untutored pursuit of a chivalric life. Although Havelok adapted well both to a life of manual labour and later chivalric enterprises, Florent is at first suited to neither career; he lacks the inclination for the former, and he lacks the education and training necessary for the latter.[11] There is a fine comic sense of incongruity when Florent, aided by his foster-parents Clement and Gladwyn, assembles rusty armour and a sword in preparation to fight a giant. The disused sword can scarcely be drawn from its scabbard:

> Clement the swyrde drawe owt wolde,
> Gladwyn his wyfe schoulde the scabard holde,
>   And bothe faste they drowe;
> When the swyrde owt glente,[a]
> Bothe to the erthe they wente:
>   There was game ynowe!
>
> (889–94)
>
> [a] 'shot'.

The specifically comic treatment of the dispossessed youth also appears in the related romances of the 'Fair Unknown' type, such

---

[11] Florent first reveals his innate nobility, as well as his naive gullibility, when he trades two oxen for a hawk and likewise £40 for a horse—much to the chagrin of his foster-father who instructed Florent to make profitable business transactions; whereas the merchant father demonstrated his skill in bargaining when he reduced the price to be paid for adopting Florent (577–88), Florent knocks the price of the horse up, giving £40 instead of the required £30 (727–32). Florent's action demonstrates his own estimation of the high worth of chivalry and a mind that is 'above' mercantile considerations.

as *Lybeaus Desconus* and *Sir Perceval*, and it seems to reflect the apocryphal representation of the young Jesus. In *Cursor Mundi*, Jesus as a boy is an *enfant terrible* possessed of great innate powers but, compared to his maturity, ignorant of their proper application; he has a tendency to strike dead playmates who spoil his mudpies (Trinity, 11933–50), and only after a counselling session from Mary does he agree to restore one dead companion to life by ungraciously kicking him (Trinity, 11973–81). While maintaining conviction in the hereditary character of nobility, or high *parage*, *Octavian* and the 'Fair Unknown' romances place greater emphasis than the related romances considered thus far on the detrimental effect of the hero's lack of education and the partly ludicrous nature of his chivalric aspirations in the context of his upbringing. This addition to the story of the dispossessed youth will be of interest when we consider the impact of the tradition on Book I of *The Faerie Queene*.

Sir Eglamour of Artois (mid fourteenth-century), a well known and liked romance judging by the evidence of its survival, is memorial in two senses: it is a composite of the characters and story-types considered so far, and it is also a tale 'Of eldirs þat byfore vs were' (Lincoln, 4).[12] Eglamour loves Christabelle, the daughter of an earl. Because he is not her social equal, he must, like Guy of Warwick, prove himself worthy of her through various heroic deeds, such as killing a boar and a dragon.[13] Christabelle has a child by Eglamour out of wedlock, and she

---

[12] The edition cited is *Eglamour*, ed. Richardson; see further pp. xxx–xxxix for a detailed discussion of the work's relationship to other Middle English romances, especially those of the 'Constance' and 'Eustace' kinds. *Sir Eglamour* survives in four medieval manuscripts, one Elizabethan manuscript, and the seventeenth-century Percy Folio. It was printed at least five times in the sixteenth century, the latest known occurrence being *c.* 1570. On its popularity and influence, see ibid. pp. xli–l.

[13] The author of *Sir Eglamour* may be recalling *Bevis* when he notes that the dragon fought by Eglamour is 'At grete Rome' (Lincoln, 697). In the earlier Auchinleck text (and subsequent witnesses) of *Bevis*, there are two dragons: the one which Bevis fights, and another which has flown 'To seinte Peter is brige of Rome; / Þar he schel leggen ay, / Til hit come domes dai' (A-text, 2642–4). The *Eglamour*-poet conceivably takes up the challenge, as well as the narrative opportunities, of this other, reputedly invincible dragon which Bevis does not fight, thus arguing for the valour of Eglamour through his victory over the dragon of Rome. The text of *Eglamour* in CUL ff.2.38, which also contains *Bevis*, has additional descriptive details of the dragon which appear to be drawn from *Bevis*: 'Hys body gretter then a tvnne' (see note to 785 of the Cotton text of *Eglamour*), comparable to *Bevis*, 'His bodi ase a wintonne' (A-text, 2673) and 'Hys body was gretter þen a tunne' (CUL ff.2.38, reconstructed from Kölbing's textual variants on p. 132).

and her unbaptized child are consequently put out to sea in a boat by her father.[14] The child, Degrebelle, is abducted by a griffin; like Bevis, Havelok, and Florent, he becomes an exile, though Degrebelle is fortunate in being found by the king of Israel, who recognizes that 'This childe es comen of gentill blode' (Lincoln, 863). Meanwhile, Eglamour resembles Isumbras or Octavian, though without their need for penance, in his laborious and prayerful quest to unite his family.[15] But the main emphasis of the story is on Christabelle, whose experiences are providentially guided—'speke we of his modir mylde, / In what land our Lorde hir lent' (Lincoln, 878–9)—to a just resolution. The sense of providential control or assistance is balanced against an anxiety stemming from the potential for tragedy. Degrebelle unknowingly marries his mother and challenges his father to combat; the poet's use of the terms of family kinship, 'fadir' and 'sone', during this battle when the characters are still ignorant of their relationship creates dramatic irony and intensifies anxiety (Lincoln, 1243ff.). True identities are discovered before the marriage is consummated or any serious violence done; Degrebelle's attraction towards his parents proves to be natural rather than Oedipal. Providence has not manifested itself miraculously, as it does in *Havelok* or *Guy*, to ensure the fulfilment of a romance narrative, but the sense of divine orchestration is palpable within the unfolding of the human drama. When the confusions are resolved and the family reunited, the narrator wryly comments:

> It es sothe sayd, by God of heuen,
> Þat ofte metis men at vnsett steuyn:
> Forsothe, sa did þay thare.
> (Lincoln, 1309–11)

(It is truly said, by God of heaven, that people often meet unexpectedly. Truly, they did so there.)

The slandered woman, the displaced youth who struggles to follow his innate inclination towards a higher life, and the penitential search of husband for wronged wife are the fundamental stories of two other romances which were well known and printed in the

---

[14] In accordance with the generally pious tone of this romance, there is an emphasis on the importance of baptism (Lincoln, 806–25).

[15] Eglamour dwells for fifteen years in the 'Haly Land', where incidentally and unknown to Eglamour his son also resides.

sixteenth century, *Sir Triamour* and *Sir Torent of Portyngale*.[16] In *Sir Triamour*, Queen Margaret refuses the advances of a false steward, 'As sche was woman trewe' (99). The steward slanders the Queen, and consequently her husband, King Ardus, banishes her. Margaret is pregnant at the time of her exile, and she gives birth to Triamour in a forest. When Triamour has grown up, he returns to his father's court (though their relationship is unknown to both) and displays strength superior to his father's in a tournament. This 'Sohrab and Rustum' incident, though without the latter's tragic consequence, recalls the moment in *King Horn* where Horn's swordplay reminds his opponents of Horn's father, King Mury;[17] the meeting of father and son is emblematic of the son's progression to his proper chivalric identity despite the lack of fitting education and paternal guidance. The interest in birth versus upbringing emerges clearly when Triamour asks a knight to lend him armour so that he can enter a tournament (685–7). At first the knight believes that Triamour is incapable of handling weapons, but Triamour insists and eventually the knight recognizes the innate chivalry of the youth:

> Syr Barnard seyde, 'What haste thou thoght?
> Of justyng[a] canste thou ryght noght,
> For thou art not of age.'
> 'Syr,' he seyde, 'What wott ye
> Of what strenkyth that y bee,
> Or[b] y be prevyd in felde wyth the sage?'[c]
>
> Barnarde seyde, also hynde,[d]
> 'Tryamowre, syn ye wyll wynde,[e]
> Ye schall wante ne wede:
> For y schall lende the all my gere—
> Hors and harnes, schylde and spere—
> And helpe the at thy nede.'
>
> (688–99)

[a] 'jousting';   [b] 'before';   [c] 'experienced (warriors)';
[d] 'very graciously';   [e] 'go'.

[16] *Sir Triamour* is cited from *Love and Chivalry*, ed. Fellows; it survives in two medieval manuscripts (one of which, a fragment, is now missing) and the Percy Folio, and it was printed at least five times in the sixteenth century, the latest issue being *c.* 1565. (Like Perceval, considered shortly, Triamour is raised by his mother (i.e., he does not lose both parents, unlike Havelok or Bevis), and she keeps secret from him the identity of his father). *Torent of Portyngale*, ed. E. Adam, EETS ES 51 (London, 1887); *Sir Torent* survives in one manuscript and two sixteenth-century printed editions.

[17] It also recalls, obviously, Degrebelle's encounter with his father Eglamour.

Like Florent, Triamour must fight in borrowed armour, a circumstance necessitated by his removal from his proper home.[18]

(II) *SIR DEGARE, SIR PERCEVAL, AND LYBEAUS DESCONUS*

Sir Degare, *Sir Perceval*, and *Lybeaus Desconus* are three works which, despite their close association with various French traditions and sources, relate to, and in some respects adapt themselves to, the recurring motifs of native romance. *Sir Degare* (before 1325) appears in two manuscripts which also contain texts of *Guy* and *Bevis*.[19] This work combines the influence of the Breton *lai*, a romance form introduced into English in the early fourteenth century, with a focus characteristic of much Middle English romance on the growth to maturity of a noble but displaced youth. A lady is raped by a faerie knight and left pregnant. When the child is born, his mother secretly conveys him to foster-parents who raise the child, Degare, in ignorance of his true parentage. These details—the forest as a place of enchantment, the faerie knight, the dilemma faced by the woman, and the secret birth of the child—are characteristic of the Breton *lai*.[20] But whereas a 'pure' Breton *lai* would, with typical brevity, focus on the emotional and moral crisis which arises from the love-incident, *Sir Degare* moves to a long representation of the displaced youth who, like Florent and Triamour, must realize his proper identity and social position through the symbolic act

---

[18] *Torent of Portyngale* is so close to *Sir Eglamour* in its plot and themes that an individual treatment would be superfluous; see Severs (gen. ed.), *Manual*, 126. *Torent*'s main interest is to reinforce the sense of tradition and intertextuality in relation to Middle English romance.

[19] The text is cited from *Middle English Metrical Romances*, ed. Walter Hoyt French and Charles Brockway Hale, 2 vols. (New York, 1964). *Sir Degare* survives in four medieval manuscripts, one Elizabethan manuscript, and the seventeenth-century Percy Folio. There were at least three printings of the romance in the sixteenth century. On the later versions of *Degare*, see Jacobs, *Later Versions of Degarre*.

[20] G. V. Smithers, 'Story-Patterns in Some Breton Lays', *MÆ* 22 (1953), 61–92, offers a classification of the characteristic narratives of the *lais*: *Sir Degare* conforms to Smithers' 'Type II'.

of locating his true parents.[21] Degare achieves victories which prove his chivalric nature, such as slaying a dragon. Like Degrebelle, he unknowingly marries his mother and matches swords against his father. Similarly and with the same significance, recognition follows before the marriage is consummated or the fight undertaken.

The direct source for *Sir Perceval of Gales* (*c.* 1330–1340) is undoubtedly French; nevertheless the story of Perceval would appeal to any reader interested in the tales of displaced youths in *Horn, Havelok, Bevis, Sir Triamour, Octavian, Sir Degare*, and other works.[22] Like Bevis, Perceval is a hero whose father, a knight, was slain when Perceval was an infant. His mother, anxious that Perceval does not follow his father's chivalric lifestyle to the same end, raises the boy in a forest and keeps him ignorant of chivalry, isolated from wherever 'dedez of armez schall be donne' (167). Just as Havelok adapted well to being a cook's apprentice, so too Perceval initially seems 'at home' in the forest:

> Thus he welke[a] in the lande,
> With hys darte in his hande,
> Under the wilde wodde wande;[b]
> He wexe[c] and wele thrafe.[d]
> He wolde schote with his spere
> Bestes and other gere,
> As many als he myghte bere;
> He was a gude knave.
>
> (209–16)

    [a] 'roamed';   [b] 'branches';   [c] 'grew';   [d] 'developed'.

Nevertheless, his upbringing in the forest, exiled from his true social milieu, has left him ignorant of more than pertains to the profession of arms. When his mother asks Perceval to pray for God's protection, the boy asks ' "Whatkyns a godd may that be / ... That I schall to pray?" ' (242–4). Bevis, brought up in pagan lands, was unaware of the occasion of Christmas day, though he

---

[21] The plot of *Sir Degare* is similar to Marie de France's *Yonec*, a 'true' Breton *lai*, but *Yonec* differs in its very brief, undeveloped consideration of the dispossessed child and the process by which he recovers his proper identity and social position.

[22] The text is cited from *Ywain and Gawain, Sir Percyvell of Gales, The Anturs of Arther*, ed. Maldwyn Mills (London and Rutland, Vermont, 1992). *Sir Perceval* survives in one manuscript, the Lincoln Thornton MS.

did remember to maintain his Christian identity and reject conversion to Islam. The effects of exile on Perceval are more detrimental, and there is comedy and failure as the hero struggles to
overcome the disadvantages of his upbringing in order to become
a Christian knight.[23] Perceval's experiences in the forest have left
him animalistic—an instinctive hunter ignorant of religion—and
the pressure of an innate chivalric and Christian identity to bur-
geon is at first very faint. Even more so than Florent with his rusty
armour and sword, Perceval's efforts to achieve his natural identity are frequently misguided.[24] When Perceval first encounters
knights, he is instinctively attracted to them, as Florent was
attracted to the hawk and horse that he bought. At the same
time, the narrator emphasizes the great disparity between Perceval and the knights, demonstrated here by their respective attires:

> In riche robes thay ryde;
> The childe hadd nothyng that tyde
> That he myghte in his bones hyde,
> Bot a gaytes[a] skynn.
>
> (265–8)

> [a] 'goat's'.

Perceval's assumption that one of these knights must be the
mysterious God whom his mother mentioned—'He said,
"Wilke of yow alle three / May the grete Godd bee...?"' (281–
2)—connects his ignorance of both religion and chivalry, at the
same time indicating his natural attraction towards and high
estimation of knighthood. His task is to remember not only his
chivalric identity but his Christian faith. Despite his comic blun-
ders here and later, he continues to progress towards the realization of his natural identity and birthright; when his mother sees

---

[23] Note the frequency with which Perceval and the forest are described as 'wilde';
175, 290, 596, 1353, 1497, 1583, 1677. Arthur comments that, considering Perceval
has had his 'techyng' in the forest 'with the wilde dere', 'Littil wonder it were / Wilde if
he ware!' (1572–83). On the theme of the forest in romance in general, see: Corinne J.
Saunders, *The Forest of Medieval Romance* (Cambridge, 1993). Ad Putter, *Sir
Gawain and the Green Knight and French Arthurian Romance* (Oxford, 1995), 22
notes the deliberate connections in medieval romance between forests and religious
heathenism. Perceval's wildness contrasts pointedly with the reasonable and courteous demeanour of Gawain, who in the face of Perceval's brashness 'was meke and
mylde / And softe of ansuare' (291–2).
[24] On the quixotic element in Perceval, see: Caroline D. Eckhardt, 'Arthurian
Comedy: The Simpleton-Hero in *Sir Perceval of Galles*', CR 8 (1974), 205–20.

him return home on a horse, the first essential of a knight, she realizes that in spite of her efforts 'the kinde wolde out sprynge' (355).

Perceval avenges his father and proves himself noble in upholding the cause of the Lady Lufamour of 'Maydenlande' (956) in an episode which reveals similarities to *Lybeaus Desconus*, discussed next. The Lady Lufamour's messenger tells how his lady is besieged by a sultan who has murdered her father, uncle, and brothers and taken all her lands. Perceval undertakes this adventure, despite the messenger's refusal of his services (1013–16), defeats the sultan, and marries the Lady Lufamour. Although the narrator makes (infrequent) comments such as 'Late we Percyvell the ynge / Fare in Goddes blyssynge' (1057–8), he does not allow an overt sense of providence working to restore the hero. In contrast to Havelok or Bevis, Perceval in this version receives no miraculous signs which indicate that he is under the guardianship of God; that notion is not denied, but certainly veiled.

Perceval's arrival at Arthur's court and his demand to be knighted not only recall Triamour's plea for arms; these details also connect him to the tradition of the 'Fair Unknown', of which the major Middle English representation is *Lybeaus Desconus* (*c.* 1325–50), also Arthurian in setting.[25] Lybeaus Desconus (the name is a corruption of 'Le Bel Inconnu', or 'The Fair Unknown') is in fact Gingelein, the illegitimate son of Sir Gawain, and his mother has brought him up, comparable to Perceval, in seclusion and ignorant of his noble identity. Despite his lack of education,

---

[25] The edition cited is *Lybeaus*, ed. Mills. *Lybeaus* survives in five medieval manuscripts and the Percy Folio, apparently a transcription of an early (now lost) printed edition; see Severs (gen. ed.), *Manual*, 248. For another piece of evidence that *Lybeaus* was printed in the sixteenth century, see Meale, 'Caxton, de Worde, and Publication of Romance', 286, f. 10. Further proof of the popularity of *Lybeaus* are the references to it in Chaucer's *Sir Thopas* (900) and Skelton's *Philip Sparrow* (649–50). Furthermore, Malory used some form of the legend in his tale of Sir Gareth. Despite an earlier version (*c.* 1190) of the Lybeaus story in French (Renaut de Beaujeu's *Le Bel Inconnu*, ed. G. Perrie Williams, CFMA 38 (Paris, 1967)) *Lybeaus* never appears to have achieved the same popularity in France. *Le Bel Inconnu* survives in only one manuscript, compared to the above evidence for *Lybeaus*' considerable popularity and influence in England; see further Loomis (gen. ed.), *Arthurian Literature*, 512. *Lybeaus* is related to *Le Bel Inconnu*, but the differences between the two works are significant and extensive; both texts presumably descend collaterally from a lost French or Anglo-Norman work: ibid., 513. On the tradition of the 'Fair Unknown' in medieval literature, see *Lybeaus*, ed. Mills, 42–50.

Lybeaus is drawn to knighthood, and he travels to Arthur, asking the king to knight him and give him the first adventure which is required of the court. This scene at the court, where Lybeaus undertakes the quest of a maiden who seeks help for her imprisoned mistress, the Lady of Synadon, will deserve fuller examination at a later stage when considering Book I of *The Faerie Queene*. What is immediately noteworthy is the climax of the quest when Lybeaus enters the enchanted castle—'J-wrought with ffayreye' (Lambeth, 1768)—where the Lady of Synadon is held captive. After various miraculous occurrences, Lybeaus encounters in the castle a dragon with a woman's face who kisses him (Lambeth, 2076–84). With that kiss, the dragon-woman suddenly transforms into a beautiful lady, none other than the Lady of Synadon. She explains that she was changed into draconian form through 'chauntement' (Lambeth, 2103):

> 'Tyll [J] had kyssed Gaweyne,
> That is doughti knyght, certayne,
> Or some of his kynde.'
>   (Lambeth, 2106–8)

Because he has broken the spell, Lybeaus now realizes his true noble identity, as the kin of Sir Gawain. The tension between what the hero has been given through birth and what he seeks to achieve for himself is here satisfyingly tight: on the one hand, Lybeaus' efforts and courage have been the cause of his successful completion of this quest, but on the other hand his birth as the kin of Gawain was an obligatory prior-condition without which he never could have succeeded. So even as he earns a victory, he learns that his victory has been given to him. Put another way, the identity which he appears to achieve is in fact the identity with which he was born.

(III) THE FIFTEENTH CENTURY

The fifteenth century was a period of intense activity in relation to the reading and writing of romance in England. Although the romances considered thus far all originated in the thirteenth or fourteenth century, there is a need to emphasize their continued presence and influence in the fifteenth century. For one, a significant majority of Middle English romances survive only in fifteenth-century copies, even though they were first composed in earlier centuries.[26] Nor was the copying of romance in the fifteenth century a mechanical labour; *Guy* and *Bevis* received completely new versions, and the texts of other romances underwent substantial changes. As we have seen, romances were collected into large manuscript-anthologies by readers such as Robert Thornton, and at the very end of the century romance came into print, overlapping with a continued and vital manuscript culture. Derek Pearsall aptly summarizes the vitality of romance in the fifteenth century, indicating the significance of the history of reading for the understanding of romance as a tradition:

This is the first point to stress about the fifteenth century, that it is the great age of fourteenth-century romance, not because it instills in us a proper gratitude to fifteenth-century scribes, but because the way a work is read and used contributes significantly to its place in literary history, and because the work of copying is, with these poems, often a work of re-composition.[27]

New tendencies in romance emerge in the English literary culture of the late fourteenth and fifteenth centuries. Pearsall notes that 'there is a movement in fifteenth-century verse-romance towards a greater sophistication and a more self-consciously "literary" mode of treatment and address'.[28] The influence of Chaucer should be seen as an important element within wider developments in literary culture, such as changing reading habits, availability of texts, rising literacy, and the slowly

[26] H. S. Bennett, 'The Production and Dissemination of Vernacular Manuscripts in the Fifteenth Century', *The Library*, 5th ser. 1 (1946–47), 167–75 (167–8) notes that 65 (out of 84) romances appear only in fifteenth-century copies. Furthermore, Edwards and Pearsall, 'Manuscripts of Major Poetic Texts', in Griffiths and Pearsall (eds), *Book Production and Publishing*, 257 note that the seventy-five years on either side of 1400 witnessed a dramatic change in the rate and nature of vernacular book production, with a spectacular increase in non-religious works after 1400.

[27] Pearsall, 'English Romance in the Fifteenth Century', 58. An excellent overall discussion of the manuscripts and texts of Middle English romance in the fifteenth century is Helen Cooper, 'Romance after 1400', in David Wallace (ed.), *The Cambridge History of Medieval English Literature* (Cambridge, forthcoming), 690–719. I am grateful to Professor Cooper for allowing me to read the text of her chapter prior to its publication.

[28] Pearsall, 'English Romance in the Fifteenth Century', 67.

widening gap between author and scribe/compositor.[29] A cursory
look at the composition of new romances in the fifteenth century
reveals some differences in comparison with the earlier romances
which were still current. For one, English romances making their
initial appearance in the fifteenth century are often the work of
named authors, such as John Lydgate, William Caxton, Henry
Lovelich, Thomas Malory, Henry Watson, and John Metham,
and their texts tend to be fairly stable in comparison to romances
such as *Bevis*, *Guy*, *Degare*, and others. Furthermore, many
fifteenth-century romances are fairly compendious, such as the
Laud Troy Book, Lydgate's *Troy Book*, Lovelich's Arthurian
romances, the prose *Merlin*, and Malory; although some of the
pre-fifteenth-century romances were long, the shorter length of
the majority of the romances probably reflected the desire for a
tale which could be recited or performed to a family or group in
one or two sittings. Fifteenth-century romances suggest in their
length the expectations of prolonged private reading, and that
expectation is also reflected in the increased use of prose rather
than verse, better suited to recitation. These larger, sometimes
authorial romances also tend to be 'scholarly', in Chaucerian
fashion indicating their *auctoritee* and consciously grounding
themselves in older literary and historical traditions. Because in
the fifteenth century English emerged as the language of crown
and court, these new romances were potentially directed at more
aristocratic tastes, or at least sought to include these interests
within a broader appeal. *Partonope of Blois*, whose narrative
replicates the Cupid and Psyche myth though with a reversal of
gender, is a dilatory romance which combines aristocratic behaviour with an interest in faerie and fantastic marvels. Chaucer's
influence is revealed in its descriptive scenes and its emphasis on
the narrator's persona, though *Partonope*, like Lydgate's
romances, does not reproduce Chaucer's irony or verbal eco-
nomy. It offers a reading experience radically different from the
vigorous narrative of *Horn* and *Havelok*, or even the longer but
still briskly paced *Guy* and *Bevis*.[30]

[29] See further: V. J. Scattergood, 'Literary Culture at the Court of Richard II', in V.
J. Scattergood and J. W. Sherborne (eds), *English Court Culture in the Later Middle
Ages* (London, 1983), 29–43.
[30] *Partonope of Blois*, ed. A Trampe Bödtker, EETS ES 109 (London, 1912).
Partonope survives in two versions, represented in all by six manuscripts. See further:

The aspiration of much fifteenth-century romance to represent—or to teach—aristocratic tastes is reflected in the physical
characteristics of a few manuscripts which differ in their profes-
sional execution, decoration, and costliness from the less osten-
tatious manuscript-anthologies, such as the Thornton MS, MS
Ashmole 61, and CUL MS ff.2.38, containing the older verse
romances. The Morgan Library MS of *Generydes*, manuscripts of
Lydgate's romances, and the manuscript of John Metham's
Amoryus and Cleopes contribute visually to the sense of
fifteenth-century romance as a 'mirror' offering the reader an
elegant reflection.[31] Bodleian Library MS Digby 185 is a more
complex instance of new developments alongside established
tendencies. The romance in MS Digby 185 is *King Ponthus*
(*c.* 1400–50), which is a prose translation of the French *Ponthus
et la belle Sidoine* (*c.* 1390).[32] *Ponthus* is traditional in the sense
that its immediate source was a reworking of the Anglo-Norman
Horn et Rimenild, the story of King Horn. But *Ponthus* represents
new directions in English romance in that it, following its French
source, reflects the notion that romance should 'exemplify the
rules of behaviour proper to a gentleman'.[33] The manuscript
context in which *Ponthus* survives similarly reflects the old and
the new: *Ponthus* is joined in MS Digby 185 by a text of the prose
Brut, the traditional 'history' of Britain derived from Geoffrey of
Monmouth with added material including the tale of Havelok,
but the manuscript also contains a text of Hoccleve's *De regimine*

B. J. Whiting, 'A Fifteenth-Century English Chaucerian: The Translation of *Partonope
of Blois*', *Mediaeval Studies* 7 (1945), 40–54; Pearsall, 'English Romance in the
Fifteenth Century', 68; Barry Windeatt, 'Chaucer and Fifteenth-Century Romance:
Partonope of Blois,' in Ruth Morse and Barry Windeatt (eds), *Chaucer Traditions*
(Cambridge and New York, 1990), 62–80. See *Partonope*, 4853–72 for its nature as a
'mirror of chivalry'.

[31] See further: John Metham, *The Works of John Metham*, ed. Hardin Craig, EETS
132 (London, 1916), p. vii for a description of the manuscript; Guddat-Figge, *Catalogue*; Carol M. Meale, 'The Morgan Library Copy of *Generides*', in Mills, Fellow,
and Meale (eds), *Romance in Medieval England*, 89–104 (this 'de luxe' manuscript,
New York Pierpont Morgan Library MS M.876 (*c.* 1460), also contains a copy of
Lydgate's *Troy Book*).

[32] *King Ponthus and the Fair Sidone*, ed. Frank Jewett Mather (Baltimore, 1897).
There may have been two English prose translations of *Ponthus* in the fifteenth
century, since the manuscript version differs from the version printed by de Worde.
Ponthus survives in two manuscripts and three sixteenth-century printed editions.

[33] Severs (gen. ed.), *Manual*, 22.

principum, an example of the 'advice to princes' genre which accords with the secular didacticism of fifteenth-century romance. *Ponthus* itself tends to read like a handbook to chivalry, in the sense of a code of martial conduct which adheres to fair play. For example, when Ponthus spares the life of a defeated opponent, the narrator interjects:

Sawe ye not the gret benignite—howe that he wold not touche the knyght, but cause he sawe hym hurte, and how he had two tymes releved hym? (50)

Ponthus is 'the floure of knyghthode and of curtesy... the best manered' and a 'myrroure of all noblenes and largenes' (67–8). Like many fifteenth-century romances, *Ponthus* is more interested in manners and morals than in the pious representation of God's providence acting in human lives, a theme which was generally characteristic of thirteenth- and fourteenth-century romance. The physical appearance of MS Digby 185 reflects *Ponthus'* interest in chivalry and courtly refinement, as well as suggesting an owner of some rank and wealth, through the heraldic devices which adorn its *litterae notabiliores*.[34] Printed editions of fifteenth-century romances could also present themselves—accurately or not—as appropriate for an upper-class readership. Caxton advises that his *Eneydos* (1490) 'is not for a rude vplondyssh man to laboure therin... but onely for a clerke & a noble gentylman that feleth and vnderstondeth in faytes of armes, in loue, & in noble chyualrye'.[35]

Size, learnedness, elegance, and the use of romance as a mirror to noble action, rather than a hybrid genre shading into hagiography, are features characteristic of a number of romances composed in English in the fifteenth century. But 'composed' should be replaced by 'translated', for many fifteenth-and sixteenth-century romances are fairly close translations of Continental romances of the thirteenth century and later. Whereas English

---

[34] See the facsimile plates in *Ponthus*, ed. Mather. The heraldic devices refer to actual families of gentry and minor aristocratic rank; on their identification, see ibid., pp. xxiv–xxv. *The Three King's Sons* (*c.* 1500) survives in a magnificently illuminated manuscript, indicating a wealthy or upper-class readership; Severs (gen. ed.), *Manual*, 163.

[35] William Caxton, *Caxton's Eneydos*, ed. W. T. Culley and F. J. Furnivall, EETS ES 57 (London, 1890), 3.14–17.

redactions of French and Anglo-Norman romances in the thirteenth and fourteenth centuries, such as *King Horn*, *Octavian*, *Ywain and Gawain*, *Lybeaus*, and *Sir Perceval*, reveal an excisive treatment of source-material,[36] fifteenth- and early sixteenth-century translations, such as Henry Lovelich's *Merlin* and *The History of the Holy Grail*, the prose *Merlin*, *King Ponthus*, and Lord Berners' translations *Huon of Bordeaux* and *Arthur of Little Britain*, are fairly faithful to their French originals.[37] This changing attitude in the treatment of French romances may reflect the emergence of a courtly English readership in the fifteenth century (who previously read Anglo-Norman and French literature in the original), but English bourgeois readers may also have developed an interest in this form of romance, particularly in light of the opportunities it afforded for social amelioration.

The increasingly authorial and aesthetic character of romance in the fifteenth century did not result in romance being remote from historical concerns or unrelated to contemporary political and social events. The refined Burgundian and French worlds of Caxton's romances, or the anachronistically chivalric worlds of Troy, Thebes, and Alexander in several works, were less superfluous to the historical realities of fifteenth-century England than one might suppose, and because of their historical and political interest they deserve to be seen as a signficant chapter in the romance tradition extending from *Horn* to *The Faerie Queene*. Lydgate's *Troy Book* (1410), for example, interestingly links English and Trojan history. The work is dedicated to Prince

---

[36] See Mehl, *Middle English Romaces*, 48–51 (*Horn*), 72 (*Lybeaus*), 111 (*Octavian*). Concerning the English redactor's treatment of Chrétien's *Yvain*, the editors of *Ywain and Gawain* note that 'Whole episodes are lopped off, while others are telescoped into a few lines. As a result, the 6,818 lines of Chrétien's poem are reduced to 4,032 lines in the English version... The elegant and dilatory court romance of Chrétien has become in the hands of the English minstrel a rapid-paced story of love and gallant adventure'; *Ywain and Gawain*, ed. Friedman and Harrington (1964), pp. xvi–xvii (the full discussion is pp. xvi–xxxiv).
[37] Sir John Bourchier (Lord Berners), *The Boke of Duke Huon of Burdeux*, ed. S. L. Lee, EETS ES 40, 41, 43, 50 (London, 1882, 1883, 1884, 1887); Lord Berners, *The History of the Valiant Knight Arthur of Little Britain*, ed. E. V. Utterson (London, 1814); Henry Lovelich, *Merlin*, ed. Ernst A. Kock, EETS ES 93, 112, OS 185 (London, 1904, 1913, 1932); Henry Lovelich, *The History of the Holy Grail*, ed. Frederick Furnivall, EETS ES 20, 24, 28, 30 (London, 1874, 1875, 1877, 1878); *Merlin*, ed. Henry B. Wheatley, intr. William Edward Mead, EETS 10, 21, 36, 112 (London, 1865, 1866, 1869, 1899).

Henry, the future Henry V, with the advice that it is a mirror in which the prince can fashion himself (Prol.166–70). The specific model for Henry in this work is Hector:

> ...of knyȝthod spring & welle,
> Flour of manhod, of strengþe per[e]les,
> Sadde & discret & prudent neuere-þe-les,
> Crop & rote, grounde of chiualrie,
> Of cher demure, and of curtesye
> He was example—þer-to of sobirnes
> A verray merour, & for his gentilnes
> In his tyme þe most[e] renomed,
> To reknen al, and of goodlyhed
> Þe most[e] famus, [and] in pes & werre
> Ferþest spoke of, boþe nyȝe & ferre.[38]

The closing wish of the *Troy Book*, that England and France will be at peace under the rule of Henry V (v.3411–42), suggests a comparison between these two countries and the subject of the work, Greece and Troy: the implication is that Henry must overgo Hector and succeed, where Hector failed, to unite two mighty nations. Furthermore, Helen Cooper has perceptively revealed how the Tudor *Blanchardyn and Eglantine* (1489–91), in Caxton's subtle revisions of his source, gives imaginative support to Henry VII's tenuous accession.[39] As Cooper observes in the same context, the bitter factionalism and competing dynastic claims of the fifteenth century must have given heightened meaning to the romances of exiled youths who struggle to regain their patrimony. In Havelok, Bevis, or Florent, a fifteenth-century reader might have seen Henry VI or Edward IV. Youths striving to regain their correct social position exist also in new fifteenth-century romances, such as Caxton's popular *The Foure Sonnes of Aymon* (1489–91).[40] Arthur is perhaps the supreme example of this figure, and considering the doubtfulness of his legitimacy and

---

[38] John Lydgate, *Lydgate's Troy Book*, ed. Henry Bergen, EETS ES 97, 103, 106, 126 (London, 1906, 1908, 1910, 1935), II.4802–12. Cf. other encomiums of Hector: II.244–65; III.484–96. See also Prol.166–70 on the use of romance as a mirror in which one sees the 'truth' concerning one's ancestors and a moral pattern in which to fashion oneself.

[39] Cooper, 'Romance after 1400', in Wallace (ed.), *Cambridge History of Medieval Literature*.

[40] William Caxton, *The Right Plesaunt and Goodly Historie of the Foure Sonnes of Aymon*, ed. Octavia Richardson, EETS ES 44, 45 (London, 1884, 1885).

his claim to the throne, he was a particularly 'Tudor' hero. The historical and political relevance of Malory's work will be considered in the following chapter, though it is interesting to note in this context the strong interest in Arthur in John Hardyng's *Chronicle* (1457), written at the height of England's internecine strife. The designation of this work as historical writing rather than romance is tenuous, and what the *Chronicle* perhaps best represents is the tendency of fifteenth-century texts to comment, directly or obliquely, on the tumultuousness and political hardships affecting contemporary England.

Approaching the same topic from the opposite end, the fifteenth-century tendency to write recent history as romance—to us, propaganda—has roots in the efforts of earlier romance texts to explore a sense of English nationhood:

> The well of knyghthode, withouten any pere,
> Of all erthely prynces thowe were the lode-sterre!
> Be-holde & rede, herkyn well and hyre!
> In gestis, in romansis, in Cronicles hygh & ferre,
> Well knowen it is, þer can no man it deferre,
>   Perelees he was, and was here yestirday.
>   All men of Englond ar bounde for hym to pray.[41]

These lines could easily apply to Guy, Bevis, or Arthur, but in fact they commemorate Edward IV. Another Yorkist poem constructs the familiar romance narrative in which the rightful heir— again, Edward IV—has regained his 'heritage', from which he was unfairly displaced by Henrys IV, V, and VI— 'Unrightful heyres by wrong alyaunce / Usurpyng this Royaume caused gret adversitey'.[42] Like Godard in *Havelok*, Henry IV seized the throne 'undir the colour of fals periury' (10). But, the poet concludes, 'Scripture saith, "heritage holdyn wrongfully / Schal never cheve"' ('succeed'; 43–4). The biblical attribution is false, but these lines could be taken as an epigrammatic summary of the romances of displaced youths, and they suggest an historical context in which older romances could still be read with a sense of their relevance to a conception of national identity and political experience.

---

[41] 'The Death of Edward IV (1483)', in *Historical Poems of the XIVth and XVth Centuries*, ed. Rossell Hope Robbins (New York, 1959), 112.29–35.
[42] 'A Political Retrospect (1462)', in ibid., 222.3–4.

Whatever their different literary aspirations and authority, fifteenth-century romances often resonate on the narrative level with the older romance texts, and therefore it is not surprising that romance-readers in the late Middle Ages could and did read both forms, the old verse romances and the new authorial works. *Ipomedon* in its tail-rhyme version is a long and complicated romance which both recalls established motifs and also seems to anticipate the colourful, heraldic chivalry of the Elizabethan Accession Day Tilt or *The Faerie Queene*.[43] The most familiar scene in the work occurs when Ipomedon, who is really a king, disguises himself as a fool and goes to the court in Sicily, voluntarily undertaking the service of a scornful maiden—a manufactured instance of the 'Fair Unknown' story, analogous to *Perceval* and *Lybeaus*, and in the detail of the maiden's contempt closely anticipating Malory's 'Tale of Sir Gareth'. The new aspect of this romance is its freedom from Christian didactic controls. Ipomedon's disguise is not part of a process of achieving his identity through the working of providence, but rather a demonstration of modesty and *sprezzatura*. The emphasis of the work is entirely on courtly manners and the appearance and conduct of a gentleman; among many adventures, Ipomedon wins a three-day tournament, disguised in a different colour of armour each day.[44] The secular emphasis here on chivalric self-effacement and courtly conduct is emblematic of a work which has been profitably analysed as a courtesy manual in narrative.[45]

Generydes also suggests the continuity of traditional matter in newer forms.[46] *Generydes* reflects the new interest in romance as

[43] *Ipomedon* survives in three versions: tail-rhyme (late fourteenth-century), rhyming couplets (early fifteenth-century), and prose (*c.* 1460). The three versions survive in one manuscript each, and the couplet version also survives in two sixteenth-century prints. All versions are edited in *Ipomedon in drei englischen Bearbeitungen*, ed. Eugene Kölbing (Breslau, 1889). The ultimate source of all versions is the Anglo-Norman *Ipomédon* (*c.* 1190) by Hue de Rotelande.

[44] In *Sir Gowther* (*c.* 1400), the hero fights against pagans, disguising his identity by wearing consecutively three different colours of armour. Unlike Ipomedon, Gowther's anonymity is part of a Christian, penitential ordeal.

[45] Carol M. Meale, 'The Middle English Romance of *Ipomedon*: A Late Medieval "Mirror" for Princes and Merchants', *RMS* 10 (1984), 136–82.

[46] *Generydes*, ed. W. Aldis Wright, EETS 55, 70 (London, 1873, 1878). *Generydes* exists in two independent versions, a couplet version and a stanzaic version that is less pictorial and more given to moralistic proverbs. *Generydes* survives in two manuscripts and the fragmentary remains of a third. Two sixteenth-century printed editions

a mirror of courtly manners, rather than the quasi-hagiographical or penitential form which romance took in a number of four-teenth-century texts.[47] Nevertheless, the plot of *Generydes* reads like a summation of narrative motifs of the 'popular' verse romances, particularly close to *Degare*: a king lost in a forest during a hunt encounters a faerie lady and leaves her with child; this unknown youth comes to court; a treacherous steward attempts to betray the youth; the father and son, ignorant of each other's identity, engage in combat as part of the process by which the orphaned son overcomes the disadvant-ages of exile.

Henry Watson's prose translation of a French source, *Valentine and Orson*, also belongs to the category of new romances gen-erally concerned with courtly and secular conduct and at the same time offers a narrative which would appeal to readers of older romances, such as the 'Eustace–Constance–Florence–Gri-selda' group.[48] It contains familiar plot-motifs: a slandered woman gives birth in a forest to twins; one of the children is abducted by a bear and raised as a 'savage man' in the forest, a more extreme version of the dispossessed youth than Perceval or Florent, but nevertheless analogous; and the other child, raised in the court of king, like Horn falls in love with a lady and, because of his condition as a foundling, is a 'squire of low degree'. Simi-larly, Lord Berners' *Huon of Bordeaux* would be inviting to readers familiar with the earlier verse romances. Like Bevis and other heroes, Huon is a dispossessed and exiled youth who falls in love with the daughter of a pagan lord. Clariet, the daughter of Huon, is a Constance-figure. Croissant, the fourth generation, is analogous to Sir Isumbras.

---

survive; furthermore, Thomas Purfoote was licensed to print a book called *Generydes*, presumably the same work, in 1568; Severs (gen. ed.), *Manual*, 148.

[47] See, for example, 3305–18 in the stanzaic version.

[48] Henry Watson, *Valentine and Orson*, ed. Arthur Dickson, EETS 204 (London, 1937). The romance survives in three sixteenth-century prints. Valentine and Orson appeared as characters in the coronation pageant of Edward VI in 1547; R. Withington, *English Pageantry* (Cambridge, Mass., 1918), I. 185. Sidney mentions Pacolet's horse, a creature from *Valentine and Orson*, in the *Defence* (66). Records survive of a sixteenth-century play apparently based on this romance: *A Transcript of the Registers of the Company of Stationers of London, 1554–1640*, ed. Edward Arber, 5 vols. (London, 1875–94), II. 298; Philip Henslowe, *Henslowe's Diary*, ed. W. W. Greg, 2 vols. (London, 1904–8), I. 90, II. 195.

Thus far, Middle English romance has emerged with a number of characterizing tendencies, the hallmarks of its memorial, traditional, and intertextual nature. We have seen that romance writers are interested in the associations between their narrative worlds and the sort of historical discourse which roots events in particular places—places which may even still bear the signs of those earlier historical events. In a number of the seemingly most popular and influential native romances, the romance world offers a mirror-version of the reader's experience, and the more idealized character of that mirror-world may be justified as true through its providential origins, or it may simply represent a more desirable way of thinking about national history and identity. And we have also seen, as characteristic of a large number of native romances, an interest in the story-patterns of displaced youths and slandered women; these stories resonate with biblical narrative, and they often work within the context of the other tendency—the historical and specifically English nature of the romance world.

These texts exploring personal and national identity, the nature of nobility and faith, and the role of providence in human affairs were to have a profound affect on Sir Thomas Malory as he reworked his French Arthurian sources. *Le Morte Darthur* is the great predecessor to *The Faerie Queene* in a way that Henry Lovelich's *History of the Holy Grail* (*c.* 1420) and *Merlin* (*c.* 1425) or the anonymous prose *Merlin* are not.[49] Under the influence of Middle English romance and historical traditions, Malory created a work with a complexity and richness equal to the great French exemplars of Arthurian romance, but one that is also deliberately rooted in native literary traditions and which offers a mirror for contemporary England.

---

[49] *The History of the Holy Grail*, which is acephalous, is a close translation of the first part of the thirteenth-century Vulgate prose cycle, *Lestoire del saint graal* (in *The Vulgate Version of the Arthurian Romances*, ed. H. Oskar Sommer, 8 vols. (Washington, D.C., 1908–16)). Lovelich's *Merlin* is a translation of the first half of *Merlin*, the second part of the Vulgate cycle (*Merlin*, ed. Alexandre Micha, TLF 281 (Geneva, 1967)). The *Prose Merlin*, *c.*1450, is also a translation of the Vulgate version of *Merlin*. See further: Dorothy Kempe, *The Legend of the Holy Grail*, EETS ES 95 (London, 1905); Robert W. Ackerman, 'Henry Lovelich's *Merlin*', PMLA 67 (1952), 473–84; Karen Stern, 'The Middle English *Prose Merlin*', in Alison Adams et al. (eds), *The Changing Face of Arthurian Romance*, AS 16 (Cambridge, 1986), 112–22 (not on Lovelich's text, but the prose *Merlin*).

5
Malory's *Le Morte Darthur*: Remembering Native Romance

Malory's response to both Continental sources and the native romance tradition so resembles the approach to these same texts taken by Spenser a century later that the preceding study of Middle English romance could be offered as a means to appreciate Malory's nativeness, and end there. Rather than enumerating the relatively few occurrences where Spenser's work demonstrates a specific textual debt to *Le Morte Darthur*, there is a need to view Malory as Spenser's predecessor in his handling of Continental and native source materials. From that perspective, the similarities between Malory and Spenser become striking. Although the *Morte* and *The Faerie Queene* differ in their didactic methods and moral vision, they are comparable in their revision of Continental sources to accord with the structure, tone, and mimetic character of the native romance tradition.[1] This chapter aims to establish the nativeness of the *Morte Darthur*, first by considering Malory's use of native romance sources, and then by looking at how Continental sources were, in his handling, influenced by his memory of native romance. Two concerns in particular will arise, both connecting Malory to the native tradition while also anticipating his relevance to Spenser: one is Malory's concern with stories of noble youths who are displaced or disguise their identity, and the other is Malory's

[1] The instances of specific relationship between Spenser's works and the *Morte* are discussed in Mark Lambert's entry on Malory in Hamilton (gen. ed.), *Spenser Encyclopedia*. In considering the relationship between *The Faerie Queene* and *Le Morte Darthur* Lambert acknowledges that 'the vital thing is not motif or locution or structure but tone and sensibility'. Rosemond Tuve, *Allegorical Imagery* (Princeton, 1966), 336 notes that the 'bane of studies relating Spenser to romances [which in her intention includes Malory] has been the hunt for borrowed story-motifs'. A welcome attempt to examine the relationship between Malory and Spenser in terms of a large-scale similarity, or intertextuality, is Paul R. Rovang, *Refashioning 'Knights and Ladies Gentle Deeds'* (Madison and London, 1996).

problematized attempt to fuse history and romance into an idealized version of England.

(I) 'SOMME IN ENGLYSSHE, BUT NOWHER NYGH ALLE': MALORY'S USE OF NATIVE ROMANCE

The study of native romance and historical writings provides an
important context in which to locate Malory as an English writer
whose 'Frenchness' has been over-represented by his two principal
editors, William Caxton and Eugène Vinaver. Caxton's 'Preface'
places an emphasis on Malory's Frenchness which reflects the
printer's enthusiasm for French and Burgundian culture and his
apparent lack of interest in native verse romance; he writes that
Malory took his Arthurian subject-matter 'oute of certeyn bookes
of Frensshe and reduced it into Englysshe'.[2] At the same time that
Caxton appeals to the patriotic inclinations of his readers—
Arthur 'was a man borne wythin this royame and kyng and
emperour of the same' (p. cxliv.7–8)—he ironically sells his
work to an upper-class and socially aspirant readership interested
in the matter of '*Frensshe*' books.[3] His edition also diminishes the
sense of Malory's connections to native literature through
the alternative, non-alliterative version of Arthur's defeat of the
emperor Lucius of Rome which it offers.[4] Vinaver's edition similarly presents a 'French' Malory, a writer whose central interest
lies in his engagement with the thirteenth-century prose Vulgate
Cycle of Arthurian romances and other Continental sources.[5]

---

[2] Sir Thomas Malory, *The Works of Sir Thomas Malory*, ed. Eugène Vinaver, rev.
P. J. C. Field, 3rd edn., 3 vols. (Oxford, 1990), p. cxlv.28–9.

[3] Caxton directs the *Morte* 'unto alle noble prynces, lordes, and ladyes, gentylmen
or gentylwymmen' (p. cxlvi.19–20).

[4] The version in Caxton's edition of Arthur's campaign against the emperor of
Rome may be the work of either Caxton or Malory. John Withrington, 'Caxton,
Malory, and The Roman War in *The Morte Darthur*', *SP* 89 (1992), 350–66 and
Shunichi Noguchi, 'The Winchester Malory', *Arthuriana* 5 (1995), 15–23 see it as
Caxton's work; Charles Moorman, 'Desperately Defending Winchester', *Arthuriana* 5
(1995), 24–9 regards it as Malory's own revision. See also P. J. C. Field, 'Caxton's
Roman War', *Arthuriana* 5 (1995), 31–60. Whether the revision of the Roman War
episode was by Malory or Caxton, the fact remains that in this respect Caxton's
edition makes an effort (not entirely successful, I will argue shortly) to disguise a
more obvious connection between Malory's work and native romance.

[5] Malory, *Morte*, ed. Vinaver, pp. lvii–lxiv provides a discussion of Malory's handling of the alliterative *Morte Arthure*. But Vinaver's main interest lies in Malory's

Vinaver's famous hypothesis based on the treatment of the text by the scribes of the Winchester MS—that Malory wrote separate works which Caxton has misrepresented as a single work, *Le Morte Darthur*—makes his edition closer in structure to the Vulgate Cycle, which is composed of five separate parts.[6] One scholar has commented that, in establishing his text, Vinaver is guided by 'the assumption that Malory must be trying to say what the French text says'.[7] Despite the very considerable merits of their editions, neither Caxton nor Vinaver reveal how Malory's treatment of French source materials was influenced by the characteristics of native romance; nor is a great deal of attention paid to his use of native romances and historical writings as primary sources.[8]

treatment of the French sources. His notes provide the basis for considering how Malory changes these sources in favour of native style and interest, though that perspective is not a priority for Vinaver.

[6] For Vinaver's arguments, see Malory, *Morte*, ed. Vinaver, pp. xxxv–li. A strong contingency of scholars have disagreed with Vinaver's interpretation both of Malory's structure and of the representation of the work embodied in the Winchester MS. On the unity of the *Morte*, see: D. S. Brewer, '"the hoole booke"', in J. A. W. Bennett (ed.), *Essays on Malory* (Oxford, 1963), 41–63; C. S. Lewis, 'The English Prose *Morte*', in ibid., 7–28; Robert M. Lumiansky (ed.), *Malory's Originality* (Baltimore, 1964), passim; Murray J. Evans, '*Ordinatio* and Narrative Links: The Impact of Malory's Tales as an "hoole booke"', in James W. Spisak (ed.), *Studies in Malory* (Kalamazoo, 1985), 29–52; Carol M. Meale, '"The Hoole Book": Editing and the Creation of Meaning in Malory's Text', in Elizabeth Archibald and A. S. G. Edwards (eds), *A Companion to Malory* (Cambridge, 1996), 3–17. Much of the more recent work concerning the putative authorial structure of Malory's work rests upon an interpretation of the physical presentation of Caxton's print and the Winchester MS, both published in facsimile: *The Winchester Malory*, intr. N. R. Ker, EETS ss 4 (London, 1976); *Sir Thomas Malory: Le Morte D'Arthur, Printed by William Caxton in 1485*, intr. Paul Needham (London, 1976).

[7] Terence McCarthy, 'Malory and his Sources', in Archibald and Edwards (eds), *Companion to Malory*, 75–95 (85). Vinaver's editorial intrusiveness, making Malory subordinate to the French romances, is more alarming in his anthology of selections from Malory: *King Arthur and his Knights*, ed. Eugène Vinaver (London, 1968). Here he places the 'Knight of the Cart' episode, which in Malory comes after the Grail quest, according to the sequence of events in the French romances (i.e., before the Grail quest). See further: McCarthy, 'Malory and Sources', in Archibald and Edwards (eds), *Companion to Malory*, 87–8.

[8] It must be admitted that Malory is guilty of giving a stronger sense than is justified of his reliance on 'the Freynsshe booke', and he is silent concerning his debt to Middle English texts; see R. H. Wilson, 'Malory's French Book Again', *Comparative Literature* 2 (1950), 172–81 for Malory's deceptive references to what the 'Freynsshe booke' says in passages that are in fact his own contributions. See further: D. S. Brewer, 'Malory: The Traditional Writer and the Archaic Mind', in Richard Barber (ed.), *Arthurian Literature I* (Cambridge, 1981), 94–120; McCarthy, 'Malory and Sources', in Archibald and Edwards (eds), *Companion to Malory*, 78.

The character of the *Morte* is arguably closer to *Guy of Warwick* than the extremes of either the French *Lancelot* or *La queste del saint graal*. These two French works were major sources for Malory; *Guy*, on the other hand, is not known to have been a definite source, even if Malory must have been familiar with this exceptionally well-known romance.[9] But the direction in which Malory changed his French sources is towards the character of Guy's world—geographically and historically English, concerned in the first instance with chivalry as a practical code of conduct, and interested secondly in exploring Christian knighthood in a way which eschews mysticism and extreme asceticism, still allowing for armed combat in God's cause.[10] Malory would have known of, and may even have known

[9] He certainly encountered Guy, as the slayer of Colbrond, in a work which is known to have been a source for the *Morte*—John Hardyng's *Chronicle*; see Richmond, *Legend of Guy*, 135–6. But it is a fair supposition, based on the extreme popularity of the work, that Malory knew the Guy legend in its fuller form as a Middle English verse romance.

[10] Beverly Kennedy's categories of Heroic Knight and True Knight, employed in her analysis of knighthood in the *Morte*, could be applied respectively to the first and second parts of Guy's career; Beverly Kennedy, *Knighthood in the Morte Darthur*, AS 11, 2nd edn. (Cambridge, 1992). Malory's belief in chivalry as a practical code of honour by which to live and maintain the peace has been well documented, particularly in regard to his amelioration of Lancelot in comparison to the French texts and his transformation of the Grail quest in order to preserve the value of earthly chivalry. Because this subject has, quite rightly, been the central interest of a great deal of Malorian scholarship, I will not repeat its arguments here. Suffice it to say that the practical chivalric code set forth in the *Morte* accords with the moral, pious, yet 'down to earth' character of *Havelok, Bevis, Octavian*, and even penitential romances, such as *Sir Isumbras* and *Guy*. See further: P. E. Tucker, 'Chivalry in the *Morte*', in Bennett (ed.), *Essays on Malory*, 64–103; Mary Hynes-Berry, 'A Tale "Breffly Drawyne Oute of Freynshe"', in Toshiyuki Takamiya and Derek Brewer (eds), *Aspects of Malory*, AS 1 (Cambridge, 1981), 93–106; Stephen C. B. Atkinson, 'Malory's Lancelot and the *Queste of the Grail*', in Spisak (ed.), *Studies in Malory*, 129–52; Dhira B. Mahoney, 'The Truest and Holiest Tale: Malory's Transformation of *La Queste del Saint Graal*', in Spisak (ed.), *Studies in Malory*, 109–28; Kennedy, *Knighthood*, esp. 111–27. The following passages in the *Morte* reflect a practical belief in chivalry as an honourable social code, not unrelated to chivalric handbooks and biographies of the fifteenth century, such as Caxton's translation of Ramon Llull's *Book of the Ordre of Chyvalry* and *Le livre des faits de Jacques de Lalaing*, a life of the famous Burgundian knight: 106.23–5, 120.17–24, 160.33–5. On the theory that the *Morte* may have been one of a series of books that Caxton printed in collaboration with Anthony Woodville, 2nd earl Rivers, intended as an educational programme for the young Prince of Wales, see George D. Painter, *William Caxton* (London, 1976), 87–8. Original contributions by Malory enhancing Lancelot as a paragon of chivalry are: 270.16–8, 348.32–349.2, 534.4–10, 745.15–20, 863.28–31, 896.1–11, 948.28–9, 1018.3–6, 1045.3–31, 1145–54 (the healing of Sir Urry), 1259.9–21.

personally, Richard Beauchamp, earl of Warwick. Beauchamp strove to emulate his legendary ancestor, and *The Beauchamp Pageants* (between 1485–90), fifty-three line drawings with captions charting the chivalric career of Richard Beauchamp, recognizes that this fifteenth-century earl is 'lynealy of blood descended of noble Sr. Gy of Warwyk'.[11] Although this document is too late to have been an influence on the *Morte*, Beauchamp's life and example may have helped mould Malory's belief in the applicability of chivalry to life, either through personal contact or depictions of the earl similar to that in the *Beauchamp Pageants*.[12] More generally, native romances such as *Guy* appear to have exerted a strong influence on the direction in which Malory turned his French sources—towards an unravelling of their interlaced structure, a reduction of amorous sentiment, magic, mysticism, and psychological introspection, and the augmentation of a sense of native location and historicity. Terence McCarthy aptly notes that 'the English sources have had an effect far and beyond the precise passages which they have inspired'.[13]

Malory's interest in native romance emerges most forcefully in the version of Arthur's Roman War preserved in the Winchester MS, which draws heavily on the alliterative *Morte Arthure* for

[11] *Beauchamp Pageant*, ed. Dillon and St John Hope, f. 9.v. See also Richmond, *Legend of Guy*, 118–20.

[12] A case has been made for the influence of Beauchamp's life on Malory's 'Tale of Sir Gareth'; see Joseph R. Ruff, 'Malory's Gareth and Fifteenth-Century Chivalry', in Larry D. Benson and John Leyerle (eds), *Chivalric Literature*, Studies in Medieval Culture 14 (Kalamazoo, 1980). The identification of Sir Thomas Malory with the knight of that name from Newbold Revel, Warwickshire, was formerly the basis for arguing that Malory served under Beauchamp in foreign and domestic wars, but that supposition has recently been questioned on the basis on chronology; see P. J. C. Field, *The Life and Times of Sir Thomas Malory*, AS 29 (Cambridge, 1993), 54–64. Accepting that argument, the life of the famous earl would still have been a 'mirror of chivalry' which could have influenced Malory's depiction of chivalry in the *Morte*.

[13] McCarthy, 'Malory and Sources', in Archibald and Edwards (eds), *Companion to Malory*, 95 (see further 93–5). Malory's use of the English forms of names and his use of names known to exist only in English romances suggests a wide reading in native romance; see Larry D. Benson, *Malory's Morte Darthur* (Cambridge, Mass., and London, 1976), 40–3. John Hardyng's *Chronicle* was also a native source employed by Malory; see further Kennedy, 'Malory and English Sources' in Takamiya and Brewer (eds), *Aspects of Malory*. McCarthy, in Archibald and Edwards (eds), 76 argues that Hardyng's *Chronicle* encouraged Malory 'to distance himself from the more overtly literary approach of his French sources, with their concerns for amorous

both style and narrative content.[14] Although Spenser is unlikely to have encountered this text in the Winchester MS,[15] the Winchester 'Roman War' episode is still relevant to this study as an instance of Malory's interest in native literature; the primary emphasis of this chapter is on Malory's place within the romance tradition which precedes and is contemporary with him. The prose of the Winchester MS version of the Roman War episode retains the forceful alliteration, even alliterative lines, of its source-text. For example:

'And thow be aferde,' seyde kyng Arthure, 'I rede the faste fle, for they wynne no worshyp of me but to waste their toolys; for there shall never harlot have happe, by the helpe of Oure Lord, to kylle a crowned kynge that with creyme is anoynted.'

(227.19–23)[16]

Malory's retention of alliteration cannot be dismissed as submissiveness before his sources or an indication of early, immature work.[17] On the contrary, he handles alliteration with skill, familiarity, and obvious relish, demonstrated by his tendency to com-

---

intrigue and private motivation, and may have helped him to focus his own more historical vision of the Arthurian world'.

[14] This is Vinaver's Tale II, 185–247. On Malory's Roman War episode, see: R. H. Wilson, 'Malory's Early Knowledge of Arthurian Romance', *Texas Studies in Literature* 32 (1953), 33–50; Mary E. Dichmann, '"The Tale of King Arthur and the Emperor Lucius": The Rise of Lancelot', in Lumiansky (ed.), *Malory's Originality*, 67–90; Edward D. Kennedy, 'Malory's Use of Hardyng's *Chronicle*', NQ 16 (1969), 167–70; L. Benson, *Malory's Morte*, 39–59; Kennedy, 'Malory and English Sources', in Takamiya and Brewer (eds), *Aspects of Malory*, 27–55; Terence McCarthy, 'Malory and the Alliterative Tradition', in Spisak (ed.), *Studies in Malory*, 53–85; Elizabeth Archibald, 'Beginnings: *The Tale of King Arthur* and *King Arthur and the Emperor Lucius*', in Archibald and Edwards (eds), *Companion to Malory*, 133–51; McCarthy, 'Malory and Sources', in ibid.

[15] Spenser presumably read Malory in one of the three sixteenth-century printed editions: 1529, by Wynkyn de Worde; 1557, by William Copland; c. 1585, by Thomas East. For a list of editions, see Eugène Vinaver, *Malory* (Oxford, 1929), 189–9.

[16] Cf. *Morte Arthure*, ed. Brock, 2438–47.

[17] Lewis, 'English Prose *Morte*', in Bennett (ed.), *Essays on Malory*, 26 condemns Malory's prose style in the Roman War episode as 'a noisy rumble'. Vinaver regarded the Roman War episode as the first and stylistically 'least polished' (p. lv) of Malory's tales; Malory, *Morte*, ed. Vinaver. The argument that the Roman War episode was Malory's first venture in the Arthurian stories and that it is stylistically weak is effectively dismissed as subjective and anachronistic by Kennedy, 'Malory and English Sources', in Takamiya and Brewer (eds), *Aspects of Malory*, 31–3 and Terence McCarthy, 'The Sequence of Malory's Tales', in ibid., 107–24.

pose additional passages in alliterative style.[18] Furthermore, the influence of the alliterative *Morte Arthure* extends beyond the Roman War episode; Ector's threnody to the dead Lancelot at the very end of Malory's work appears to be adapted from the eulogy given to Gawain in the alliterative poem.[19]

The version of the Roman War episode in Caxton's print and the printed editions of the sixteenth century, which Spenser would have known, remains a text which derives from a native romance source and which reflects its characteristic structure, historical interests, and narrative tone. Although the text in Caxton's print does reduce alliteration, it does not eliminate it entirely. It becomes instead a subtle but persistent thread running throughout the text:

And as the kyng laye in his caban in the shyp he fyll in a slomerynge and dremed a merueyllous dreme hym semed that a dredeful dragon dyd drowne moche of his peple and he cam fleynge oute of the west and his hede was enameled with asure and his sholders shone as gold his bely lyke maylles of a merueyllous hewe his taylle ful of tatters his feet ful of fyne sable & his clawes lyke fyne gold And an hydous flamme flewe oute of his mouthe lyke as the londe and water had flammed all of fyre.[20]

Caxton's account of Arthur's war against Lucius preserves other essential features of the Winchester version, features which derive from and signal an interest in native romance and historiographical traditions. For one, it retains the linear narrative structure characteristic of Middle English romance, and it also presents an 'historical' subject-matter, reflecting Geoffrey of Monmouth's *Historia* and derived texts such as Hardyng's *Chronicle*. Most importantly, Caxton's version of the Roman War preserves the specific detail which Malory found in Hardyng—Arthur's coronation as emperor of Rome. The climax of Arthur's foreign conquests comes when he is 'crouned emperour by the popes hand

---

[18] McCarthy, 'Sequence of Tales', in Takamiya and Brewer (eds), *Aspects of Malory*, 111–3. See also McCarthy, 'Malory and the Alliterative Tradition', in Spisak (ed.), *Studies in Malory*, 53–85.

[19] Cf. Malory, 1259 with *Morte Arthure*, 3872–8. See further Kennedy, 'Malory and English Sources', in Takamiya and Brewer (eds), *Aspects of Malory*, 40.

[20] The text of Caxton's edition is printed in Malory, *Morte*, ed. Vinaver as a parallel text (at the bottom of the page). I have reproduced this passage (196.4–11) as Vinaver presents it, without marks of punctuation.

with all the ryalte that could be made' (Caxton's text; 245.1–2).[21]
Malory has removed the tragic ending of the alliterative *Morte*,
preferring to place Arthur's Roman conquest as an early achievement in his career.[22] Both texts of the Roman War also omit
details from the alliterative *Morte* which portray Arthur as
cruel, bloodthirsty, and culpable of sin.[23] As a result, Malory's
reworking of the *Morte Arthure*, in Caxton's version as well as
the Winchester MS, provides an uninhibited vision of England
replacing Rome as God's chosen nation. It is a politically charged
use of romance-as-history which anticipates Spenser's own
application of romance, or a providential view of history, to the
Elizabethan nation. Indeed, because of the potential of Arthur's
defeat of Rome to be good Protestant allegory, Spenser might
have incorporated Arthur's Roman campaign into the projected twelve Books dealing with the period after Arthur's
coronation.[24]

Malory's 'memory' of the alliterative *Morte Arthure* is obvious.
Other recollections of native romance in his work cannot be

[21] Caxton appears to have regarded this detail as significant, since he specifies in his
'Preface' that Arthur was 'kyng and emperour' of Britain (p. cxliv.8). The text of the
Winchester MS is here closely similar; Arthur is 'crowned Emperoure by the Poopys
hondis, with all the royalté in the worlde to welde for ever' (245.7–8). The coronation
is anticipated in the alliterative *Morte Arthure* (3183–6), but it does not occur because
of the disruption caused by Mordred's usurpation. On Malory's use of Hardyng's
Chronicle, see: Kennedy, 'Malory's Use of Hardyng'; Malory, *Morte*, ed. Vinaver,
1405. On the thematic significance of the coronation scene in Malory, see Elizabeth
T. Pochoda, *Arthurian Propaganda* (Chapel Hill, 1971), 89.
[22] In Hardyng's *Chronicle*, the Roman war precedes the Grail quest; it also occurs
early in the Vulgate Cycle, in the *Estoire de Merlin*. In Geoffrey's *Historia* and
Laȝamon's *Brut*, Arthur receives the news of Mordred's rebellion before reaching
Rome; he returns immediately to Britain and his death.
[23] William Matthews, *The Tragedy of Arthur* (Berkeley and Los Angeles, 1960),
176.
[24] Malory possibly intends Arthur's foreign conquests to allude to the French
victories of Henry V; see Malory, *Morte*, ed. Vinaver, 1367–8, 1396–8. Terence
McCarthy, *An Introduction to Malory*, AS 20 (Cambridge, 1991), 17–18 emphasizes
the sense of historicity in Malory's account of the Roman war. Similarly, Arthur in the
alliterative poem may be intended as a representation of Edward III, another king who
conducted campaigns on the Continent; see Sir Thomas Malory, *The Morte Darthur:
Parts Seven and Eight*, ed. D. S. Brewer (London, 1968), 7. Arthur's Roman expedi-
tion was used by the medieval English (not without being queried) to support political
claims; Kendrick, *British Antiquity*. Two articles by A. Kent Hieatt argue that Spenser
would have included the Roman conquest for the period of Arthur's kingship because
of the natural opportunities it offered for Protestant allegory; 'The Projected Continuation of *The Faerie Queene*: Rome Delivered?', *SS* 8 (1990), 335–42; 'Arthur's
Deliverance of Rome? (Yet Again)', *SS* 9 (1991), 243–8.

determined with such specificity, but only because they relate to areas of intertextual complexity within the tradition. Furthermore, Malory's recollections of native romance often provide the bare ingredients from which he returns an innovative contribution to the developing tradition. This is particularly the case with the 'Tale of Sir Gareth', which has no known source, only analogues and traditions to which it is related.[25] Rather than imagining a lost direct source among French literature[26] it is reasonable to consider, on the basis of Malory's established interest in native romance and his inventive response to source materials and traditions, that 'Sir Gareth' is a composite memory of several heroes of the native tradition examined in the preceding chapters—namely, displaced youths who are raised in surroundings which contrast or conflict with their vocational longing (derived from birth) towards chivalry and Christian faith. This story-type provides a framework for different kinds of thematic and narrative exploration, as we have seen: an emphasis on providential guidance and fulfilment for both the individual and the nation, an insistence that chivalry is in the blood, and a comic treatment of the youth's noble pretensions lacking the authority of training. Malory and Spenser both adapt the framework to their own concerns, and for Malory the story provides narrative focus for an examination of the nature of chivalry. Malory's recollection of this story-type contains the individual stamp of his particular interest: an élitist emphasis on the relationship between chivalry and noble blood and a concern to define chivalry not just as a martial code but in relation to a broader range of human behaviour and character traits. Because Malory's 'Tale of Sir Gareth' both relates his work to traditional Middle English verse romances and foreshadows the career Redcrosse, it deserves fuller consideration.

Like Lybeaus and Perceval, Gareth arrives abruptly at Arthur's court and requests of the king various favours, including knighthood and the undertaking of the first adventure required of the

---

[25] On the possible sources for Sir Gareth, see further: R. H. Wilson, 'The Fair Unknown in Malory', *PMLA* 58 (1943), 1–21; Benson, *Malory's Morte*, 92–108; P. J. C. Field, 'The Source of Malory's *Tale of Gareth*', in Takamiya and Brewer (eds), *Aspects of Malory*, 57–70; T. L. Wright, 'On the Genesis of Malory's *Gareth*', *Speculum* 57 (1982), 569–82.

[26] This is the view considered by Vinaver: Malory, *Morte*, ed. Vinaver, 1427–34.

court. Whereas Lybeaus and Perceval were genuinely ignorant of their aristocratic identities, Gareth, who is the son to King Lot and brother to Sir Gawain, has deliberately chosen, like Ipomedon, to disguise his noble birth. On his arrival at the court, Gareth's good looks (294.29–30) and courteous speech (294.3–11) lead Arthur and others to believe that he is 'com of men of worshyp' (294.19–20). For Kay, however, Gareth's initial request—food and drink for a year—is too basic to be the priority of a knight:

'I undirtake he is a vylane borne, and never woll make man, for and he had be come of jantyllmen, he wolde have axed horse and armour, but as he is, so he askyth'.

$$(294.36–295.3)^{27}$$

Sir Kay may be wrong in his estimation of Gareth's birth and character, but his essential point-of-view—that 'a vylane borne... never woll make man'—receives the full support of the other characters and the text. For example, before Lancelot agrees to knight Gareth, or Bewmaynes as Kay has derisively named him, he orders that 'ye tell me your name of ryght, and of what kyn ye be borne' (299.21–2). When Lancelot hears what he earlier suspected, that Bewmaynes is in fact of noble birth, he is pleased to knight him: 'for evir me thought ye sholde be of grete bloode, and that ye cam nat to the courte nother for mete nother drynke' (299.29–31). Lancelot's values are the same as Kay's; he is simply more astute in realizing that Gareth really must be of noble birth, even if disguised, because of his deeds and appearance. Indeed, Lancelot's faith in the evidence of Gareth's deeds as signifiers of noble birth argues a more élitist estimation of the value of noble birth and knighthood than Kay's scepticism, which suggests in turn that knighthood can be successfully impersonated by a 'vylayne'. Lancelot later makes clear that Gareth could never earn entry to his order without the prerequisite of correct birth; Gareth, Lancelot says, 'is com of full noble bloode... or ellys I wolde not have yeffyn hym the hyghe Order of Knyghthode' (326.23–9). The damsel, Lynet, who accompanies

[27] A knightly contempt for food is carefully displayed by Don Quixote; Miguel de Cervantes Saavedra, *The Adventures of Don Quixote*, tr. J. M. Cohen (Harmondsworth, 1950), 70–1 (Part 1, Ch. 8).

Gareth on his quest to aid the Lady Lyonesse demonstrates a growth in perspicacity in relation to her companion-knight, from the prejudices of Kay to the perception of Lancelot. At first, she scorns the 'impostor' Bewmaynes, even though he defeats his opponents fairly and effectively:

'What wenyste thou?' seyde the lady, 'that I woll alow the for yondir knyght that thou kylde? Nay, truly, for thou slewyst hym unhappyly and cowardly. Therefore turne agayne, thou bawdy kychen knave! I know the well, for sir Kay named the Beawmaynes. What art thou but a luske, and a turner of brochis, and a ladyll-waysher!'

(300.7–14)

Later, she realizes that Gareth's deeds are truly noble, the sure indications of noble birth:

hit may never be other but that ye be com of jantyll bloode, for so fowle and shamfully dud never woman revyle a knyght as I have done you, and ever curteysly ye have suffyrde me, and that com never but of jantyll bloode.

(312.30–4)[28]

'The Tale of Sir Gareth' has a dialogic relationship with other incidents in the *Morte*. Although these incidents were embedded in Malory's French sources, they are drawn into the work's nativeness through their similarities to the 'Tale of Sir Gareth'. Early in 'Sir Gareth', Lancelot connects Bewmaynes to one of these analogous figures when he rebukes Kay: 'so ye gaff the good knyght Brunor, sir Dynadans brothir, a name, and ye called hym La Cote Male Tayle, and that turned you to anger aftirwarde' (295.15–18). Both Bewmaynes and La Cote Male Tayle are given their derisive pseudonyms by Kay. Both knights appear abruptly at Arthur's court and request to be knighted. Both knights undertake the quest of a damsel who appears at the court. Like Bewmaynes, La Cote Male Tayle is scorned by the damsel.[29] In both cases, there is a concern with the lineage of the new knight; in the case of Sir La Cote Male Tayle, he states at the outset 'within shorte space ye shall know that I am comyn of goode kynne'

---

[28] There are other insistences that Bewmaynes' actions reveal, and by implication stem from, his noble blood, such as 315.19–20, 326.19–21, 330.4–9.

[29] She later reveals that she rebuked him because of her love for him—to dissuade him from undertaking an adventure for which she supposed him too young and tender (471.16–23).

(459.9–10) and later Sir Lancelot comments 'I doute nat but he shall preve a noble man' (471.13–14). And both knights retain some of the comic or rustic behaviour of displaced heroes such as Bevis, Florent, and Perceval: Lynet taunts Gareth for being, like Havelok, a 'bawdy kychen knave' and 'ladyll-wayssher', and 'La Cote Male Tayle' has an eponymous ill-fitting garment.

The account of La Cote Male Tayle, despite its French origins, becomes a memory of native romance through its resemblance to Sir Gareth. Similarly, other parts of the *Morte* begin to look more at home in the Middle English romance tradition through their sympathetic resonance with 'Sir Gareth'. The emphasis in 'Sir Gareth' upon the priority of birth applies also to Arthur and connects the king to all the romances, such as *Bevis* and *Havelok*, in which displaced heirs regain their proper patrimony in accordance with providential guidance. Arthur believes that Sir Ector, rather than King Uther Pendragon, is his father. The trial of the sword in the stone reveals his innate, indelible royalty, a thing which cannot be earned or acquired; despite strenuous efforts, all the other knights fail the test (14.32–40). The damsel's initial scorn of Bewmaynes is matched in the reaction of the barony to Arthur's success at the trial of the sword in the stone; they 'saide it was grete shame unto them all and the reame to overgovernyd with a boye of no hyghe blood borne' (15.23–5). As with Sir Gareth, Arthur's subsequent actions justify the barons' point-of-view, though not to the detriment of Arthur: 'hyghe blood' is indeed essential to chivalry and rule, and Gareth and Arthur only succeed because they do in fact possess this gift of birth, even if it is at first not recognized. Similarly, the account of Torre maintains an élitist insistence on the link between noble birth and noble, or knightly, character. A cowherd who believes that Torre is his son brings him to court, complaining that Torre is unlike his other sons. Torre's siblings labour in the fields, but Torre 'woll be shotynge, or castynge dartes, and glad for to se batayles and to beholde knyghtes' (100.7–9). In fact, Torre is revealed to be the son not of the cowherd but of King Pellinor.[30]

---

[30] Torre's habit of shooting darts, despite his rearing by a cowherd, is a detail in Malory's text which does not appear to derive from his source, the *Suite de Merlin*; see Malory, *Morte*, ed. Vinaver, 1325–6. It may be an echo of *Sir Perceval*, where the hero's favourite weapon is the 'darte' (210).

(II) 'THERE WAS A KYNG OF THYS LANDE NAMED ARTHUR': THE UNION OF HISTORY AND ROMANCE IN THE *MORTE*

Malory's use of native source-materials is one important element in the creation of a work which is in no sense a smaller English Vulgate Cycle. His treatment of the French sources also reveals the shaping influence of native romance, whose most character-istic tendencies have impacted on the French sources in Malory's reception. In particular, Malory's adaptation of the French texts reveals his greater interest, concurrent with native romance, in the relationship between the romance mode and the representa-tion of national history, locality, and experience.

By 1485, the historicity of Arthur, or at least of certain aspects of his career, had been opened to challenge. Ranulph Higden, in the fourteenth century, and other medieval historians were troubled by their failure to locate in Continental and Anglo-Saxon historical writings confirmation of Arthur's overseas and domestic campaigns.[31] Caxton's 'Preface' to the *Morte* is a docu-ment belonging to the debate concerning Arthur's historicity and his appropriateness as a national figure—even if the views of the 'Preface' chiefly derive from a desire to sell the work. Concerning Arthur's historicity, Caxton writes:

Fyrst, ye may see his sepulture in the monasterye of Glastyngburye; and also in Polycronycon ... where his body was buryed, and after founden and translated into the sayd monasterye ... Also Galfrydus, in his Bru-tysshe book, recounteth his lyf. And in dyvers places of Englond many remembraunces ben yet of hym and shall remayne perpetuelly, and also of his knyghtes: fyrst, in the abbey of Westmestre, at Saynt Edwardes shryne, remayneth the prynte of his seal in reed waxe ... item, in the castel of Dover ye may see Gauwayns skulle and Cradoks mantel; at Wynchester, the Rounde Table; in other places Launcelottes swerde and many other thynges.

(p. cxliv.20–36)

---

[31] Caxton's initial scepticism to the 'noble jentylmen' who required him to print Arthurian literature was that 'somme cronycles make no mencyon ne remembre hym noothynge' (p. cxliv.14–15). In fact, query of the historicity of the Arthurian stories began much earlier, with William of Newburgh, but from the late fifteenth century onwards it intensified. In his English translation of Higden's *Polychronicon*, John Trevisa attempted to restore the historical credibility of the Arthurian legends; see further Kendrick, *British Antiquity* and R. H. Fletcher, *Arthurian Material in Chroni-*

Caxton's proofs recall the technique of romances such as *Have-lok, Guy, Bevis, Horn Childe* and *Athelstan*— the appeal, either directly or allusively, to something which is 'still there', connecting our world to the romance world and thus 'proving' that the events in the romance really happened. Malory himself gives an example of the appeal to something 'still there' in his account of Gawain's death:

And so at the owre of noone sir Gawayne yelded up the goste. And than the kynge lat entere hym in a chapell within Dover castell. And there yet all men may se the skulle of hym, and the same wounde is sene that sir Launcelot gaff in batayle.

$$(1232.16-20)^{32}$$

Furthermore, the origins of the religious foundation at Mont-St-Michel are explained by Arthur's battle with a giant at this site: Arthur 'commaunded his cosyn, sir Howell, to make a kyrke on that same cragge in the worshyppe of Seynte Mychael' (Winchester text, 205.14–16).[33] The narrator does not go so far as to say that the church is 'still there', but that is unnecessary due to the fame of the site. Caxton's phrase—'many remembraunces ben yet of hym and shall remayne perpetuelly'—could equally apply here.

One of the strongest connections between the *Morte* and the native romance tradition is Malory's effort to present his work as historical and by implication a guide to national self-understanding. The blatant appeal to something 'still there' is not his principal method of attaining historical credibility. Rather, Malory employs the more subtle rhetorical technique of

---

cles for useful summaries of the critical reception of the Galfridean tradition of British history.

[32] The passage appears to be Malory's own addition. It is not in *La mort le roi Artu*; see 224 for Gawain's death-scene. Nor is it in the stanzaic *Morte Arthur*, 3066–73, 3136–43.

[33] The source for this passage is in the alliterative *Morte Arthure*:

> He comande hys cosyne, with knyghtlyche wordez,
> To make a kyrke on the cragg, ther the corse lengez,
> And a couent there-in, Criste for to serfe,
> In mynde of that martyre, that in the monte rystez.
>
> (1218–21)

The passage also occurs in the text printed by Caxton: 'And after that kynge Arthur sayd and commaunded his Cosyn howel that he shold ordeyne for a chirche to be bylded on the same hylle in the worship of saynte Mychel' (205.6–8).

assuming historical credibility, and reflecting that assumption in his prose without special pleading. Historical veracity is taken for granted in the work's beginning:

Hit befel in the dayes of Uther Pendragon, when he was kynge of all Englond and so regned, that there was a myghty duke in Cornewaill that helde warre ageynst hym long tyme, and the duke was called the duke of Tyntagil.

(7.1–4)

Malory's style has been characterized as a chronicle style.[34] The hallmarks of the historical mode in writing are a specificity of time, place, and persons. In the opening passage of the *Morte*, events are fixed to a period of time, which is the reign of a king, the name of the king and also of the involved duke are given, and reference is made to actual geography. These characteristics obtain throughout the work. Added localization in particular is a pervasive feature of Malory's treatment of his French sources. For example, Malory writes that 'at Saynt Albons ther mette with the kynge a grete hoost of the North' (11.27–8). The French text makes no mention of St Albans; it merely states that Arthur's enemies 'vinrent contre lui'.[35] As another example, here Malory assumes the posture of an historian doing the best he can by his sources: 'Soo in the grettest chirch of London—whether it were Powlis or not the Frensshe booke maketh no mencyon—...' (12.26–8). Similarly, concerning the location of Joyous Gard, Lancelot's castle, the narrator confesses to a lack of information, thus implying that such historical information is relevant and could be obtained by diligent searching: 'Somme men say it was Anwyk, and somme men say it was Bamborow' (1257–27–8).[36] All true historical records, Eumnestes' chamber reminds us, have occasional 'canker holes'.

---

[34] P. J. C. Field, *Romance and Chronicle* (London, 1971), 37–9. See also: Jeremy Smith, 'Language and Style in Malory', in Archibald and Edwards (eds), *Companion to Malory*, 97–113.

[35] See Malory, *Morte*, ed. Vinaver, 1286. Vinaver proposes that Malory is alluding to the battle of St Albans of 1455. If Vinaver is correct, then this localization would have offered its fifteenth-century readers an even stronger sense of historical relevance.

[36] See further Vinaver's commentary to this passage (1660) for another possible reference to the Wars of the Roses.

Passages such as these are reminiscent of the English redactor's interpolation in *Bevis* of a battle in the streets of London, where geographic localization is accurate and detailed, or of the emphasis in the Auchinleck text of *Guy* placed on the English location and cause of Guy's final battle with the giant Colbrond. Like these other romance redactors, Malory tends to specify actual English placenames when the French sources are vague regarding locality. It is a characteristic of English romance which arguably has roots in the adaptation of Geoffrey of Monmouth's *Historia*, a work which abounds in toponymy and geographical references. Through the vernacular adaptations of Laȝamon, the prose *Brut*, Thomas Castelford's *Chronicle*, and Hardyng's *Chronicle*, the manner of 'historical' writing became increasingly available to and part of texts that partook of the romance mode, especially those treating Arthurian subject-matter. The numerous instances of localization in Malory are part of this tradition. Malory's identification of Camelot with Winchester, perhaps due to its 'Round Table', is another example.[37] A more detailed localization occurs in the episode of the 'Fair Maid of Ascolat', where Ascolat is identified as Guildford (1065.28). Malory places the court at the time of the story at Westminster, and Elayne floats down the river Thames (thirteen miles from Guildford) on her funeral barge to the court:

And whan she was dede the corse and the bedde all was lad the nexte way unto the Temmys, and there a man and the corse, and all thynge as she had devised, was put in the Temmys. And so the man stirred the bargett unto Westmynster, and there hit rubbed and rolled too and fro a grete whyle or ony man aspyed hit.

(1095.9–14)[38]

The rhetorical point to this passage is that the journey could still be done; all readers are able to gain access to Elayne's world.

---

[37] Caxton mentions the Round Table at Winchester in the passage from the 'Preface' cited above. Hardyng also mentions its presence, which may have given Malory the idea to link Camelot with Winchester. See further: Ellen Holbrook, 'Malory's Identification of Camelot as Winchester', in Spisak (ed.), *Studies in Malory*, 13–27.

[38] See further: George R. Stewart, 'English Geography in Malory's "Morte D'Arthur"', *MLR* 30 (1935), 204–9 (esp. 206–7); Malory, *Morte*, ed. Vinaver, 1604. More examples of Malory's specification of English placenames are: 61.6–7, 127.23, 635.23–4. Malory is also inclined to name characters who are nameless in his sources, a habit which augments the sense of concrete, 'historical' reality; see, for

Malory's tendency to specification, relating the action of the romance to accessible points of reference, is persistent throughout the *Morte*, and it has a cumulative force which relates the work strongly to the world of its contemporary readers. Because of the historicity and Englishness of the Arthurian world in the *Morte*, Malory is able to present its occurrences as directly relevant to a contemporary sense of national self-understanding, as he does in this famous passage:

Lo ye all Englysshemen, se ye nat what a myschyff here was? For he that was the moste kynge and nobelyst knyght of the worlde, and moste loved the felyshyp of noble knyghtes, and by hym they all were upholdyn, and yet myght nat thes Englyshemen holde them contente with hym. Lo thus was the olde custom and usayges of thys londe, and men say that we of thys londe have nat yet loste that custom. Alas! thys ys a greate defaughte of us Englysshemen, for there may no thynge us please no terme.

(1229.6–14)

Like many of the native romances already discussed, the Arthurian legends in Malory's treatment become not only more credible but also, borrowing Gower's phrase, a 'bok for Engelondes sake'.

A detailed sense of place and linear narrative structure are realistic, 'historical' elements within the *Morte,* but the work cannot be described in all its aspects as realistic. Perilous forests, giants, dwarves, bridges where one meets knightly challengers, enchanted ships and castles, the Holy Grail, and idealized, exaggerated human achievements are pronounced features of Malory's text. Like *Guy, Bevis,* and other romances (as well as contemporary historical writings and hagiography), the *Morte* combines the representative modes of romance and history, allowing for both the curtailing law of nature and the liberating force of the supernatural. But the *Morte* differs from texts considered thus far in its greater emphasis on the realistic mode, particularly after the Grail episode. Its world contains the political upheavals, prevarications, and treacheries of our own experience. It is ultimately a world in which, unlike the divinely assisted worlds of Guy and Bevis, time occasionally does run out; even in the case of an early episode, the story of Balyn and Balan, the

example, 1066.23 and Vinaver's commentary (1601) as well as R. H. Wilson, 'Malory's Naming of Minor Characters', *JEGP* 42 (1943), 364–85.

brothers' mutual recognition only occurs after they have wounded each other mortally. Considering the length of the work and numerousness of its incidents, it is inevitable that the *Morte* cannot represent one continuous, providentially guided movement of the historical world to romance completion, such as we find in *Guy*. Each of its 'completions' threatens to unravel as the narrative eye returns to areas of its world still lacking completion. The strong sense in Malory's work of the corruptibility of human nature, enacted above all in the loss of the Round Table through baronial factionalism and conflict, means that the early hopes in the *Morte* that human, or specifically English, experience might be fulfilled providentially give way to a bleak and realistic view of human lives as undirected, caught in cycles or less predictable rhythms of rise and fall. When Lancelot hears of Mordred's rebellion against Arthur, he rushes 'in all haste that myght be' (1250.5) to aid the king. But he is too late:

> Than sir Launcelot spyrred of men of Dover where was the kynge becom. And anone the people tolde hym how he was slayne and sir Mordred to, with an hondred thousand that dyed uppon a day.
>
> (1250.9–12)

Time has run out, a thing which never happened in the 'historical' native romances. In Malory, the things which are 'still there', such as Gawain's skull with its wound marks, truly attest to the victory of time, the failure of the world's events to shape themselves into the idealized patterns of romance.

Although the *Morte* in its ending does not represent the providential guidance of England towards a romance fulfilment, Malory's handling of Arthur's death does involve an ambiguity which recalls the providential sense which the king acquired in the earliest stages of his career. The principal sources for Malory's treatment of Arthur's ending were the stanzaic *Morte Arthur* and the final segment of the Vulgate Cycle, *La morte le roi Artu*, though he also retained a familiarity with the alliterative *Morte Arthure* and Hardyng's *Chronicle* and they may have shaped his own version of Arthur's ending.[39] Any writer treating Arthur's ending is faced

---

[39] On Malory's treatment of his sources in relation to Arthur's death, see: R. H. Wilson, 'Malory, The Stanzaic "*Morte Arthur*" and the "*Mort Artu*"', *MP* 37 (1939–40), 125–38; E. Talbot Donaldson, 'Malory and the Stanzaic *Le Morte Arthur*,' *SP* 47 (1950), 460–72; Robert M. Luminansky, 'Arthur's Final Companions in Malory's

with a decision, easily defined by these opposites: death or projected return, Glastonbury or Avalon, time or timelessness, history or romance. The alliterative *Morte Arthure* and *La morte le roi Artu*, Chapter 2 argued, offer historical representations of Arthur's demise, in which the king's death is the necessary price to pay for historical credibility. The stanzaic *Morte Arthur*, however, divorces itself from the ineluctable process of time, but in doing so it ceases to be history. Malory's achievement is to urge on his readers both belief in Arthur's historicity and an uncritical sense that he might be capable of returning. He does this by creating a 'grey area' in which those who are willing to suspend rational scrutiny can be satisfied that there is a connection between the England they know and a romance world of healing. Disjunction, ambiguity, and confusion create the necessary middle ground in which the barrier between history and romance is obscured or sublimated. To begin with, Arthur's last words are modelled on the stanzaic *Morte Arthur*: 'For I wyll into the vale of Avylyon to hele me of my grevous wounde. And if thou here nevermore of me, pray for my soule!' (1240.32–5).[40] The expectation of healing is part of the strategy with which the stanzaic poem, and Malory's work, resists the historical closure of death. But Arthur's second sentence in the quotation from Malory—'And if thou here nevermore of me, pray for my soule!'—is significantly not in the stanzaic poem. Malory is here working with a sense of detail, refining his words to achieve an exact effect. This addition opens up the possibility of an alternative ending, namely an historical one where Avalon is Glastonbury, a place where Arthur's tomb can still be seen: proof that these things happened but also proof that they are irrevocably behind us. Deliberate ambiguity makes it impossible to determine which ending will prevail; Arthur uses only the name Avalon, and the chapel visited later by Sir Bedyvere is '*besydes* Glassyngbyry' (1242.31; my emphasis), which is perhaps less precise than it could be. At one point, the narrator appears to be favouring the historical version of Arthur's death:

Morte Darthur', *Tulane Studies in English* 11 (1961), 5–19; C. David Benson, 'The Ending of the *Morte Darthur*', in Archibald and Edwards (eds), *Companion to Malory*, 221–38. A collection of essays on the death of Arthur in Arthurian literature in general is *The Passing of Arthur*, ed. Christopher Baswell and William Sharpe (New York and London, 1988).

[40] Cf. the stanzaic *Morte Arthur*, 3515–17.

Now more of the deth of kynge Arthur coude I never fynde, but that thes ladyes brought hym to hys grave, and such one was entyred there whych [the] ermyte bare wytnes that sometyme was Bysshop of Caunturbyry.

(1242.15–18)

But then Malory adds the ambiguity which creates a chink in the temporal process without eradicating historical credibility: 'But yet the ermyte knew nat in sertayne that he was veryly the body of [kyn]ge Arthur' (1242.18–20).[41] Our eye-witness authority for Arthur's death has failed us. He may be in the tomb in Glaston-bury, or he may not. Glastonbury may be a finite place, or it may be in the process of becoming Avalon. Malory acknowledges that 'som men say in many p[art]ys of Inglonde that knyge Arthure ys nat dede, but h[ad] by the wyll of Oure Lorde Jesu into another place; and men say that he shall come agayne, and he shall wynne the Holy Crosse' (1242.22–5). The attempt to join history to romance was achieved in works such as *Havelok* and *Guy* through an emphasis on God's providence as the agent which creates this reconciliation; Malory's notion that Arthur may be kept alive 'by the wyll of Oure Lorde Jesu' employs the same strategy. Divine Providence, coupled with ambiguity, allows for the possibility of two contradictory understandings of Arthur and his ending appearing to be reconciled. Malory's judgement neces-sarily retains a uncertainty of language and thought:

Yet I woll nat say that hit shall be so, but rather I wolde sey: here in thys worlde he chaunged hys lyff.

(1242. 25–7)

'Chaunged hys lyff' is a phrase which can take either the historical or the romance reading—the sense either of death or of transform-ative rebirth. Malory's inclusion of the sepulchral epitaph—HIC IACET ARTHURUS, REX QUONDAM REXQUE FUTURUS (1242.29)— is justified given the 'double ending' of his Arthur. The division of the treatments in various works of Arthur's ending between his-tory and romance could also be described as a division between *quondam* and *futurus*. But Malory's treatment suggests a para-dox: a king who was, and who may yet be. That hope is all the more luminous in the final stages of the *Morte* considering the

---

[41] Perhaps Malory's inspiration here comes from the Archbishop of the stanzaic *Morte Arthur*, who is completely ignorant of who is in the tomb (3537).

bleak failure, from the human perspective, of providence which is the context for Arthur's 'death'.

Guy of Warwick and other native romance heroes, who left a multitude of traces attesting to their historicity and who also achieved idealized adventures and, in the case of Guy, a sanctified death, come closer to the duality in Malory's treatment of Arthur than any French text. Most significantly, in turning now to Spenser, Malory has demonstrated the adaptability of Continental romance materials to accommodate native concerns. For one, story-types such as the 'Fair Unknown', which are characteristically native, and native sources such as the alliterative *Morte Arthure* can be combined with Continental sources, providing an overall sense of a native version. Furthermore, Continental Arthurian romances can be adapted, according to the influence of both Middle English romance and historical texts such as Hardyng's *Chronicle*, to explore a sense of English history and identity and to examine the possibility of connecting that historical world to an idealized, romance version of itself; Malory searches for that fulfilment, but ultimately recognizes its difficulty. He has sensed and responded to the chief characteristics and concerns of native romance. Spenser must now be considered from the same perspective.

6

The 'Reformation' of Native Romance in *The Faerie Queene*, Book I

In Book I of *The Faerie Queene*, Spenser draws heavily upon native romance to give narrative representation to a Protestant paradigm of 'Holiness'. He does not just depend upon native romance for language, incident, and descriptive details, though all of these are important, but for the full narrative scope of Book I, for the careers of Redcrosse and Una. Book I's saturation with imagery from the Book of Revelation and Protestant works which expound that text, such as John Bale's *The Image of Bothe Churches* (1548), is so engaging that it has led to a general neglect of the underlying narrative structures of native romance on which that imagery and doctrine are positioned.[1] But Book I could not have attained its present form without access to those narrative structures, and Spenser's Legend of Holiness would have been a different work without his use of native romance. Put another way, investigating the use of native romance in Book I is fundamental to understanding Spenser's strategy in creating a Protestant romance-epic.

The adaptation of native romance to Protestant theology entailed certain difficulties. The heroic exploits which are an expected feature of the romance mode would seem more adaptable to the representation of Catholic spirituality, where the good works of the individual can be efficacious or co-operative with God's grace in reducing purgatory and eventually attaining salvation.[2] It is difficult to imagine a romance where the hero is

---

[1] I am indebted to these works which increase understanding of Spenser's relationship with Protestant literature: King, *Spenser and Reformation Tradition*; Hume, *Spenser*; Richard Mallette, *Spenser and the Discourses of Reformation England* (Lincoln, Nebraska and London, 1997). I hope that my work assists theirs by providing a sense of how Spenser imported Middle English romance narrative as a 'reformed' native tradition with which to present Protestant theology as a dynamic drama.

[2] This is not a statement of the Pelagian heresy. But there is a strong distinction between the Calvinist notions of predestination and election, where the salvation of

powerless. A passage which provides an important, if not the key, theological orientation in Book I also seems antithetical to the celebration of human prowess characteristic of the romance mode, even though romance heroes such as Guy, Bevis, and others pray to and thank God for deliverance throughout the course of their adventures:

> What man is he, that boasts of fleshly might,
>   And vaine assurance of mortality,
>   Which all so soone, as it doth come to fight,
>   Against spirituall foes, yeelds by and by,
>   Or from the field most cowardly doth fly?
>   Ne let the man ascribe it to his skill,
>   That thorough grace hath gained victory.
>   If any strength we haue, it is to ill,
> But all the good is Gods, both power and eke will.
>   (I.x.i)[3]

This passage places a Calvinist emphasis on God's grace as the sole agent of salvation, with the implied notion that humans can do nothing to alter the fixed determination of their salvation or damnation, decreed by God before time.[4] The tension between romance of an heroic ethos and Protestant spirituality emerges in Redcrosse's approach to Despair's cave. The scene is loaded with

the individual rests with God alone and is an impenetrable mystery, and the Catholic emphasis on works of mercy, penance, confession, pardons, and priestly absolution as the means through which the individual, under the aegis of the Church, might attain remission for sins and salvation. See further: Duffy, *Stripping of Altars*, 357–62.

[3] Mallette, *Spenser and Discourses of Reformation England*, 42–3 notes that this passage is usually isolated as the doctrinal heart of Book I, while other passages, such as I.x.10, which appear to allow the human will a degree of co-operative agency, are necessarily ingnored by the critic; cf. III.iii.25 and III.v.27. Mallette's argument, that *The Faerie Queene* does not provide a unified doctrinal statement but rather reflects the complex polyvalence of Reformation theological discourse, particularly as reflected in homiletic literature, is salutary. Even allowing for that complexity, combining the extreme Protestant soteriology of Calvin and Cranmer with the more moderate views of Erasmus and Hooker, Book I places pre-eminent emphasis on God's grace as the chief agent of salvation, and this fact is potentially resistant to its representation in a romance narrative.

[4] Calvin writes: 'We call predestination God's eternal decrees, by which he determined with himself what he willed to become of each man. For all are not created in equal condition; rather, eternal life is foreshadowed by some, eternal damnation for others. Therefore, as any man has been created to one or the other of these ends, we speak of him as predestined to life or to death'; John Calvin, *Institutes of the Christian Religion*, ed. John T. McNeill, tr. Ford Lewis Battles, Library of Christian Classics 20, 21 (Philadelphia, 1960), III.xxi.5; p. 926.

images traditional to romance encounters between a hero and a terrifying beast in its lair.[5] The fact that Redcrosse is upbraided for his handling of Despair, by whom he is nearly defeated, provides a marked contrast to the outcome of such encounters in romances. Redcrosse's mettlesome approach to Despair— 'With firie zeale he burnt in courage bold' (i.ix.37)—proves ineffectual, and his sense of self-sufficiency needs to be changed into a willing acceptance of absolute dependence upon God. Una instructs: 'In heauenly mercies hast thou not a part? / Why shouldst thou then despeire, that chosen art?' (i.ix.53).[6] An heroic attitude is commendable in Arthur when, in the alliterative *Morte,* he attacks the giant of Mont St Michel, or in Bevis when he kills a dangerous boar, scenes which are in many ways similar to the Despair episode. But Book I adopts a radically different perspective, under the influence of Calvinist theology as received by Spenser, in which only human actions which are specifically directed by God can be effective and admirable.

Potentially, then, chivalric romance could be an inappropriate narrative form in which to express the tenets of Protestant theology. There are two aspects to Spenser's solution, resulting in a 'reformation' of native romance. The first has been the major

---

[5] For example: (1) Redcrosse's heroic resolution to meet this famous adversary (i.ix.32) is echoed in the heroic determination of Bevis, setting out to kill a dangerous boar (*x*-text, cited throughout this footnote, 619–20), Arthur, resolving to fight the giant of Mont St Michel (the alliterative *Morte Arthure,* 876–9), as well as Florent in *Octavian* (865–77) and Guy (15th-c. version, 7845–7), both also undertaking to fight giants. (2) The approach to Despair's cave is strewn with corpses (i.ix.34); this ominous sign of proximity to the enemy appears also in *Bevis* (629–36) and the alliterative *Morte* (1045–52). (3) The wasted look of Despair (i.ix.35) fits the traditional attributes of the disease, as described by Burton (*The Anatomy of Melancholy,* ed. Floyd Dell and Paul Jordan-Smith (New York, 1955), i.3.i.2; pp. 327–8), but it is also a monstrous appearance that chimes with the unappealing looks of the adversaries met by Bevis (639–42) and Arthur (1045–52). Most scholarship on Despair focuses on Despair's rhetoric and pays little attention to the way in which the encounter is introduced according to the formulas of romance. C. S. Lewis is the only critic who has drawn attention to the palimpsest of a romance encounter in the scene: 'St George goes to Despair as a knight goes to an ogre, to avenge a previous victim... it is a simple matter of physical adventure' (C. S. Lewis, *Spenser's Images of Life,* ed. Alastair Fowler (Cambridge, 1967), 30).

[6] A similar rejection of the heroic ethos which is central to many romances occurs in the Error episode. Una warns Redcrosse to 'Be well aware... / Least suddaine mischiefe ye too rash prouoke' (i.i.12). Nevertheless, Redcrosse attacks the monster with the kind of courage that is appropriate in chivalric romance but here hybristic: 'But full of fire and greedy hardiment, / The youthful knight could not for ought be staide' (i.i.14).

concern of Spenserian scholarship—allegory. The following Pauline passage is a key text for the use of romance and its militaristic imagery for spiritual allegory:

Put on the whole armour of God, that ye may be able to stand against the assauts of the deuil. For we wrestle not against flesh and blood, but against principalities, against powers, *and* against the worldlie gouernours, *the princes* of the darkenes of this worlde, again*s*t spiritual wickednesses, *which are* in the hie places ... Stand therefore, and your loines girde about with veritie, & hauing on the brest plate of righteousnes, And your fete shod with the preparation of the Gospel of peace. Aboue all, take the shield of faith, wherewith ye may quench all the fyrie dartes of the wicked, And take the helmet of saluation, and the sworde of ye Spirit, which is the worde of God.[7]

As chivalric knight, Redcrosse dons the armour of God. In the application of allegory to romance, human actions can be redefined as the operations of divinity upon humanity.[8] The second aspect of Spenser's use of the chivalric romance mode has received less attention; it is Spenser's insightful perception that the native romances offer specific narrative patterns which are uncannily appropriate for a dramatization of both the Calvinist paradigm of salvation and the Protestant historical interpretation of the English Reformation.

The development of these points relating to the second aspect of Spenser's 'reformation' of native romance is the main concern of this chapter. I wish to begin with one spectacular instance of Spenser's use of native romance in Book I, the dragon-fight. Then the figures of Redcrosse and Una need to be considered for their intertextual relation to comparable figures from native romance.

(I) 'THAT FIRE-MOUTHED DRAGON, HORRIBLE AND BRIGHT': REDCROSSE AND BEVIS OF HAMPTON

Thomas Warton first noted that the battle between Redcrosse and the dragon at the climax of Book I is indebted to the Middle

---

[7] *The Geneva Bible*, intr. Lloyd E. Berry (Madison, 1969), Ephes. 6:11–17. This is a facsimile of the 1560 edition.
[8] See further Richard A. McCabe, *The Pillars of Eternity* (Dublin, 1989), 177–8 and the quotation therein from Calvin, based on this Pauline passage.

English romance, *Bevis of Hampton*.[9] This borrowing needs to be examined in close detail, to shed more light on both how and why Spenser used native romance. Therefore I quote in full the episode from Thomas East's print of *Bevis* from *c.* 1585, the closest surviving print in date to *The Faerie Queene*:

[f. 121.v, l.22]
... but Beuis rode foorth and sought,
And when the Dragon that foule is, had a sight of sir Beuis,
He cast vp a loud cry, as it had thundred in the sky.
He turned his belly toward the sun, it was bigger then any tunne,
His scales wes brighter then the glasse,] harder they wer then any brasse,
betweene his shoulder and his tayle, was forty foote without fayle,
He weltred out of his den, and Beuis pricked his steede then,
And to him a speare he thrust, that all to shiuers it brust,
The Dragon gan Beuis assayle,] smot sir Beuis with his tayle,
Then downe went horse and man, two ribbes of Beuis brused than,
Up start Beuis with good will, and after ranne the Dragon till,
And good Morglay out brayd, and on the Dragon fast he layd,
but for no stroke that he did strike, would not Morglay on him bite,
The Dragon was greeued sore, and smote at Beuis more and more
And gaue him many a great wound, and felled him oft to the ground,
What for wery and what for faint, sir Beuis was neere attaint,
The Dragon sewed on Beuis so hard, y[t] as he would haue fled
    backw[a]rd,

---

[9] Thomas Warton, *Observations on the Fairy Queen of Spenser*, 2nd edn. (London, 1807), 1.66–75. Warton's discussion of this borrowing is quoted in part in *Variorum Spenser*, 1.395–6. Other sources for Spenser's dragon are: Rev.12:7–8, 20:1–2; the St George story in several versions, including those of Jacobus de Voragine, Lydgate, and Mantuan (translated by Barclay); and Ovid's tale of Cadmus and the serpent in *Metamorphoses*, III.1–67. On sources, see further: *Variorum*, 1.379–89, 395–6, 401–4. M. Pauline Parker, *The Allegory of The Faerie Queene* (Oxford, 1960), 101–2 erroneously states that in his description of the fight between St George and the dragon, Spenser follows closely Richard Johnson's *The Seven Champions of Christendom* (STC 14677). Johnson's work was in fact printed in 1596, later than the publication of Book I in 1590. Parker's confusion may stem from the fact that Johnson's work also draws, in places verbatim, upon the dragon-fight in *Bevis*, a borrowing first noted in 1762 by Thomas Percy; Fellows, 'St George', 48–53 quotes the dragon-fight from both Johnson and *Bevis*. Discussions of Spenser's dragon-fight in relation to either its indebtedness to romance or its Protestant allegory are: Carol V. Kaske, 'The Dragon's Spark and Sting and the Structure of Red Cross's Dragon Fight: *The Faerie Queene*, I.xi.-xii', *SP* 66 (1969), 609–38; *Bevis*, ed. Fellows, 1.134–6; Michael Leslie, *Spenser's 'Fierce Warres and Faithfull Loves'* (Cambridge, 1983), 105–18; Alan Sinfield, *Literature in Protestant England 1560–1600* (London, 1983), 44–5; Hume, *Spenser*, 102–6; King, *Spenser and Reformation Tradition*, 197–9.

[f. 122.r]
There was a well as I weene, and he stumb[l]ed right therein,
Then was Beuis afrayed and woe, lest the Dragon should him slo,
Or that he might away passe, when he in that well was,
Then was the well of such vertue, through the might of Christ Iesu.
For sometime dwelled in that lond, a Virgin full of Christs sond,
That had bene bathed in that well, that euer after as men tell,
Might no venimous worme come therein, by the verture of that Virgin,
Nigh it seauen foote and more, then Beuis was glad therefore,
When he sawe the Dragon fell, had no power to come to the well,
Then was he glad without fayle, and rested a while for his auayle,
And dranke of that water his fill, and then he lept out with good will,
And with Morglay his brand, assayled the Dragon I vnderstand,
On the Dragon he smote so fast, where that he hit the scales brast,
The Dragon than faynted sore, and cast a galon and more,
Out of his mouth of venime strong, and one [sic] sir Beuis he it flong,
Which was so venimous ywis, that when it was on sir Beuis.
His armour burst in that stound, and he fell dead to the ground,
There was no life on him seene, he lay as a dead man on the greene,
The Dragon smot him without faile, that he tourned top and tayle,
but thereoff he tooke no keepe, he lay as a dead man on sleepe,
He smote Beuis as I you tell, the dint smote him into the well,
That was of great vertue that time, for it would suffer no venime,
Through vertue of the Virgin, that once was bathed therin,
When Beuis was at the ground, that water made him whole ⌉ sound,
And quenched all the venim away, this well saued Beuis that day,
When he feelt him whole and light, and knew that well of great might
Then was he a ioyfull man, he was as fresh as when he began,
He kneeled downe in that place, to Iesu Christ he called for grace,
That he would send him might, to slay the Dragon in fight,
Beuis blessed him and foorth yode, and lept out with hart full good,
And Beuis to the Dragon gone is, and the Dragon also to Beuis,
Long and hard was the fight, betwext the Dragon and the knight,
But euer when Beuis was hurt sore, he went to y͏ᵉ wel ⌉ washed him thore,
He was as whole as any man, ⌉ euer as fresh as when he began,
The Dragon saw yᵗ might not auayle, beside the well to hold battaile,
He thought he would with some wile, out of that place Beuis beguile,
He would haue flowen then away, ⌉ Beuis lept after with good Morglay,
And hit him vnder the wing, as he was in his flying,
[f. 122.v]
There he was tender without skale, and Beuis thought to be his bale,
He smote after as I you say, with his good sword Morglay,
Up to the hilts Morglay yode, through hart, liuer, bone and bloud,

To the ground fell the Dragon, great ioy sir Beuis begon.
Under the scales all on hight, he smote his head foorth right,
And put it vpon a speare, and vnneth he might it beare,
He went to Colaine that tide, with great ioy and much pride,
When they of the citie sawe Beuis, come with the dragons head ywis,
All the bells gan they ring, priestes and clearkes then did sing,
And brought Beuis to the towne, with procession and renowne,
Then was Beuis name in honour, euery man had him in fauour,
In euery land is spred, sir Beuis price and laud,
Glad was the Bishop tho, that sir Beuis had borne him so.

(East, ff. 121.v.22–122.v.6; Cf. κ, 2420–594)[10]

This passage provided a direct source for the battle between Redcrosse and a dragon at the climax of Book I:

It fortuned (as faire it then befell)
　　Behind his backe vnweeting, where he stood,
　　Of auncient time there was a springing well,
　　From which fast trickled forth a siluer flood,
　　Full of great vertues, and for med'cine good.
　　Whylome, before that cursed Dragon got
　　That happie land, and all with innocent blood
　　Defyld those sacred waues, it rightly hot
The well of life, ne yet his vertues had forgot.

For vnto life the dead it could restore,
　　And guilt of sinfull crimes wash cleane away,
　　Those that with sicknesse were infected sore,
　　It could recure, and aged long decay
　　Renew, as one were borne that very day.
　　Both *Silo* this, and *Iordan* did excell,
　　And th'English *Bath*, and eke the german *Spau*,
　　Ne can *Cephise*, nor *Hebrus* match this well:
　　Into the same the knight backe ouerthrowen, fell…

Redcrosse emerges from the well with new strength and attacks the dragon again:

[10] STC 1990: *Syr Beuis of Hampton*, pr. T. East [*c.* 1585]. I follow East's layout in printing each couplet as a single line. East's text corresponds roughly to the lower of the two texts (the *x*-text) in *Bevis*, ed. Kölbing. This text in Kölbing's edition is based on Manchester Chetham's Library MS Mum.A.6.31 (olim 8009), the manuscript-text which is closest to the text preserved in the sixteenth-century prints. Each citation from East's edition will be followed by a reference to the comparable lines in Kölbing's edition, designated as κ in parentheses directly following the quotation, as above.

The heate whereof, and harmefull pestilence
    So sore him noyd, that forst him to retire
    A little backward for his best defence,
    To saue his bodie from the scorching fire,
    Which he from hellish entrailes did expire.
    It chaunst (eternall God that chaunce did guide)
    As he recoyled backward, in the mire
    His nigh forewearied feeble feet did slide,
And downe he fell, with dread of shame sore terrifide.

There grew a goodly tree him faire beside,
    Loaden with fruit and apples rosie red,
    As they in pure vermilion had beene dide,
    Whereof great vertues ouer all were red:
    For happie life to all, which thereon fed,
    And life eke euerlasting did befall:
    Great God it planted in that blessed sted
    With his almightie hand, and did it call
The tree of life, the crime of our first fathers fall.

In all the world like was not to be found,
    Saue in that soile, where all good things did grow,
    And freely sprong out of the fruitfull ground,
    As incorrupted Nature did them sow,
    Till that dread Dragon all did ouerthrow.
    Another like faire tree eke grew thereby,
    Whereof who so did eat, eftsoones did know
    Both good and ill: O mornefull memory:
That tree through one mans fault hath doen vs all to dy.

From that first tree forth flowd, as from a well,
    A trickling streame of Balme, most soueraine
    And daintie deare, which on the ground still fell,
    And ouerflowed all the fertill plaine,
    As it had deawed bene with timely raine:
    Life and long health that gratious ointment gaue,
    And deadly woundes could heale, and reare againe
    The senselesse corse appointed for the graue.
Into that same he fell: which did from death him saue.

For nigh thereto the euer damned beast
    Durst not approch, for he was deadly made,
    And all that life preserued, did detest:
    Yet he it oft aduentur'd to inuade . . .

Then freshly vp arose the doughtie knight,
  All healed of his hurts and woundes wide,
  And did himselfe to battell readie dight ...

  ... The weapon bright
Taking aduantage of his open iaw,
Ran through his mouth with so importune might,
That deepe emperst his darksome hollow maw,
And back retyrd, his life bloud forth with all did draw.
                 (I.xi.29–30, 45–9, 52–3)

The most salient parallel between the two dragon-fights is, as
Warton observed, the heroes' 'miraculous manner of healing' (I,
69). In both texts the hero falls into a well, he does so uninten-
tionally, and the well's water is miraculously revitalizing. There is
a structural similarity too in the fact that Bevis falls into the well
twice and defeats the dragon on the third encounter; in Spenser,
the second fall into the well is replaced for purposes of allegory
with the Tree of Life, but the narrative pattern remains the same.
Warton also notes that:

The circumstance of the dragon not being able to approach within seven
feet of this well, is imitated by our author st. 49 below, where another
water is mentioned, which in like manner preserves the knight.

                                   (I, 74)

This other water in Spenser is in fact 'a trickling streame of Balme'
which flows from the Tree of Life 'as from a well' (I.xi.48). In
Bevis, there is an area around the well which its special properties
protect: 'Might no venimous worme come therein, by the vertue
of that Virgin, / Nigh it seauen foote and more' (East, f. 122.r.7–8;
Cf. K, 2465–7). In Spenser, the pool flowing from the Tree of Life
similarly exudes a special inviolability:

  For nigh thereto the euer damned beast
  Durst not approch, for he was deadly made,
  And all that life preserued, did detest.

                (I.xi.49)

  More details, not mentioned by Warton, can be added to support his argument for direct textual dependence. In Spenser, the
dragon 'all with brasen scales was armd, / Like plated coate of
steele' (I.xi.9); in *Bevis*, the dragon's 'scales wes brighter then the
glasse, ⌐ harder they wer then any brasse' (East, f. 121.v.26; Cf. K,

2427–8). Redcrosse's first effective blow against the dragon penetrates 'Close vnder his left wing' (I.xi.20); Bevis delivers a fatal stroke 'vnder the wing' (East, f. 122.r.38; Cf. к, 2527). Another echo which is suggestive of textual dependence comes at the height of the battle in *Bevis*: 'What for wery and what for faint, sir Beuis was neere attaint' (East, f. 121.v.37; Cf. к, 2449). 'Wery' and 'faint' are given prominence in the line by the syntactical parallelism. At a comparable moment of feverish pitch in his battle with the dragon, Redcrosse is described as *'Faint, wearie, sore, emboyled, grieued, brent'* (I.xi.28; my emphasis). Furthermore, before Bevis falls into the well a second time, the dragon casts so much venom on him that 'His armour burst in that stound' (East, f. 122.r.17; Cf. к, 2485); before his immersion in the Well of Life, Redcrosse is so scorched by the dragon's fire that he 'thought his armes to leave, and helmet to vnlace' (I.xi.26). Another interesting parallel between Book I and *Bevis* is found in the text of *Bevis* in Caius College Cambridge MS 175.[11] The manuscript-text reads 'Aboue Þe tayl ffyue ffoot & more / He hew ffrom Þe body Þore'.[12] Similarly, Redcrosse cuts off five 'units' of the dragon's tail: 'Of his huge taile he quite a sunder cleft, / Fiue ioynts thereof he hewd, and but the stump him left' (I.xi.39). A final piece of evidence for textual dependence is the passage in *The Faerie Queene* where Redcrosse searches for the dragon for the first time:

> With that they heard a roaring hideous sound,
>   That all the ayre with terrour filled wide,
>   And seemd vneath to shake the stedfast ground.
>   Eftsoones that dreadfull Dragon they espide,
>   Where stretcht he lay vpon the sunny side
>   Of a great hill, himselfe like a great hill.
>
> (I.xi.4)

Bevis contains a close parallel to this passage; the details of the thundering roar which leads to the sighting of the beast, the dragon's exposure to the sun, and its prodigious size all occur in the same order:

---

[11] This passage is not found in any of the printed editions, but that does not prohibit its potential relevance to Spenser. I have already argued for the continued presence of Middle English romance in manuscript in the sixteenth century.

[12] Lines 99–100 of the minuscule text in *Bevis*, ed. Kölbing (1885, 1886, 1894), p. 134.

The Dragon cast vp such a yell, that would haue feared the diuel of hell,
Ascapart said with heauy cheere, hearest thou what I do heare,
Yes said Beuis haue no doubt, the Dragon is heere about...
... but Beuis rode foorth and sought,
And when the Dragon that foule is, had a sight of sir Beuis,
He cast vp a loud cry, as it had thundred in the sky.
He turned his belly toward the sun, it was bigger then any tunne.

(East, f. 121.v.11–13, 22–5; Cf. K, 2397–402, 2420–6)

The comment of the editors of the *Variorum Spenser*, that such details 'are hardly more than the stock in trade of dragon fights',[13] seems excessively cautious in the light of such close and consistent similarity.

The relationship between the two dragon-fights is paradoxical: what needs emphasis is both how completely Spenser has incorporated the popular romance episode into his own work and how radically different the dragon-fight is in Spenser's retelling. As an example of the 'matter of iust memory', Spenser's recollection of the dragon-fight demonstrates the subjectivity of any memory and its implication in its own particular time, place, and ideologies.[14] Although Spenser maintains, and even intensifies, the narrative excitement of the dragon-fight as depicted in *Bevis*, thereby drawing attention to the influence of native romance on his work, he also emphasizes that this dragon-fight must be considered as different from all other battles in literature. Redcrosse is '*Not* that great Champion of the antique world...' (I.xi.27; my emphasis) and the well into which he falls is differentiated from Siloam, Jordan, Bath, and other healing waters (I.xi.30).[15] Rather than being like all previous classical and romance heroes, Redcrosse is somehow different. Spenser has chosen in Bevis' dragon-fight one of the most famous English heroes and exploits, and he now asks his readers to remember

[13] *Variorum*, 1.396.
[14] Other, earlier English descriptions of St George's battle with the dragon are Alexander Barclay, *The Life of St George*, ed. William Nelson, EETS 230 (London, 1955), 862–75 and Lydgate's *The Legend of St George*, in *The Minor Poems of John Lydgate*, ed. Henry Noble MacCrachen, EETS ES 107, OS 192 (Oxford, 1911, 1934), 99–105. Neither account offers the strongly narrative description of the dragon and the battle that is characteristic of Spenser's treatment. On the effective power of Spenser's description of the dragon-fight, see Hume, *Spenser*, 103–4.
[15] Comparably, concerning the Tree of Life, 'In all the world like was not to be found' (I.xi.47).

that scene according to a point-of-view which they have never likely adopted before. That memory will be revelatory, accompanied by a sense that the truth has always been present in native thought, even romance, and now can be recalled correctly.

All details of the dragon-fight enforce the lessons learnt with Error and Despair—that human nature is completely fallen and only God's grace can redeem that nature and restore it to its original perfection. Article XI, 'Of the Justification of Man' of 'The Thirty-Nine Articles', is the doctrine which the dragon-fight enacts: 'We are accounted righteous before God, only for the merit of our Lord and saviour Jesus Christ by Faith, and not for our own works or deservings.'[16] When the dragon is killed, the weapon, which is part of the armour of God, acts independently and without human agency: '...The weapon bright / Taking aduantage of his open iaw, / Ran through his mouth...' (1.xi.53).[17] Furthermore, the last lines of the Canto contain a deliberate ambiguity, involving the possessive adjective 'his', which allows the literal meaning that St George killed the dragon as well as the Protestant understanding that the victory was achieved through God's grace: 'Then God she praysd, and thankt her faithful knight, / That had atchieu'd so great a conquest by his might' (1.xi.55).[18] The episodes which above all uphold the Protestant doctrine inscribed in Article XI are Redcrosse's collisions with the Well and Tree. The fall into the Well is also the greatest debt which Spenser's scene owes to *Bevis*, and the two passages need fuller consideration to mark how Spenser has adapted the romance to fit the Calvinist doctrine of salvation.

[16] See further Calvin, *Institutes*, III.xi.2; pp. 726–7.

[17] Spenser's careful representation that the weapon, and not Redcrosse, kills the dragon is remarked by Leslie, *Spenser's 'Fierce Warres'*, 105, f.7 and King, *Spenser and Reformation Tradition*, 199, as well as in the annotations of *The Faerie Queene*, ed. Hamilton. Calvin's denial of human free will in the light of God's providential control of events is relevant to this passage, even if it is a view which other parts of *The Faerie Queene* challenge: in the *Institutes* Calvin writes that 'providence means not that by which God idly observes from heaven what takes place on earth, but that by which, as keeper of the keys, he governs all events' (1.xvi.4; pp. 201–3); and 'the plans and intentions of men...are so governed by his providence that they are borne by it straight to their appointed end' (1.xvi.8; p. 207).

[18] A. C. Hamilton, 'Our New Poet: Spenser, "Well of English Undefyled"', in Hamilton (ed.), *Essential Articles*, 488–506 (503).

It has long been recognized that the 'Well of Life' and the 'Tree of Life' which save Redcrosse derive their value as Christian symbols from Revelation:

And he shewed me a pure riuer of water of life, cleare as crystal, proceding out of the throne of God, and of the Lambe. In the middes of the strete of it, and of ether side of the riuer, was the tre of life, which bare twelue maner of frutes, & gaue frute euerie moneth: & the leaues of the tre *serued* to heale the nations with.

(Rev. 22:1–2; Geneva Bible)

The Well and the Tree function in Book I as gifts necessary for Redcrosse to fulfil God's will in the destruction of the dragon. Anthea Hume regards Spenser's Well and Tree as having a value more complex and inclusive than equative symbols of baptism and the Eucharist; in her view, the Well and Tree are rich, allusive manifestations of 'Christ's doctrine and Christ himself'.[19] Her broader interpretation accords both with Spenser's allegorical method, which shuns simple equations, and also with the Protestant emphasis on the individual's communion with Christ's teaching and grace rather than the mediating role of the Church.[20] Bale's *Image of Bothe Churches*, a Protestant exegesis on Revelation, offers an interpretation of the Well in Revelation 22:1 which illuminates interpretation of Spenser's Well:

None other can I suppose thys ryuer to be by the serche of the scriptures, but the flowing verite, the worde of saluacion, or the effectual doctrine of Christes holy sprete. That is the swete flood of Eden, which plesauntly floweth throughe Paradyse, and visiteth the .iiij. quarters of the worlde. This is that wholsome and dilectable water, which dayly conforteth and preserueth the spirituall Hierusalem from all contagyouse maladies … This running flood with hys ryuers on euery syde, reioyseth ye cytie of God which is the habitacion of the hyghest … The nature of this water is none other but euermore to clense, euermore to reuyue, and euermore to make whol and perfight … I will poure cleare water vpon

[19] Hume, *Spenser*, 104–5. See also O'Connell, *Mirror and Veil*, 66 who sees the Well and Tree as 'different symbols for the spiritual events of which the sacraments are themselves symbols'. O'Connell's interpretation draws upon the Pauline emphasis on Christians dying with Christ to be born anew, a doctrine that is supported by the nearly dead condition of Redcrosse when he encounters the Well and the Tree.

[20] The Geneva Bible's gloss to 'middes' in the passage just quoted from Revelation is significant: 'Meaning y^t Christ who is the life of his Church, is commune to all his and not peculiar for any one sorte of people'.

you (saith the Lord in Ezechiel)] ye shall be cleane from all filthynesse. A
new hart wil I geue you. A new sprete wil I plante in you, and so clense
you from all your Idols.[21]

Focusing on the Well in Book I as Spenser's narrative reveals it, it
clearly offers a profoundly restorative grace which the knight
cannot earn or achieve by his own will. He falls into it 'vnweeting'
(I.xi.29), with the same lack of human agency which marks the
eventual slaying of the dragon, and the effect of the Well is to
make him a new man.[22] Bale's view of the Well in Revelation goes
beyond baptism as a sacrament of the Church and a specific
moment in one's life; rather, he sees the Well as a spiritually
cleansing, renewing power which, like a spring, flows unceas-
ingly throughout one's life. In this respect Bale's reading of
Revelation and Spenser's Well are closely similar symbols. Bale
emphasizs that the Well of Christ's doctrine serves 'euermore to
clense, euermore to reuyue, and euermore to make whol and
perfight'. Similarly, Spenser's Well 'vnto life the dead . . . could
restore . . . / It could recure, and aged long decay / Renew, as one
were borne that very day' (I.xi.30).

Since the nature or function of Spenser's Well corresponds so
strongly with the Well of Life in Revelation, particularly as illuminated by Bale's commentary, one might think that the contribution of *Bevis* to the scene is insignificant. However, that view
would overlook Spenser's careful syncretism and his strong desire
to present *The Faerie Queene* as the product of a native literary
tradition. It would also ignore the possibility that *Bevis* contributes something to the scene which does not derive from Revelation and its Protestant reception. What does the well in *Bevis*
mean, and how greatly did Spenser change it?

[21] John Bale, *The Image of Bothe Churches*, The English Experience 498 [facsimile
edition of STC 1297] (Amsterdam, 1973), pp. [oo.vii^v-oo.viii^v]. For a placement of
Bale in the religious and literary milieu of the Henrican and Edwardian Reformation,
see King, *English Reformation Literature*, 61–6. Complementary with Bale's text is
this passage from the homily 'Of the Miserie of Al Mankynd', from the *Book of
Homilies* (1547): Christ 'is that flowyng and moste plenteous fountain, of whose
fulnesse all we have received'; *Certain Sermons or Homilies (1547) and a Homily
Against Disobedience and Wilful Rebellion (1570)*, ed. Ronald B. Bond (Toronto,
1987), 75.
[22] Similarly, 'It chaunst' that Redcrosse fell against the Tree of Life, but 'eternall
God that chaunce did guide' (I.xi.45). See Calvin, *Institutes*, I.xvi.2; pp. 198–201 for
the denial of fortune and accident within God's providential scheme. The major study
of the role of providence in *The Faerie Queene* is McCabe, *Pillars of Eternity*.

The dragon-fight in *Bevis* is not an allegory where the dragon is representative of an abstract value, particularly in relation to the psyche of Bevis. It is true that Bevis prays to God 'for grace, / That he would send him might, to slay the Dragon in fight'; but the emphasis, particularly in the texts of the printed editions, is on a secular romance adventure in which Bevis overcomes a terrifying opponent, to his own glory.[23] Bevis' victory is accredited to himself, not God, and his prayers to God do not add up to a sense that Bevis' role is negligible and 'all the good is Gods'; after the defeat of the dragon, 'Than was Beuis name in honour, euery man had him in fauour, / In euery land is spred, sir Beuis price and laud'. In this context, the well is a crucial support in Bevis' victory; twice it refreshes and heals him. On the second occasion, the seriousness of Bevis' injuries have rendered him unconscious: 'His armour burst in that stound, and he fell dead to the ground, / There was no life on him seene, he lay as a dead man on the greene'.[24] The well not only restores Bevis—'. . . that water made him whole] sound, / And quenched all the venim away . . . / . . . he was as fresh as when he began'—but it clearly has a moral dimension of its own; it will not cure *anyone's* wounds, and the dragon for one 'had no power to come to the well'. The well is not just used in a good cause, but it is intrinsically virtuous. The source of the well's efficacy is that a virgin 'full of Christ's sond' ('message') bathed in it. The purity and godliness of the virgin are qualities which she has imparted to the well, which is above all a source for miraculous physical healing aligned with a Christian sense of right and wrong.[25]

[23] The text of the Auchinleck MS generally provides a more pious framework for the dragon-fight than the textual tradition from which the printed editions descend. See, for example, Auchinleck, 2693–700, 2784, 2838–40, 2867–70, 2910. In the tradition of the printed editions, the tone is markedly more secular. The Auchinleck MS version interestingly anticipates Spenser's association of Bevis and St George, though from the other direction: when Bevis is in the well for the first time, 'A nemenede sein Gorge, our leuedi kniȝt' (2817). See further: Fellows, 'St George'.

[24] The word 'dead' here is not to be understood in its literal sense; it was a commonplace word for 'unconscious' (see OED, adj., A.I.2), comparable to the use of 'lifeless' in the eighteenth and nineteenth centuries.

[25] The importance of virginity is stressed throughout the romance by Josian's (successful) efforts to remain a virgin, despite being married under coercion, until she can marry Bevis. Bevis agrees with the Patriarch of Jerusalem ' Þat he neuer toke wif, / Boute ȝhe were clene maide' (Auchinleck, 1968–9).

Can the well in *Bevis* be taken as a symbol for baptism, emblematic of the spiritual grace which supports Christians against all things which oppose or weaken their faith? Other romances offer the point of view that physically healing waters might be aligned with a notion of baptism, however the ironic nature of that alignment precludes a genuinely spiritual symbol. In *Guy of Warwick*, for instance, Guy wryly comments that a giant whom he is fighting has 'baptized' him when the giant knocks Guy into a river.[26] The scene was borrowed in *Lybeaus Desconus*, where the reference to baptism recurs.[27] Both references to baptism are jocose; the revitalizing power of water is acknowledged by hot and thirsty warriors, but the humour lies in the perception that baptism is very different, a spiritual rather than a physical cure. These scenes, in addition to the narrative details of *Bevis*, suggest the *potential* of the well to become a symbol for baptism, something closer to Spenser's handling of the scene. But the well in *Bevis* remains a miraculous physical object rather than a symbol. For one, no details concerning the virgin or the nature of her message, which could be the basis for understanding the well and its cure as symbolic, are given. Moreover, the well cures Bevis in one specific moment, but there is no justification for thinking that its efficacy will endure throughout his life or that this moment is a distinct turning-point in the hero's spiritual pilgrimage. Rather, the well in *Bevis* belongs to medieval popular religion—faith which sees a sanctity or magical efficacy in physical objects themselves, rather than perceiving the object as merely representational of an abstract quality which can only be arrived at through faith, grace, and prayer.[28] Chaucer's Pardoner appeals to belief in this primitive magic:

[26] Caius MS 107: 'In cold water hast thow bathid me, / But name had I none for the' (8516–7). CUL MS ff.2.38: 'Thou haste me baptysed, hyt ys þy schame. / But ȝyt þou haste not chaunged my name' (8267–8). The reference to baptism is in the Anglo-Norman *Gui de Warewic* (8824–6). The incident occurs in the Auchinleck MS text of *Guy* without the reference to baptism (st. 113–29).

[27] *Lybeaus*, ed. Mills, Cotton 1357–62, and see Commentary.

[28] Duffy, *Stripping of Altars*, 280–2 describes how the objects used in the sacrament of baptism, such as the water, were perceived to have an objective power, though he argues against the view of late medieval religious practice as superficial or concerned with 'magic'. See also: G. R. Owst, *Preaching in Medieval England* (Cambridge, 1926), 109–10; Francis Oakley, *The Medieval Experience*, Medieval Academy Reprints for Teaching 23 (Toronto, 1988), 67–8. Calvin argues in the *Institutes* against the medieval and Catholic view of baptismal water as intrinsically holy and efficacious:

> If that this boon be wasshe in any welle,
> If cow, or calf, or sheep, or oxe swelle
> That any worm hath ete, or worm ystonge,
> Taak water of that welle and wassh his tongue,
> And it is hool anon.
>
> (VI.353–7)

Like the well mentioned here by the Pardoner, the healing power of the well in *Bevis* is an automatic consequence of the virgin bathing there, involving a sense of the supernatural; this is 'holy water', belonging to the world of the Compestella, and a thoroughly 'un-Protestant' moment in *Bevis*.[29]

Wells which have magical capabilities through associations with virgins appear in other romances. Spenser gives an example of such a well, with classical contextualization, early in Book II, when Guyon tries to wash the bloody hands of Amavia's child. The origin of this well was a virgin nymph who, being chased by Faunus, implored Diana's aid. She was consequently changed into the well:

> And yet her vertues in her water byde:
> For it is chast and pure, as purest snow,
> Ne lets her waues with any filth be dyde,
> But euer like her selfe vnstained hath been tryde.
>
> (II.ii.9)

The contrast between this secular, intrinsically magical well and the well of the dragon-fight is that the former is ineffectual in removing the spiritual decay symbolized in the Babe's bloody hands. A magical well, indeed the general magical and supernatural potentials of the romance mode when conceived of as secular rather than providential, are not enough to aid Spenser's knights. Their assistance, Redcrosse's well makes clear, must come from God. Spenser has transformed the nature of the well in *Bevis* to illustrate this difference, changing the well through allegory from magical object to spiritual, Christian symbol.[30]

'Paul did not mean to signify that our cleansing and salvation are accomplished by water, or that water contains in itself the power to cleanse, regenerate, and renew; nor that here is the cause of salvation, but only that in this sacrament are received the knowledge and certainty of such gifts' (IV.xv.2; p. 1304).

[29] In the Auchinleck MS, the well is described as 'holi' (2807).

[30] In the *Legenda aurea*, as well as in Barclay's and Lydgate's dependent versions of the St George legend, a baptismal well springs from the ground after George has

We are now in a position to understand why Spenser incorporated *Bevis* into a scene which derives its imagery and meaning from Revelation and Protestant exegesis and which depends for its characters and events on the life of St George. *Bevis* added three aspects which complete the meaning of Spenser's scene and raise it above simplistic religious allegory. For one, recounting the adventure of a dragon-fight from a romance text offered a wider scope for the impact of the narrative. By invoking the sense of romance, Spenser could meet the generic expectations of detailed, enthralling descriptions of the adversary and the encounter. Such detail is comparatively absent from Barclay's and Lydgate's versions of the life of St George, perhaps because it would generate an excitement in the reader which might diminish the reception of the work as a saint's life.[31] For Spenser, however, the narrative description drawn from the romance accords with his didactic, theological vision: the danger and the difficulty of the dragon emphasize the need for assistance, or grace, to overcome it. The Protestant doctrine that salvation can only be achieved through God's grace is demonstrated, or 'proven', by the dragon's terror: how else could such a formidable beast possibly be destroyed?

The second contribution which *Bevis* made to Spenser's scene relates to Redcrosse's identity as a saint. The palimpsest of Bevis in Redcrosse's battle with the dragon was a means of removing George firmly out of the catalogue of saints in a pre-Reformation sense.[32] The Spenserian George's reliance on God's grace to defeat the dragon changes him from a potential intercessionary figure to a Protestant 'Everyman'. His perceived relationship with Bevis adds to this 'humanization'. Redcrosse is predicted to

defeated the dragon, when the foundations are dug for a new church. This feature may have aided the development of Spenser's thought, to rewrite the well in *Bevis* as a spiritual symbol. But the well in *Bevis* remains the source for the action of Redcrosse being restored during the dragon-fight. Barclay's translation of Mantuan may incorporate verbal echoes of *Bevis*. For example, in Barclay—'Which had suche vertue / that it made hole and sounde' (1230)—compares with *Bevis*: 'Then was the well of such vertue' and 'that water made him whole] sound' (East, f. 122.r, 4, 24; cf. K, 2459, 2500).

[31] Although hagiography and romance often intersected as genres, competition existed between the two forms, particularly discernible in hagiographical collections that are defensive concerning their lack of adventures. See the prologue to *The South English Legendary*, 3.59–64.

[32] The Protestant rejection of the intercessory function of saints receives a classic formulation in Calvin, *Institutes*, III.xx.21–7; pp. 878–87.

> be a Saint, and thine owne nations frend
> And Patrone: thou Saint *George* shalt called bee,
> Saint *George* of mery England, the signe of victoree.
>
> (I.x.61)

His saintly identity is defined politically, in terms of nationhood, rather than according to a Catholic understanding of sainthood. The adaptation of one of the most famous of English heroes, Bevis, to the legend of St George allows the redefinition of the patron saint as a folk hero.

The third significance of Spenser's adaptation of *Bevis* relates in a precise sense to the character of *The Faerie Queene* as 'matter of iust memory'. Spenser's use of the popular romance would have stimulated contemporary readers to recognize that memories—specifically collective cultural and literary memories, embodied in native literature—provide an understanding of how an individual (or the nation) has evolved to the present. In the case of *Bevis*, a memory which may be potentially embarrassing, the recollection of a wayward period of youth, turns out instead to be comprehensible as an important stage of growth in the 'right' direction. Creative, revisionary, and redemptive memories of the past (such as Foxe also gives) are of course subjective manipulations taking place in the present, but their effect is precisely the opposite: they establish that the present identity, in this case Protestant religion, has not been merely constructed in the here and now but rather has a valid and objective existence because it apparently existed before the sixteenth-century English recognized its rightness. Memory refers to truth, the things that really happened, rather than 'painted forgery' (II.Proem.1); in several Middle English romances, the things which are 'still there' prove that the romance really happened and at the same time offer the present reader a mythopoeic past from which to construct present identity. In the case of the dragon-fight, *Bevis* itself, along with the archaic description which Spenser uses to describe the fight, are objects which are 'still there' in the literary and cultural landscape of the nation, represented by *The Faerie Queene*. For Elizabethan readers, *The Faerie Queene* is their corporate memory, holding their collective experience of the past and explaining whence they have come. Middle English romance can be a positive element in that memory, rather than the source of a guilty conscience for past misdeeds. As *The Faerie Queene* urges us to remember it, *Bevis* is not a work of 'bold bawdry and open manslaughter' but a narrative in which the triumph of Protestant St George was adumbrated. The memory of Bevis in Redcrosse's encounter with the dragon suggests that Holiness was not a new achievement for the Reformed English nation, but the correct remembering of something much older and derived from God rather than human invention. The well is 'auncient' (I.xi.29) in all senses.

(II) REDCROSSE, FAIR UNKNOWNS, AND DISPLACED YOUTHS

The dragon-fight is a specific scene in which *The Faerie Queene* reveals itself to be the 'matter of iust memory'. But the theme of memory applies further to Redcrosse; he is a character who is based on a number of related heroes from Middle English romance. In particular, Redcrosse demonstrates the same experience of earlier native heroes who discover their true identity, conferred by noble birth but obscured by the circumstances of their upbringing. Redcrosse's 'first' appearance, in the 'Letter to Ralegh', is the starting point:

In the beginning of the feast, there presented him selfe a tall clownishe younge man, who falling before the Queen of Faries desired a boone (as the manner then was) which during that feast she might not refuse: which was that hee might haue the atchieuement of any aduenture, which during that feaste should happen, that being graunted, he rested him on the floore, vnfitte through his rusticity for a better place. Soone after entred a faire Ladye in mourning weedes, riding on a white Asse, with a dwarfe behind her leading a warlike steed, that bore the Armes of a knight, and his speare in the dwarfes hand. Shee falling before the Queene of Faeries, complayned that her father and mother an ancient King and Queene, had bene by an huge dragon many years shut vp in a brasen Castle, who thence suffred them not to yssew: and therefore besought the Faery Queene to assygne her some one of her knights to take on him that exployt. Presently that clownish person vpstarting, desired that aduenture: whereat the Queene much wondering, and the Lady much gainesaying, yet he earnestly importuned his desire. In the end the Lady told him that vnlesse that armour which she brought, would serue him (that is the armour of a Christian man specified by

Saint Paul v. Ephes.) that he could not succeed in that enterprise, which being forthwith put vpon him with dewe furnitures thereunto, he seemed the goodliest man in al that company, and was well liked of the Lady. And eftesoones taking on him knighthood, and mounting on that straunge Courser, he went forth with her on that aduenture: where beginneth the first booke ... (738)

In Book I, Una repeats this narrative from her perspective:

> Forwith to court of *Gloriane* I sped ...
> There to obtaine some such redoubted knight,
> That Parents deare from tyrants powre deliuer might.

> It was my chance (my chance was faire and good)
> There for to find a fresh vnproued knight,
> Whose manly hands imbrew'd in guiltie blood
> Had neuer bene.
>
> (I.vii.46–7)

Earlier scholarship has remarked that the description of Redcrosse at Gloriana's court and Una's arrival there are indebted to Middle English romances of 'Fair Unknowns' and displaced youths, such as Lybeaus Desconus, Malory's Sir Gareth and Sir Torre, and Ipomedon.[33] Lybeaus Desconus is the closest analogue to Redcrosse; like Spenser's knight, Lybeaus is genuinely ignorant of his true birth and identity. Both are rustic youths who appear in the court requesting to undertake the first adventure; in both cases, they undertake the quest of a damsel, appearing on behalf of her besieged lady. *Lybeaus* may be Spenser's direct narrative model for Redcrosse, particularly as he appears in the 'Letter to Ralegh'. Malory's Sir Gareth offers a variation in that the protagonist is aware of but deliberately hides his true identity; but the narrative outline is the same. Redcrosse shares with Sir Gareth, or Bewmaynes, an apparent rusticity; the detail of Redcrosse sitting on the floor, 'vnfitte through his rusticity for a better place', corresponds to Bewmaynes, who 'sette hym downe amonge boyes and laddys ... and lay nyghtly as the kychen boyes dede' (295.26–37). The arrival of the damsel, her petition, and her reaction to the proposed champion are also details which the 'Letter to Ralegh' shares with *Lybeaus* and 'Sir Gareth'. Comparable to the description of Una's arrival at Gloriana's court, the damsel in *Lybeaus* appears at Arthur's court on a 'Milke white'

---

[33] See: *Variorum*, 1.391–5; Rovang, *Refashioning Knights*, 23–38.

mount (Lambeth, 129) accompanied by a dwarf. The damsels in 'Sir Gareth' and *Lybeaus* are highly critical of their proposed champion; in *Lybeaus* the maid describes the youth as 'witles and wylde' (Lambeth, 185). Spenser's language is less strong here, but there is a corresponding detail in 'the Lady much gainesaying'. Una's critical admonitions to Redcrosse during the course of their adventures, such as 'Be well aware . . . least suddaine mischiefe ye too rash prouoke' (I.i.12) and 'Fie, fie, faint harted knight' (I.ix.52), recall the criticisms of the damsels in 'Gareth', Malory's related adventure of Sir La Cote Male Tayle, and *Lybeaus*. Redcrosse's impetuous undertaking of the lady's quest—'Presently that clownish person vpstarting'—echoes *Lybeaus,* possibly even at the verbal level: 'Vppe startte that yonge knight' (Lambeth, 166).[34] Redcrosse's armour is another detail which associates him with the 'Fair Unknown' figures of Middle English romance. His armour is borrowed, but when he put it on 'he seemed the goodliest man in al that company'. The resemblance to Gareth is unmistakable: 'So whan he was armed there was none <or> but fewe so goodly a man as he was' (297.24–9).[35]

The 'Letter to Ralegh', and to a lesser extent Una's recollection of her arrival at court, define Redcrosse as a cousin of the 'Fair Unknown' figure. We need to go a step further and consider how

[34] Spenser may also be recalling *Ipomedon*, where the word occurs at the same moment: 'Vp sterte the fole anon . . .' (1691) and 'The fole sterte vp *with* oute delaye' (1703).

[35] In addition to the romances of 'Fair Unknowns' preserved in prints and manuscripts, another interesting piece of evidence survives as a possible analogue to Spenser's conception of Redcrosse's history and character—an Accession Day Tilt speech, probably written by Elizabeth's champion, Sir Henry Lee, before 1590. The speech is given by a hermit on behalf of a knight who is 'clownishly clad', reminiscent of Redcrosse's appearance as a 'clownish younge man'. In both the Accession Day speech and in *The Faerie Queene*, the character appears at an annual feast and in the presence of a queen. Sir Henry Lee's speech petitions the Queen that the knight and his rustic company might partake in the chivalric exercises of the day. This speech reveals a nearly contemporary use of the 'Fair Unknown' story and thus provides evidence for the fame of the story and Spenser's presumed expectation that readers would recognize the imprint of native romance in his text. The speech is preserved in British Library MS Add. 41499A, ff. 2.r–3.v. See further: I. L. Schulze, 'Elizabethan Chivalry and the Faerie Queene's Annual Feast', *MLN* 50 (1935), 158–61; Yates, *Astraea*, 99–101; Roy Strong, *The Cult of Elizabeth* (London, 1977), 140, 211. Furthermore, another Elizabethan example of the 'Fair Unknown', occurring just after *The Faerie Queene*, is Christopher Middleton's *Chinon of England* (1597). Chinon is an oafish, rustic youth who succeeds in heroic combats and is rewarded by Oberon with faerie armour; Christopher Middleton, *The Famous History of Chinon of England*, ed. William Edward Mead, EETS 165 (London, 1925).

the whole career of Redcrosse throughout Book I represents a reformed memory of that popular figure of native romance. In this investigation, the theme of memory operates on two levels: as the sense of literary tradition which is invoked in the intertextual relationship between Redcrosse and earlier heroes, and as a process by which the displaced hero regains or remembers his true identity, bestowed on him at birth. The closer textual parallels offered by *Lybeaus*, 'Sir Gareth', and *Ipomedon* should not preclude consideration of other related romances—namely, those texts which are concerned with a displaced youth's struggle to attain the situation which is his birthright. Horn, Havelok, Bevis, Florent, Triamour, Degrebelle, and Perceval are all relevant as male youths who feel compelled to grow into their father's image and higher social position, despite the father's absence as a guide.

Ingeniously, Spenser perceived that this story could be told, or remembered, according to an teleological and Calvinist perspective. From that point-of-view, its most traditional narrative elements become the means of dramatizing salvation by predestination and God's grace. For example, the insistence in the romances that nobility is a gift of birth and cannot be attained, or indeed erased, by effort chimes perfectly with the Calvinist notion of predestination and election; Redcrosse is the 'chosen' knight (1.ix.53), marked out by birth—indeed, before birth—for victory. Furthermore, the notion of the hero's exile, or displaced upbringing, is crucial not only to the romances but also to the experience of Redcrosse: the orphaned condition in which Redcrosse, as a Christian Everyman, finds himself is the fallen world. The Wood of Error establishes the profoundly fallen condition of the world at the beginning of Book I, and Redcrosse's wanderings here are comparable to Bevis' exile in pagan lands, Perceval's sojourn in the forest, and Bewmaynes' life in the kitchen. Also, just as Florent, Degrebelle, Horn, Havelok, and others have been separated from their fathers, Redcrosse has been separated from his Father, who is God. But like the heroes whose fathers are absent or dead, Redcrosse contains within him his father's spirit—in this case, the *imago Dei*—and a vocation to a higher life.[36] The orphaned

---

[36] The biblical authority for the doctrine of *imago Dei* is Gen. 1:26. See also Calvin, *Institutes*, 1.xv.3; pp. 186–9. The prominence of the concept in the Renaissance is discussed by Thomas P. Roche, Jr., *The Kindly Flame* (Princeton, 1964), 90–3.

youth's inclination to chivalry in the romances becomes, in the reformative process of Spenser's memory, the sense possessed by the elect of their call to God.

Because of the emphasis given in *The Faerie Queene* to the profound effects of the Fall, Redcrosse is one of the most displaced and dispossessed of all heroes; the Fall has almost obscured his memory of his origin *in imago Dei*, just as Bevis' exile in pagan lands causes him to forget the significance of Christmas day. But much more so than Bevis, Redcrosse's attempts to remember his identity will be a painful process of trial and error. The ludicrousness of Perceval and Florent, whose aspirations to chivalry are undermined by a lack of education, is replicated in the career of Redcrosse with greater seriousness and anxiety. Florent's borrowed armour is comically 'Rowsty' and 'All sutty, blakk and unclene' (881, 885). The borrowed armour of Redcrosse—'mightie armes and siluer shielde, / Wherein old dints of deepe wounds did remaine' (i.i.1)—involves disconcerting ambiguity when we learn 'Yet armes till that time did he neuer wield' (i.i.1). His strained effort to control his horse also links Redcrosse to the practical inexperience of Perceval and Florent, while invoking a more particular tension: 'His angry steede did chide his foming bitt, / As much disdayning to the curbe to yield' (i.i.1).

Like Perceval, Florent, and others, Redcrosse leaves his ploughman stepfather and, 'prickt with courage, and...forces pryde' (i.x.66), seeks the court of Gloriana. The spiritual reorientation which Spenser has given the story of the displaced youth creates a shift in the connotation of language; 'pryde' is here negative, and it is the chief failing which Redcrosse displays throughout his quest, from his reception at the House of Pride, through to the encounter with Orgoglio, and ending with his near submission to the most insidious form of spiritual pride, Despair and suicide. Redcrosse's adventures depict the error of a continual self-reliance rather than a reliance on God's grace; he trusts his own eyes when he sees the false 'Una' in bed with a squire, he trusts his own arm when he faces Orgoglio, and he trusts his own strength when facing Despair. At the outset, we learn, '...his hart did earne / To proue his puissance in battell braue / Vpon his foe, and his new force to learne' (i.i.3). The emphasis on '*his* puissance', '*his* foe', and '*his* force' needs to be changed, as the dragon-fight has illustrated, to a sense of God's prominence in all goodness. Arthur's role in Book I, in part as an instrument of heavenly grace (i.viii.i), underscores the error of Redcrosse's presumed self-sufficiency. Una's two great outbursts to Redcrosse—'Add faith vnto your force' (i.i.19) and 'In heauenly mercies hast thou not a part?' (i.ix.53)—urge recognition of his dependence on a force outside of himself. Heroes like Lybeaus, Perceval, and Florent may appear to offer a contrastingly admirable impression of self-reliance, but their own sense of personal achievement is partly stripped from them at the end of their adventures when they learn that noble birth has 'predestined', or at least allowed, them to achieve noble deeds. Lancelot's insistence that Bewmaynes 'com of full noble bloode', or else he will not give him 'the hyghe Order of Knyghthode' (326.23–9), is a crucial element in that narrative, one which is syncretic with Redcrosse's innate, rather than achieved, condition: 'thou.. chosen art' (i.ix.53).

For both the secular heroes and Redcrosse, birth has been the greatest determination of their identity, though the different kinds of birth—aristocratic and spiritually elect—are in no way related in Spenser's text. The secular romance is simply an analogous model to illustrate the spiritual paradigm. Calvin's description of salvation could equally be said of noble birth: it 'is freely offered to some while others are barred from access to it' (III.xxi.1; p. 921). After recognition of the gift of birthright, then the manner in which an individual life is conducted becomes important. In the secular romances, the deeds of the heroes prove their worthiness to be their father's sons as well as demonstrating the 'genetic' character of nobility.[37] In Book I, Redcrosse's efforts

---

[37] Spenser also participates in this secular notion of the innate character of nobility, despite inappropriate rearing, in the Salvage Man in Book VI. These two stanzas provide an apt summary of the view taken of the relationship between noble blood and noble deeds in the Middle English romances, including Malory:

> O What an easie thing is to descry
>   The gentle bloud, how euer it be wrapt
>   In sad misfortunes foule deformity,
>   And wretched sorrowes, which haue often hapt?
>   For howsoeuer it may grow mis-shapt,
>   Like this wyld man, being vndisciplynd,
>   That to all vertue it may seeme vnapt,
>   Yet will it shew some sparkes of gentle mynd,
> And at the last breake forth in his owne proper kynd.

and inclinations to goodness, however, flawed, 'spring out necessarily of a true and lively Faith', even though they 'cannot put away our sins, and endure the severity of God's Judgement' (Article XII, 'Of Good Works'). The fear of Perceval's mother, that for all her repression of chivalric life 'the kinde wolde oute sprynge' (355) in her son, is analogous to the inclination of the righteous to seek the *imago Dei* within themselves. And despite Book I's solifidean emphasis, it is equally clear that Redcrosse must destroy the dragon, or at least be God's instrument in the destruction of the dragon; an emphasis on God's omnipotence does not negate the reality of vocation. Contemplation clearly specifies a necessary sequence of events: '*when* thou famous victorie hast wonne...' and 'thou.../*Shalt* be a Saint (I.x.60, 61; my emphases). Redcrosse's request to attain at once the heavenly Jerusalem is firmly denied: 'That may not be (said he) ne maist thou yit / Forgo that royall maides bequeathed care' (I.x.63). If sin is bequeathed to Christians, then so too is the 'true and lively Faith' upon which they must act. As in the romances, interest in Book I still centres on the experiences and actions of the hero. What Redcrosse does is important; but what is more important is who he is—one of God's elect for whom a 'blessed end' has been 'ordained' (I.x.61).

Redcrosse's movement towards realizing his true identity as one of God's elect comes through stages in which he divests himself of a sense of self-sufficiency. Recognition of that identity is an introspective process, achieved through Contemplation:

> For thou emongst those Saints, whom thou doest see,
> Shalt be a Saint, and thine owne nations frend
> And Patrone: thou Saint *George* shalt called bee,
> Saint *George* of mery England, the signe of victoree...
>
> (I.x.61)

>> That plainely may in this wyld man be red,
>>   Who though he were still in this desert wood,
>>   Mongst saluage beasts, both rudely borne and bred,
>>   Ne euer saw faire guize, ne learned good,
>>   Yet shewd some token of his gentle blood,
>> By gentle vsage of that wretched Dame.
>> For certes he was borne of noble blood,
>> How euer by hard hap he hether came.
>>
>> (VI.v.1–2)

That it is *Contemplation's* reference to the past, to Redcrosse's history as a changeling, suggests a process of memory:

> For well I wote, thou springst from ancient race
> Of *Saxon* kings, that haue with mightie hand
> And many bloudie battailes fought in place
> High reard their royall throne in *Britane* land,
> And vanquisht them, vnable to withstand:
> From thence a Faerie thee vnweeting reft,
> There as thou slepst in tender swadling band,
> And her base Elfin brood there for thee left.
> Such men do Chaungelings call, so chaungd by Faeries theft.
>
> (I.x.65)

This moment of sudden self-awareness is comparable to the climax of *Lybeaus*, when the hero learns that he is Gawain's kin. George has arrived at this knowledge of his identity as one of God's elect and the future saint of England through the exercise of memory. That was dramatically illustrated in the episode of Despair, where Despair worked to erode memory, memory of God's grace and the innate sense of deriving from God. Una's sharp injunction—'Why shouldst thou then despeire, that chosen art?' (I.ix.53)—is a direct appeal to his memory, reminding him of what he should already know. In the fuller terms of Article XVII, 'Of Predestination and Election', Redcrosse should remember that those predestined to salvation

through Grace obey the calling: they be justified freely: they be made sons of God by adoption: they be made like the image of his only-begotten Son Jesus Christ: they walk religiously in good works, and at length, by God's mercy, they attain to everlasting felicity.[38]

This Article provides almost a plot summary of not only Book I but, if its terms are converted to a secular meaning, of all the romances of displaced youths who strive to become what they have in fact been given—the image of their father. Spenser's redemption of native romance has involved his perception of the narrative opportunities afforded by the stories of Florent, Lybeaus, Perceval, Bevis, and others to enact the doctrine of predestination and election. The sons in these romances are each called into their father's image—'they be made sons ... by

---

[38] See further Calvin, *Institutes*, III.xxi; pp. 920–32.

adoption'. Their birth determines who they will be, and their own deeds demonstrate their willingness to answer that vocation.

Rosemond Tuve and others have rightly stressed that Redcrosse is not equatable with Christ but rather represents the Christian's struggle to live in imitation of Christ.[39] It is therefore interesting to remember how appropriate the 'Fair Unknown' romance is for adaptation to a Christian story. For it is not only Redcrosse who is like Lybeaus and others, incited by and striving to achieve the special identity conferred on them by birth. Christ himself can be seen as a 'Fair Unknown', and it is possible that Spenser saw the parallel between the life of Christ and that of a hero like Florent. The Incarnation is a birth in exile, away from his Father. Like Florent, Jesus had a lowly upbringing (as a carpenter's apprentice) by a surrogate father. Despite this dislocated upbringing, Jesus had an innate calling to achieve his true and higher identity as the Christ, the Son of God. He accepted his quest, which was the Passion. With the completion of that task, his identity as the saviour of humanity, foretold by the prophets, was achieved. Spenser adapts the 'Fair Unknown' romances to dramatize the Protestant Christian's quest to live in imitation of Christ and the absolute dependence of that soul upon the predestined will of God. In that adaptation, Spenser also reinforces the link between the story-pattern of the secular romances and the life of Christ.

(III) UNA AND THE CONSTANCE–FLORENCE FIGURE IN NATIVE ROMANCE

Like Redcrosse, Una is closely related to a particular type of heroine who features in some of the most popular of the Middle English romances. Though this character-type is not exclusive to native texts, its prominence in that tradition allows the view that Spenser is drawing upon Middle English romance; and in that response, Spenser again makes *The Faerie Queene* an act of revisionary memory, just as typological biblical criticism allows a clarified recollection of Old Testament narrative. Both acts of

---

[39] Tuve, *Allegorical Imagery*, 404. See also: Leslie, *Fierce Warres*, 114–15; Hume, *Spenser*, 105.

memory encode the belief that the past can only now be understood truly—now that its prophetic tendencies have been fulfilled—and that belief is particularly relevant to the reading of
Una as the true Church, embodied in the reformed Church of
England. Una's history relates to the story-type of the lady who is
separated from her husband or lover, a figure seen, with variations, in *Sir Eglamour, Octavian, Sir Torent, The Earl of Tolous*,
and *Sir Triamour*. In particular she belongs to the category of the
innocent faithful woman (though she is not Redcrosse's wife)
who is slandered. The treachery which results in her separation
from Redcrosse occurs when Archimago constructs a false Una, a
'miscreated faire' (1.ii.3), and places her in bed with a 'false other
Spright' (1.ii.3), in the likeness of a squire. Archimago then presents this sight to Redcrosse: 'Come see, where your false Lady
doth her honour staine' (1.ii.4). Redcrosse finds the 'false couple'
'In wanton lust and lewd embracement' (1.ii.5): 'Which when he
saw, he burnt with gealous fire, / The eye of reason was with rage
yblent' (1.ii.5). Because he is not in his own dwelling Redcrosse
can hardly banish Una—what happens in the Constance–Florence romances; instead he forsakes her (1.ii.6).[40]

Two Middle English romances in particular provide close analogues to this scene in *The Faerie Queene*. In *Octavian*, the
Emperor's mother puts a naked squire into bed with the sleeping
and insensible Florence and then brings her son into the room:

> The emperowrs modur awey went than;
> To hur sone swythe sche wan,
>   At masse there as he stode.
> 'Sone,' sche seyde, 'thou trowest not me;
> Now thou mayste the sothe see.'
>
>   (145–9)

As in *The Faerie Queene*, there is a misguided emphasis on the
value of ocular proof: 'Now thou mayste the sothe see', and
'Come see, where your false Lady doth her honour staine'. The
mistake of both Octavian and Redcrosse is to trust completely in

[40] When Archimago summons Redcrosse to see 'Una' and the squire in bed, 'All in
amaze he suddenly vp start' (1.ii.5). This recalls verbally the moment in the 'Letter to
Ralegh' (which in turn appears to recall *Lybeaus* and possibly *Ipomedon*) when
Redcrosse undertook Una's quest: 'Presently that clownish person vpstarting' (p.
738). The repetition invokes pathos, since Redcrosse is now failing Una rather than
serving her.

the testimony of sight in a fallen world, where appearances are often not indicative of substance. The spectacle witnessed by Redcrosse is described as 'guiltie' (1.ii.6), but that adjective really applies to Redcrosse's manner of seeing, his too easy credence in the vision presented to him. Both Octavian and Redcrosse possess a deeper knowledge or memory, which is faith in the loved one, but that inward sight is obscured by passion: with Redcrosse, 'The eye of reason was with rage yblent' (1.ii.5); similarly, when Octavian sees the couple in bed, 'Sorowe to hys herte ranne / And nerehonde waxe he wode' (152–3). Redcrosse 'would haue sleine them in his furious ire' (1.ii.5) but is restrained by Archimago; Octavian, however, 'The knave ... slewe in the bedd', spilling 'gyltles blode' (154–6).

Similarly in *The Earl of Tolous* a lady is slandered with the false evidence of a naked squire.[41] Two knights who lust after the Emperor's wife engineer this deceit. An unfortunate squire is persuaded to hide naked in the lady's chamber as a joke when she is sleeping (727). The treacherous knights then arm themselves, raise the household, and rush into the lady's chamber:

> The yonge knyght, verrament,
> Nakyd founde they thore.
> That oon thefe, wyth a swerde of were,
> Thorow the body he can hym bere,
> That worde spake he no more.
>
> (773–7)

The knights then accuse the innocent lady:

> 'We are here, thou false hore!
> Thy dedys we have aspyedd.
> Thou haste betrayed my lorde:
> Thou schalt have wonduryng in thys worde—
> Thy loos schall sprynge wyde.'
>
> (785–9)

When the Emperor returns, the two traitors tell him of his wife's supposed infidelity.[42]

---

[41] The text is in *Love and Chivalry*, ed. Fellows.

[42] *Sir Triamour* presents a related version of this sort of deception, based on hearsay rather than visual proof, but mirroring the details of the lady and lover apparently found in bed and the lover consequently killed. A false steward slanders Queen Margaret to her husband, King Ardus:

Like Redcrosse, Una not only derives from highly traditional romance narratives but also represents the 'prophetic' link between that character-type and Protestant exegetical and doctrinal beliefs. Just as Redcrosse's career provided an teleological reworking of the displaced youth, Una's experiences involve a remembering of the narrative of the slandered and outcast woman in spiritual and theological terms. Spenser has turned this story from one of faith in human relationships to a concern with correct religious faith in a fallen world. Like the Constance-Florence figure of native romance, Una is the entity in whom belief must be invested—and if lost then restored—for the narrative to reach the sort of conclusion which will define the text as romance. Perhaps to a greater extent than the Constance–Florence figures of Middle English romance, Una is a more active, effective character than she may at first appear. Not only does she save Redcrosse at crucial moments, such as from Orgoglio and Despair, but, unlike the slandered women of native romance, she determinedly seeks Redcrosse after Archimago's deception:

> Vp *Vna* rose,...
> And on...[her] former iourney forward pas,
> In wayes vnknowne, her wandring knight to seeke,
> With paines farre passing that long wandring *Greeke*,
> That for his loue refused deitie;
> Such were the labours of this Lady meeke
> Still seeking him, that from her still did flie.
>
> (1.iii.21)

Interestingly, Una is here cast as the mobile Odysseus rather than the faithful and static Penelope. Una 'wandred had from one to another *Ynd*, / Him for to seeke, ne euer would forsake' (1.vi.2). Spenser has emphasized, and even augmented, the special kind of determinancy which the Constance–Florence figure represents in order to develop the exploration of Holiness; as Una prepares for

> 'In the fyrste fourtenyght that ye were went
> Y fownde them togedur, verament,
> O[s] they ther wylle had done.
> To hym y ran wyth egur mode,
> And slew the knyght there he stode,
> Be myn owne dome.'
>
> (187–92)

Redcrosse's rescue from Orgoglio, the narrator reminds us that 'heauenly grace' (Arthur) and 'steadfast truth' (Una) constantly uphold and restore the 'righteous man'. The potential for that spiritual allegory lies in the emotional depth of the Constance–Florence stories, concerned as they are with love, betrayal, faith, and supreme forgiveness, and once again Spenser has built his meaning from those narrative blocks.

An important part of Spenser's reworking of the Constance–Florence figure as a prophetic embodiement of the true Church is his integration of the romance heroine with the Protestant interpretation of the 'woman clothed with the sunne' in Revelation (12:1).[43] Like the Florence–Constance figures and Una, the Woman Clothed with the Sun 'fled into wildernes' (Rev. 12:6) because of her persecution by evil—the shared narrative element which possibly led Spenser to exploit the 'prophetic' potential of the slandered women of romance. In the gloss of the Geneva Bible (1560), the Woman Clothed with the Sun represents 'ye Church which is compassed about with Iesus Christ the Sonne of righteousness... [and] persecuted of Antichrist'. It would be insufficient to say that by 'ye Church' the glosser, and Spenser speaking through Una, mean the Protestant English Church. In a sense, that is exactly what they mean, but according to a powerfully influential historical interpretation, represented by Bale and Foxe, they could claim that they intend the *true* Church—not an institution created out of exigencies of international and royal politics but rather perceived to descend from Apostolic authority. The 'fact' that God chose England to be his leading nation was presented as a providential grace rather than a human construct.[44] One historian writes that by the 1580s 'a generation of churchmen emerged who could... defend the Church not merely

---

[43] Una is associated with the figure from Revelation through her 'sunshyny face' (I.xii.23; cf. I.iii.4), as well as their mutual persecution by a dragon (Rev. 12:3–6). The relationship of Una to the Woman Clothed with the Sun is discussed by John N. King, *Tudor Royal Iconography* (Princeton, 1989), 203–4 and fig. 64; King, *Spenser and Reformation*, 119, 122. See also O'Connell, *Mirror and Veil*, 44–54, which relates the apocalyptic understanding of Una and Duessa to its historical context.

[44] On the Reformation theme of England as the 'elect nation', comparable to Israel, see Patrick Collinson, 'Biblical Rhetoric: the English Nation and National Sentiment in the Prophetic Mode', in McEachern and Shuger (eds), *Religion and Culture*, 15–45. Collinson demonstrates how English preachers adopted the style of Old Testament prophets to convey a sense of England as 'a special object of God's favour and concern' (23).

in obedience to the queen's will, but because they believed it to be a unique embodiement of divine truth'.[45]

Spenser achieves that sense of objective authority for his own creation, Una, precisely through her memorial relationship to traditional, native romances. Because she is not simply the product of Revelation as seen through Protestant commentators but also recognizably (to contemporary readers) the anti-type of heroines from familar old English romances, Una appears to substantiate the reality of pre-Reformation Apostolic Christianity in Britain. In her, Elizabethan Protestant readers could meet the comforting notion that their religious settlement was a resuscitation rather than a manufacturing. And at the same time, England's medieval literary heritage was (at least partly) redeemable, or worthy to be remembered, insofar as it appeared to prophesy the eventual, providentially ordained break with Rome. Elizabeth herself, denounced as heretical and illegitimate in the Papal Bull *Regnans in excelsis* (1570) and following Catholic texts, was also a slandered woman, and both the queen and Una converge in their associations with the Church of England. Cardinal William Allen's 'Admonition to the Nobility and People of England', a militant Catholic document prepared for distribution in support of the (failed) Spanish invasion of 1588, denounced Elizabeth as 'an incestuous bastard'—more Mordred than Arthur.[46] The native romance narratives upon which Spenser drew had an extraordinary applicability to Reformation history, and in emphasizing the typological dimension of these stories he added historical depth not only to the Reformation experience but also to English literature itself.

In turning now to Book II, interest regarding Spenser's incorporation of native romance shifts from the concerns of the individual to the nation, from the question of personal salvation to the projected union of history and romance in relation to Britain. The providential scheme for the determination of human lives in Book I is extended into Books II's investigation of British history. Just as native romance provided for Book I character-types appropriate for the consideration of the individual's response to

[45] D. M. Loades, *Politics and the Nation 1450–1660* (Brighton, 1974), 319. See also Loades' quotation (ibid.) from Elizabeth's address to Parliament in 1588.
[46] Ibid., 314.

providence, it also offered Spenser for Book II a well-established representation of the British nation as collectively shaped by providence according to the idealizing patterns of romance. But this sense of providence must come into conflict with the realities of historical experience, especially in a Book, dealing with temperance, which places an emphasis on human moral responsibility while maintaining a Calvinist sense of humanity's corrupt and fallen nature.

7

'It seemed another worlde to beholde': Native Romance, History, and Book II of *The Faerie Queene*

Native romance provided a necessary foundation for Spenser's representation in Book I of the English Reformation as a providential enactment. While Holiness was demonstrated in relation to an individual life, Redcrosse's identity as 'Saint *George* of mery England' (I.x.61) allows also a corporate or national perspective. Similarly, in much Middle English romance the providentially guided achievements of the hero involve not merely a personal restoration but also a vision of a wider society—often specifically the English nation—attaining a privileged moral condition through God's grace. The bridge from Book I to Book II exists in the deepening of nationalistic concerns. The questions of salvation and providence, developed through the individual in Book I, are examined in Book II in relation to Britain. In addition to native romances such as *Havelok* and *Guy*, sixteenth-century texts such as *The Actes and Monuments*, *The Image of Bothe Churches*, and also Bale's *King Johan* promoted an understanding of England as a providentially guided and chosen nation.[1] However, Spenser's reception of this tradition will be complicated in Book II, and the sources and impact of those complications deserve careful examination. How does the Calvinist emphasis on human depravity square with a vision of national redemption, especially in a Book concerned with temperance? How reliable is memory as a guide to one's sense of history as revelatory of providence? And how adaptable are the Arthurian historical materials to a providential historical discourse, particularly in the Tudor era?

---

[1] A recent, interesting study of this theme is Thomas Betteridge, *Tudor Histories of the English Reformations, 1530–83* (Aldershot, 1999).

(I) FAERIE LAND AND MIRROR-VERSIONS OF ENGLAND

Faerie land, the narrator emphasizes at the outset of Book II, is neither 'th'aboundance of an idle braine' nor 'painted forgery', even though he concedes that 'none, that breatheth liuing aire, does know, / Where is that happy land of Faery' (II.Proem.I). However, the New World discoveries—'th'Indian *Peru*', '*Amazons* huge riuer now found trew', and 'fruitfullest *Virginia*'— substantiate the view that faerie land is attainable, and like the treatment of England in the Middle English romances the analogy of actual (discovered) places suggests a very physical and geographical understanding of faerie land: 'Of Faerie lond yet if he more inquire / By certaine signes here set in sundry place / He may it find' (II.Proem.4).[2] The 'certaine signes' which promise to lead readers to faerie land seem to recall the tradition of things 'still there'. In Book I, a romance like *Bevis* is 'still there' in the dragon-fight, and by this certain sign Protestant readers might reach faerie land from England in the sense of seeing a national (literary) past which prophesied or even sanctified the religious developments of the sixteenth century. The emphasis in the Proem to Book II on faerie *land*, and the analogy of colonial territories, implies Book II's greater concern with a political identity, geographically defined. At the same time, this physical definition of faerie land reduces the teleological perspective offered in Book I, where Redcrosse viewed a still inaccessible heavenly Jerusalem beyond this world; the adaptation of the displaced youth story similarly depended upon a teleological view which placed both the beginning and the end of that story—the Father—outside of this world and time.

A native romance hero who, because of his defending England against an invading pagan and foreign army, is closer than Bevis to being a national figure appropriate to the viewpoint of Book II is Guy of Warwick. Not surprisingly, therefore, Guy is 'still there' in Guyon,[3] though how readers might use this and other 'certaine

---

[2] See further: Fichter, *Poets Historical*, 182.
[3] Guyon's derivation from Guy is clear from: (1) the similarity of names, more obvious because the form *Guyon* frequently appears in *Guy of Warwick* for the purpose of rhyme, particularly in the printed editions; (2) Guy's period of ascetic pilgrimage makes him the natural ancestor of Guyon, who resists temptations of the flesh; Guy's abandonment of Felice chimes with Guyon's destruction of the Bower of

signes' in relation to reaching Faerie land is unclear. An individual may experience, as Redcrosse does, the sign or sense of being one of the elect, but how does an entire nation, a collective political body, acquire this sense? To answer these points in relation to Book II, we need to recall native romances with a recognizably English or British setting, allowing also for the significance of generically related historical and hagiographical writings whose relevance is also to a sense of English/British nationhood. The crucial motif in these texts is the rhetorical appeal to an object or place which is 'still there'. Because of its dual existence—both in the text and in the reader's actual world—that entity defines the text as a mirror of the contemporary nation. Fifteenth-century readers know Winchester as a place, and when they look into the *Morte Darthur* it is reflected back at them—like any object when seen in a mirror, both the same and not the same. The mirror confirms the reality or veritable existence of the object which it reflects; or, going the other way with the false or jumbled logic which mirroring invariably produces, the reflection draws from the originating object the basis for belief in the *total* reality of that mirror-world—even though, as said, the mirror-world will differ even as it replicates. The world of *Guy* mirrors English places known to the readers as well as social injustices that would be part of their actual experience. But this mirror-world also shows the reader's world as shaped according to God's providential care, and although that reflection is desirable or flattering its credibility may be difficult to sustain.

Geoffrey of Monmouth's *Historia* was a seminal work in this as in so many respects, and its elaborate rhetorical strategies, in its exordium and throughout the text, conspire to erode any doubt which a reader might have concerning its truthfulness. In the Tudor period, numerous works co-operated with the ongoing romance tradition by focusing on objects both in their textual worlds and 'still there' in England for the reader to see.[4] John Hardyng's *Chronicle*, though fifteenth-century, was first printed

---

Bliss; (3) Guy relinquishes his horse and Guyon loses his; both heroes proceed on foot; (4) Guy changes from a knight to a pilgrim, and Guyon is a knight who is accompanied by a pilgrim. See further: Josephine Waters Bennett, *The Evolution of 'The Faerie Queene'* (New York, 1960), 82.

[4] Renaissance antiquarianism and local history feature in: Margaret Aston, 'English Ruins and English History: The Dissolution and the Sense of the Past', *JWCI* 36 (1973), 231–55; Mendyk, *'Speculum Britanniae'*, passim.

in 1543, with additions by Richard Grafton. Grafton writes that Hardyng's work is 'the verray trueth', and that it will, like a mirror, help the English to 'haue vnderstanding / Of all affaires touching their owne countree' (10). Hardyng offers numerous references to things 'still there', including the first reference to the Round Table at Winchester (146). John Leland takes even further the reading of physical England, as if the landscape were a mirror in which the nation's history and character might be viewed.[5] In his *Assertio inclytissimi Arturii regis Britanniae* (1544; tr. Richard Robinson, 1582), Leland depicts an almost numinous power residing in the landscape as he surveys the topographical 'memories' of Somerton, a fort south of Glastonbury reputed to have been inhabited by Arthur:

Good Lorde, what and howe many most deepe Ditches are there heere; How many vallyes are there heere out of the earth delued? Againe what daungerous steepnesse? And to end in fewe wordes, truly me seemeth it is a mirackle, both in Arte and nature . . .

> *But corne there is where* Troy *did stand,& cattle there abound,*
> *Stalled in towne with ditches deepe, in trench mounting from grond,*
> *There Yew trees grow, & subtile Foxes made their cabbins round.*

ANd in deede this is the interchaunge of human affayres. Heerehence had *Ilcester* that auncient Towne this calamitie. Heere vpon doth the customary traffique there beholde the cleere welspring with heauie eyes, and weepe their fill. There the inhabitants plow the ground, and euery yeere finde by seeking for them, Golden, Siluer, and Brasen peeces of money, expressing the images not very liuely of the *Romanes*.

(35)

Thomas Churchyard's *The Worthiness of Wales*, furthermore, rebuts Polydore Vergil's sceptical reception of the British history by pointing to the evidence of Carleon and other places 'still there' to be seen—'Which yet appeares to view of man, / To trye this tale a troth'.[6] Churchyard's main objection to Vergil, in

---

[5] John Leland, *The Assertion of King Arthure*, tr. Richard Robinson, in *Chinon*, ed. Mead. On Leland's works and career, see: McKisack, *Medieval History*, 1–11; James P. Carley, 'Polydore Vergil and John Leland on King Arthur: The Battle of the Books', *Interpretations* 15 (1984), 86–100; Hume, *Spenser*, 145–61; Christopher Dean, *Arthur of England* (Toronto, 1987). See also: John Leland, *Leland's Itinerary in England and Wales*, ed. Lucy Toulmin Smith, foreword by Thomas Kendrick, 5 vols. (Carbondale, 1964).

[6] Thomas Churchyard, *The Worthiness of Wales*, Spenser Society 20 (New York, 1876), 31.

addition to a thinly disguised suspicion of his Italian background, is that the historian has not actually seen the vestigial remains in Wales: 'For wit can not, conceiue till sight send in / Some skill to head, whereby we knowledge win' (26). Particularly relevant to Book II is Richard Lloyd's inclusion of Guy of Warwick among the Nine Worthies in 1584. Lloyd has Guy say in his own words what signs he has left:

'In Windsor forrest I did kill a Bore of passing strength,
   Whose like in England neuer was for highness, breadth, and length.
Some of his bones in Warwicke yet, within the castle lie.'

Lloyd's Guy also defeated a mad cow, and 'Hir bones also in Warwicke lie yet, for a monument, / Which vnto euerie looker on a woonder may present'; and the reader 'may behould' the earl's own remains, which 'In Warwicke lieth yet, though now consumed to mould' ([G.i.v]).

Like Doubting Thomas, the reader is urged to believe in the historical credibility of Guy's world and the Arthurian world because of the witness of his or her own eyes. William Copland's print of *Guy of Warwick* (*c.* 1565) adds a detail which is not found in earlier versions of the romance, that Guy's slaying of the dragon is depicted in a tapestry at Warwick: 'In Warwick the truth there ye shall see / In arras wrought full craftily' (5973–4).[7] Clearly, seeing is believing, and physical objects have as much, if not more, persuasiveness as records and chronicles. In addition to creating the text as a mirror, vestigial, residing objects are the physical embodiments of memory—the memory of collective, regional or national, experience. And as memories, they apparently testify to what must precede memory—a real historical event.[8]

Spenser's participation in this rhetorical strategy is, however, more complex than the examples seen so far. In *The Faerie Queene*, the narrator states that Arthur's shield was made by Merlin: 'But when he [Arthur] dyde, the Faerie Queene it brought / To Faerie lond, where yet it may be seene, if sought' (I.vii.36). Instead of directing us to an accessible remnant or relic, such as

---

[7] *Guy of Warwick*, ed. G. Schleich, *Palaestra* 139 (Leipzig, 1923).
[8] See further: Southern, 'Aspects of the European Tradition', 256. Southern's analysis is directed towards twelfth-century historians, but its earlier chronological focus only emphasizes the medieval roots of the tradition under consideration here.

Gawain's skull in Dover castle, Spenser has directed us to faerie land. The shield is 'still there' only in the romance world, not in the reader's everyday experience, and Spenser has, as he admits in the Proem to Book II, 'vouch[ed] antiquities, which no body can know' (II.Proem.1). The model of the mirror becomes problematic at this moment, and the credibility of the textual world seems fragile, despite the narrator's insistence that it is true. In a similar passage describing the location of Merlin's cave, a whimsical tone cuts against seriousness; this is very different from the assertions of literal truth which one finds in *Havelok* or the Glastonbury literature:

> And if thou euer happen that same way
>   To trauell, goe to see that dreadfull place:
>   It is an hideous hollow caue (they say) ...
>   But dare thou not, I charge, in any cace,
>   To enter into that same balefull Bowre,
> For fear the cruell Feendes should thee vnawares deuowre.
> (III.iii.8)[9]

Bearing in mind the model of Middle English romance and related texts which represent national experience as providentially guided, we need to consider further both how and why this tradition meets new complications in Spenser's reception.

(II) PHANTASTES AND ELIZABETH

The representation in Book II of Phantastes, shaper of mental images or fantasies, allows the undermining of the native literary tradition which offered a mirror-England enjoying providential support. In their tour of the macrocosmic Castle of Alma, Arthur and Guyon eventually reach three chambers comprising the brain—Phantastes, reason (unnamed as a character), and Eumnestes. The greater description and characterization given

[9] Polydore Vergil's account of Arthur's reign foreshadows Spenser's tongue-in-cheek 'they say' with its diplomatic attribution of absurdity to local legend: 'for the common people is at this presence soe affectioned, that with wonderus admiration they extol Arthure unto the heavens, alleginge ...' A crescendoing series of incredulities is completed thus: 'that finallie he slewe giauntes, and appalled the hartes of sterne and warlike menne'. *Polydore Vergil's English History*, Vol. 1, ed. Henry Ellis, CS 36 (London, 1846), 121–2.

to Phantastes and Eumnestes appropriately highlight their significance to a 'Poet historical', and in separating these faculties
Spenser is demonstrating a critical sensibility unknown to the
authors of *Guy of Warwick* or the prose *Brut*, evaded even by
Malory. The basis for understanding Phantastes as dangerous or
beguiling exists in the overall imagistic coherence of *The Faerie
Queene*. Here is Phantastes' chamber:

> His chamber was dispainted all within,
> With sundry colours, in the which were writ
> Infinite shapes of things dispersed thin;
> Some such as in the world were neuer yit,
> Ne can deuized be of mortall wit;
> Some daily seene, and knowen by their names,
> Such as in idle fantasies doe flit...
>
> (II.ix.50)

Significantly, the chamber foreshadows in its imagery aspects of
the Bower of Bliss, namely the Bower's 'painted flowres'
(II.xii.58), 'diuersitie' (II.xii.59), and above all its artificiality,
indicated by a fountain 'ouer-wrought' in all senses 'with curious
imageree' (II.xii.60). At the same time, it also recalls the Proem to
Book II, where we are told what *The Faerie Queene* is not: it is not
'painted forgery' or 'th'aboundance of an idle braine'
(II.Proem.1)—images and words which are echoed in the description of Phantastes' chamber. The comparison between Phantastes
and the Bower is particularly apposite because of the Bower's
certain erotic attractiveness; and the apparent fecundity of Phantastes, however false or sterile he may in fact be, must similarly be
attractive to a poet. The chamber may be filled with annoying
'flyes, / Which buzzed all about', but they are '*Like* many
swarmes of Bees assembled round, / After their hiues with
honny do abound' (II.ix.51; my emphasis). However deceptive,
this metaphoric faculty offers a sense of sweetness; in its alchem-
ical workings, buzzing flies become honey-laden bees.

The attack on the Bower of Bliss, which will feature at the end
of this chapter, is in part an attack on Phantastes—on the image-
imprinting aspect of the mind which causes us to see falsely, and
thus see dangerously:

> All those were idle thoughts and fantasies
> Deuices, dreames, opinions vnsound,

Shewes, visions, sooth-sayes, and prophesies;
And all that fained is, as leasings, tales, and lies.
(ii.ix.51)

The motivations for such mental distortion, Phantastes and the
Bower of Bliss imply, are desire and fear. The admission that
humans, pricked by these emotions or instincts, can see an object
for something other than what it truly is problematizes the tradition we have been considering of things 'still there', both as
testimonials to presumed events and as the basis for seeing textual
worlds as mirrors of contemporary society. Spenser's treatment of
Merlin's cave, quoted above, implicitly recognizes that this object
on its own is insignificant; its (false) significance only arises when
viewed through the eyes of Phantastes. And since Phantastes is
not the same as memory—Eumnestes' chamber is quite separate—the objects 'still there' are no longer embodiments of memory; they are merely the vehicles for wishful thinking.

Phantastes is necessary for the creation of literature, even if he
is potentially dangerous. His unreal shaping of images and fictions must be applied to the base substance of reality or fact.
Sidney's disparaging description in the *Defence* of the historian
'with old mouse-eaten records' (30.6–7) is reminiscent of
Eumnestes. The historian 'is so tied, not to what should be but
to what is, to the particular truth of things and not to the general
reason of things, that his example draweth no necessary consequence, and therefore a less fruitful doctrine' (32.6–9). The
fiction-shaping tendencies of Phantastes are therefore allowable
because they can recreate events in a way which is morally
instructive.[10] Spenser appears to be in step with Sidney's thought
in his distinction between a 'Poet historical' and an 'Historiographer':

For an Historiographer discourseth of affayres orderly as they were
donne, accounting as well the times as the actions, but a Poet thrusteth
into the middest, euen where it most concerneth him, and there

---

[10] Sidney distinguishes between two uses of imagination: 'eikastike' imagination,
'figuring forth good things', and 'phantastike' imagination, 'which doth, contrariwise,
infect the fancy with unworthy objects' (*Defence*, 54). Archimago, as his name
implies, represents an abuse of the imagination; the 'phantastic' Una which he creates
is a projection of Redcrosse's own phantasms, or fears. Behind Sidney's and Spenser's
ambivalence towards the imagination lies Plato's rejection of poets from his Republic,
discussed by Sidney, 57–61.

recoursing to the thinges forepaste, and diuining of things to come, maketh a pleasing Analysis of all.

('Letter to Ralegh', 738).

Spenser does not state explicitly here, as Sidney does, that the 'Poet historical' can and should insert a 'feigned example' (36.23) into a work dealing with historical matter, but rather suggests that the poet's business is to restructure the historical material into a meaningful sequence of events. But Spenser's description of the poet's task—'recoursing to the thinges forepaste, and diuining of things to come'—reveals his view that the 'Poet historical' depends upon Phantastes, who 'could things to come foresee' (II.ix.49) as much as Eumnestes, who 'things past could keepe in memoree' (II.ix.49). The poet's interaction with the past, with the records of history and the things which are 'still there', apparently cannot avoid the involvement of Phantastes, who impresses on that object 'still there' a (contrived) sense of access to a mirror-world of romance, or of providential fulfilment. Taken together, Phantastes and Eumnestes are a false, or human, version of the Boethian God, who can see at once both 'thinges forepaste' and 'thinges to come'.[11]

But if Spenser accepts here in the 'Letter' the activity of Phantastes when considering the past, in Book II he is less prepared to admit subjectivity into historical vision. Arthur and Guyon will read their chronicles in Eumnestes' chamber, and they obviously cannot be in Phantastes' chamber at the same time. Faerie land and Arthur's shield *do* exist, and the narrator's insistence upon their reality has none of the self-conscious irony which marks the description of Merlin's Cave in Carmarthen, Wales. Medieval romance portrayed no anxiety (and no critical judgement) when depicting national experience as providentially controlled, though Spenser has provided us with the means of evaluating the rhetorical strategies of those texts as 'phantastic'. However,

---

[11] Boethius writes: 'Eternity [the attribute of Godhead] ... is the complete, simultaneous and perfect possession of everlasting life; this will be clear from a comparison with creatures that exist in time. Whatever lives in time exists in the present and progresses from the past to the future, and there is nothing set in time which can embrace simultaneously the whole extent of its life: it is in the position of not yet possessing tomorrow when it has already lost yesterday' (v.vi; 163–4). Because God is eternal and transcends time, his inclusion of past, present, and future is genuine sight. But the 'foresight' of Phantastes is a false providence because it is positioned in a temporal process which prohibits genuine knowledge of things to come.

in building upon the Calvinist paradigm of salvation in Book I, Book II seeks to achieve a genuine, rather than phantastic, sense of election for the whole nation. Central to this quest is the figure of Elizabeth, since she possesses the point-of-view which looks into the mirror of faerie land and she may be the means by which the nation can cross through that mirror—or, in other terms, remember their history, leading to the Reformation and Elizabeth's accession, as genuinely providential. Brief consideration of some of the less thoughtful Elizabethan eulogies will sharpen awareness of Spenser's difficulty.

Many pageants and entertainments devised for the queen position her as the presence who can deliver the nation. Elizabeth is more than just a spectator; she is inscribed into the entertainments as their active, determining centre.[12] In 1574 in Bristol, for example, the Queen watched a mock-battle in which a fort was attacked. The occupants of the fort had this to say to their besiegers:

the Cortayns nor bulwarks was not their defence, but the corage of good peple, and the force of a mighty Prince (who saet and beheld all these doyngs), was the thyng they trusted to, on which answer the Enemie retired, and so condicions of peace were drawn and agreed of; at which peace both the sides shot of their artillery, in sien of triumphe, and so crying 'God save the Queen,' these triumphes and warlik pastimes finished.[13]

Elizabeth's presence scatters the enemy. In the Kenilworth pageants of 1575, Elizabeth's blessing or deliverance is invited for a landscape which is explicitly native.[14] As in Bristol,

---

[12] Most of the relevant primary materials are in *The Progresses and Public Processions of Queen Elizabeth*, ed. John Nichols, 3 vols. (London, 1823). 'Journey Through England and Scotland Made by Lupold von Wedel in the Years 1584–1585', *TRHS* n.s. 9 (1895), 258–9 offers an eye-witness account of an Elizabethan tilt. See Strong, *Cult of Elizabeth*, pl. 64 for a contemporary drawing of an Elizabethan tilt. See further: Arthur B. Ferguson, *The Indian Summer of English Chivalry* (Durham, North Carolina, 1960); Sydney Anglo, *Spectacle, Pageantry, and Early Tudor Policy* (Oxford, 1969); David M. Bergeron, *English Civic Pageantry 1558–1642* (London, 1971); Louis Adrian Montrose, 'Celebration and Insinuation: Sir Philip Sidney and the Motives of Elizabethan Courtship', *Renaissance Drama* 8 (1977), 3–35; Arthur B. Ferguson, *The Chivalric Tradition in Renaissance England* (Washington, 1980); Richard C. McCoy, *The Rites of Knighthood* (Berkeley, 1989).

[13] *Progresses*, ed. Nichols, 1.406.

[14] Master Laneham's description of the pageants dwells upon the historical richness of the site: 'the bilding and auciently of the Castl, that . . . was first reared by

Elizabeth is courted to assume the identity of an ideal, romance self, thus drawing the historical England around her into the mirror-world of the pageant. The monarch is addressed at Kenilworth by the 'Lady of the Lake', who has recently escaped entrapment because of Elizabeth's presence: 'by Merlynes prophecie, it seemed she [the Lady of the Lake] could never be delivered but by the presence of a better maide than herselfe'.[15] Thomas Churchyard's *The Queen's Entertainment in Suffolk and Norfolk* (1578) develops the mirror-image which is so important in Middle English romance and related genres. Churchyard conceives of his own report of the entertainment as a mirror in which the nation may view its better self:

And bycause I sawe most of it, or heard it so credibly rehearsed as I know it to be true, I meane to make it a mirror and shining glasse, that al the whole land may loke into, or use it for an example in all places (where the Prince commeth) to our posteritie heereafter for ever.[16]

The entertainment is in turn a mirror to those who are there, such as Elizabeth who is addressed by 'The Queene of Phayries' (II.212). Facing the 'Queene of Phayries', Elizabeth looks into the mirror of the entertainment as if she were looking at the Ditchley portrait of herself, seeing someone who is the same and not the same, the realization of herself as an ageless ideal.

Elizabeth's personal motto, *semper eadem*, allows us to align her in a moment such as this with the 'still there' objects; she is both in our world and in a textual world that, in this case, is idealized and marvellous. But the discrepancy between the ageing, heirless queen and her static, iconic mirror-portraits, particularly in the 1590s when each pole drew further apart,[17] creates a new significance for the 'still there' object; by registering the debilitating effects of time, it emphasizes more our separation

Kenulph, and hiz young sun and successor Kenelm; born both indeed within the Ream heer, but yet of the race of Saxons, and reigned Kings of Marchlond from the year of our Lord 798 too 23 yeerz toogyther, above 770 yeer ago'; *Progresses*, ed. Nichols, 1.428. Furthermore, in one of the Kenilworth pageants the goddess Diana notes that 'By sundrie signes, I now perceive we be, / In Brutus' land ... Now England short, a land of worthy fame' (1.505).

[15] *Progresses*, ed. Nichols, I.498.
[16] *Progresses*, ed. Nichols, II.179.
[17] Sir Roy C. Strong, *Portraits of Queen Elizabeth I* (Oxford, 1963) notes that portraits of the Queen in the 1590s present her as a timeless icon rather than an aging leader. See also: McCabe, *Pillars of Eternity*, 128–9.

from the mirror-world than our proximity or access to it. Only Phantastes, the governing spirit of the Bower of Bliss, will let Britons see their world and collective experience in the idealized terms represented in this pageant. Middle English romance provided a more credible experience because readers could see in *Bevis* or *Guy* an England with a great many evils only gradually becoming perfected through God's providence. But cultic representations of Elizabeth tend to leave unwritten and unnegotiated the space between the real object and her idealized reflection. Only the subtle tentativeness of Churchyard's observation—'it *seemed* another worlde to beholde' (II.181; my emphasis)—suggests a Spenserian anxiety that a view of British, specifically Tudor, history as providential may in fact be phantastic rather than informed by verifiable signs of election. Two nineteenth-century examples of mirror-worlds may help to elucidate the conceptual issues at play here.

In George MacDonald's 'fairy-novel', *Phantastes* (1858), a mirror is described as analogous to the workings of the human imagination; they share a 'wondrous affinity'.[18] The world of the imagination is like the world reflected in a mirror, 'the same and yet not the same' (154) as the historical, actual world in which we live. The mirror, or imagination, transforms the objects which it reflects, lifting them 'out of the region of fact and into the realm of art' (155). A battle-axe in the actual room becomes, when reflected in the mirror, part of a romance world of perfected and absolute definition:

that old battle-axe [i.e., the image of it reflected in the mirror] looks as if any moment it might be caught up by a mailed hand, and borne forth by the mighty arm, go crashing through casque, and skull, and brain, invading the Unknown with yet another bewildered ghost. I should like to live in *that* room if I could only get into it.

(155–6; authorial emphasis)

Like the object which is 'still there', the actual battle-axe attains an idealized identity in the imaginatively heightened world in the mirror. But unlike the Middle English romances, that mirror-world is not true in the sense of being remembered; rather, it is an imaginative world, since that is the value given here to the

---

[18] George MacDonald, *Phantastes* (London, 1858), 154.

mirror.[19] MacDonald's text suggests the subjectivity of the mirror-world and locates the fashioning of human experience into
idealized patterns of completion not in the otherness of providence but rather in the wish-fulfilment of the viewer. Looking at
the object which is 'still there', the viewer can see whatever he or
she wants. When an object 'still there' is offered as proof that
something happened, it is not so much a case of 'seeing is believing' as 'believing must come before seeing, or you will not see at
all'. Subjectivity and suspended truth become the means to enter
the mirror-world, even if that world is a delusion which, like any
mirror, can be shattered. In texts which claim to report an historical experience, memory may in fact intermingle with, or even be
usurped by, the fiction-making process of desire. Providence may
be invoked as a means of giving authority to a constructed,
imaginative version of events, but there should be an anxiety as
to the genuineness of the providential experience.

Lewis Carroll's *Through the Looking-Glass* (1872) equally
suggests that the process by which our world appears to become
fulfilled or idealized may only happen in the subjectivity of desire.
Alice says:

'Oh, Kitty, how nice it would be if we could only get through into the
Looking-glass House! I'm sure it's got, oh! such beautiful things in it!
Let's pretend there's a way of getting through into it, somehow, Kitty.
Let's pretend the glass has got all soft like gauze, so that we can get
through. Why, it's turning into a sort of mist now, I declare! It'll be easy
enough to get through—'[20]

The means of getting through the glass—'somehow'—and the
softness and mistiness of the mirror are indications of the suspended truth and logic which are required to 'realize' the perfect
version of this world as a reality. The juxtaposition in the penult-
imate sentence of the meaningless 'sort of' with the emphatic 'I
declare' represents the use of rhetoric to make the incredible
credible.

---

[19] In contrast to Spenser, who represents Phantastes as at least partly suspect or
dangerous, MacDonald represents imagination from a Romantic point-of-view: as a
positive, vibrant, life-imparting faculty.

[20] Lewis Carroll, *Alice's Adventures in Wonderland & Through the Looking-
Glass, and What Alice Found There* (London, 1978), 220.

(III) ARTHURIAN HISTORY AND ROMANCE IN BOOK II

In Book II's description of *The Faerie Queene* as 'matter of iust memory', what is now at stake is the epithet 'iust', in both of its senses of 'only' and 'righteous, correct'. An anxiety, concomitant with Calvinism, concerning the veracity of divine election at the national level has developed, understandably, from Redcrosse's personal doubts. 'Why shouldst thou then despeire, that chosen art?' (I.ix.53) may be an adequate response to counter Redcrosse' despair, but can it be said with equal confidence to the entire Elizabethan nation? The sense of being an elect nation was undermined in part by the succession crisis. The desire for government which, like the Garden of Adonis, 'is eterne in mutabilitie, / And by succession made perpetuall' (III.vi.47)[21] is at the heart of Book II's quest for a verifiable sense of the Elizabethan nation as elect. In its political and historical aspects, Book II is concerned with what MacDonald, Carroll, and Churchyard all avoid—the 'somehow' of crossing through the mirror. The faerie land in which the poem's action occurs, then, is comparable to the space between a subject and its reflection in the mirror—between a real Britain and a Britain which is providentially fulfilled. Like the narrative world of much Middle English romance, this interim space is a world of becoming rather than full attainment, and it consequently contains aspects both real and supernatural. It is a world full of the dangers and dissimulations of our own experience, but it is also, as we saw in Book I and as we see in Book II in the angel's adminstrations to Guyon (II.viii.1), a world in which human actions can be supported by divine providence towards perfection.

But there is another faerie land which is not seen in the poem, and it is the final achievement of perfection and the projected point of narrative closure. Earlier in Book II, Arthur had noted that the inanimate picture of Gloriana on Guyon's shield offers the appearance of vitality. Guyon responds:

> Faire Sir... if in that picture dead
> Such life ye read, and vertue in vaine shew,
> What mote ye weene, if the trew liuely-head
> Of that most glorious visage ye did vew?
>
> (II.ix.3)

---

[21] Dr Richard McCabe interestingly observed during my D.Phil. *viva* how these lines descriptive of the Garden apply obliquely to the Elizabethan succession crisis.

This may be intended as one of the 'certaine signes' which lead to Faerie land, but it is in fact anything but certain. It is precisely that direct experience of the ideal—'the trew liuely-head / Of that most glorious visage'—which Arthur never achieves in the poem. This second, unseen faerie land, beyond the poem's middle-ground arena of action, is the court of Gloriana in Cleopolis. Unlike Churchyard, Spenser does not directly present this mirror-opposite to his own world until the means of crossing over can be worked out. As a quasi-historical figure, Arthur in his pursuit of Gloriana represents the process by which Britain could become perfected, the same struggle of trial, error, and providence seen in the native romances. In the episode of Eumnestes' chamber, Spenser explores the problems involved in this providential vision, but an earlier scene which is preliminary to that episode is Arthur's account of Gloriana in Book I:

> For-wearied with my sports, I did alight
> From loftie steed, and downe to sleepe me layd...
> Me seemed, by my side a royall Mayd
> Her daintie limbes full softly down did lay:
> So faire a creature yet saw neuer sunny day...
>
> But whether dreames delude, or true it were,
> Was neuer hart so rauisht with delight,
> Ne liuing man like words did euer heare,
> As she to me deliuered all that night;
> And at her parting said, She Queene of Faeries hight.
>
> When I awoke, and found her place deuoyd,
> And nought but pressed gras, where she had lyen,
> I sorrowed all so much, as earst I ioyd,
> And washed all her place with watry eyen.
> From that day forth I lou'd that face diuine;
> From that day forth I cast in carefull mind,
> To seeke her out with labour, and long tyne,
> And neuer vow to rest, till her I find.

(I.ix.13–15)[22]

As a mirror-opposite to Elizabeth, Gloriana represents the form which Elizabeth would take if the world were guided to fulfilment. The most significant thing about Gloriana is that she never

---

[22] The quest for Gloriana, which is the overriding narrative arc of the poem, is reaffirmed at: II.ix.7; III.iv.54; IV.ix.17; V.xi.35; VI.viii.30.

appears; this may be due to the impossibility for the ideal to be rendered by the human artist, but it may equally be because she does not exist. Our only knowledge of her comes from Arthur's memory, and that memory might be under the influence of Phantastes. Spenser's handling of the scene admits the danger of seeing falsely. In relating his dream—or encounter?—with the Faerie Queene to Redcrosse and Una, Arthur's ambiguous language, like Malory's treatment of Arthur's death or Alice's passing through the looking-glass, reflects the uncertainty of his memory as to what actually happened. His account positions his experience between reality and its idealized mirror-opposite, a space in which an interchange *may* have taken place, though the 'somehow' remains obscure: '*Me seemed*, by my side a royall Mayd... (my emphasis). The equally ambiguous addition that 'So faire a creature yet saw neuer sunny day' could be taken literally: she is a phantasm. Arthur admits his own confusion: 'But whether dreames delude, or true it were...' The only 'proof' which Arthur has is the 'pressed gras, where she had lyen'; at least something is 'still there', but this evidence is elusive, a testimony to emptiness rather than presence.

If Gloriana is elusive and indeterminable, so too is Arthur—or at least the Arthurian historical traditions which Spenser can hardly exclude from his work, particularly considering Arthur's function in the work as a political symbol. We have already encountered something of the intractability of Arthur as a national hero in *Of Arthour and of Merlin*; that text paradoxically promotes its own Englishness and sympathizes with the British Celts, who are the natural enemies of the English. Saxons become Saracens, and other Arthurian texts (particularly those concerned to explore historical origins or represent Arthur as a national figure) face problems which highlight the complexity of 'British consciousness and identity'.[23] Not only is Arthur's national or ethnic identity confusing in the context of English literature, but he is also problematic as a dynastic hero. The Tudor rulers' much vaunted descent from the old British kings, including Brutus, Arthur, and Cadwallader, attempts to solve the

---

[23] I take this phrase from a recent collection of stimulating essays: Brendan Bradshaw and Peter Roberts (eds), *British Consciousness and Identity* (Cambridge, 1998). Further references will be made to individual contributions below. On Arthur as a national hero, see further McCabe, *Pillars of Eternity*, 80–4.

first problem—nationality—but in doing so emphasizes the second—dynastic descent. Spenser's address to Elizabeth concerning Arthur can only cause him problems at a later stage:

> Thy name O soueraine Queene, thy realme and race,
> From this renowmed Prince deriued arre,
> Who mightily vpheld that royall mace,
> Which now thou bear'st, to thee descended farre
> From mightie kings and conquerours in warre,
> Thy fathers and great Grandfathers of old.
>
> (II.x.4)

This passage stops short of asserting direct lineal descent. The difficulty in seeing Arthur as part of a providential, historical-dynastic scheme is the well known 'fact' that he died without legitimate heirs. In the prose *Brut*, Arthur, knowing that he is dying, calls Constantine, Cador's son, and bequeathes him the crown 'for-asmiche as he hade none heire of his body bigeten: and grete harme was hit þat soche a noble Kyng, and so doughty, had none childe of his body bigeten' (91.2–4). A number of Tudor Arthurian texts, in opposition to Polydore Vergil's *Historia Anglica* and in propagandistic support of the Tudor dynasty, assert an untroubled lineage. For example, Arthur Kelton's *A Chronycle with a Genealogie* (1547) claims:

> Also Galfridus, reherseth plain
> How many kynges, *successiuely*
> *One, after other*, here did remain
> *Of one dissent, lyne and progeny*
>
> Fully an hundred, as he doth specifie
> Recon from Brute, doune to Cadwaladre...
> From Cadwalader, the yere accomptyng
> As diuerse auctors, doth specify
> Untill this tyme, *doune dissendyng*
> Till our most noble, theight kyng Henry
> *Of the same stocke, lyne and progeny*
> *As by dissent...*[24]

[24] Arthur Kelton, *A Chronycle with a Genealogie Declaryng that the Brittons and Welshemen are Lineallye Dyscended from Brute*... (London, 1547), e.iiii.[r]; my emphasis. Kelton emphasizes the direct, lineal, blood descent of the Tudors from Brutus at other points in the work, such as ([e.v.r]). Similarly, Churchyard insists that Elizabeth descends 'from Arthurs rase and lyne' (*Worthiness of Wales*, 34).

Kelton's *Chronycle* includes a genealogical table in which a direct line is drawn between Arthur and Cadwallader; a marginal gloss ambiguously adds 'Betwene Arthur and Cadwalader was .ix. kynges in Britaygne' ([f.i.r–v]).[25]

By the time Spenser was writing *The Faerie Queene*, succession was critical not only in relation to Arthur but also—and obviously more so—in relation to Elizabeth. Richard Robinson's translation of Leland's *Assertio, A Learned and True Assertion of... Arthure* (1582), contains a dedicatory epistle from the translator to Lord Arthur Grey (Spenser's former employer), Sir Henry Sidney, and Thomas Smith; the three are identified respectively as '*Lord Deputie* & Liefetenant Generall for the Queenes *Maiestie in Ireland*', '*President for her Maiestie in the Marches of Wales*', and 'Chiefe Customer for her Maiestie in the Porte of London: & to the Worshipfull Societie of Archers... celebrating the renoumed memorie of the Magnificent Prince ARTHVRE & his Knightly Order of the Round Table' (3). These descriptions add up to a fairly militant image of 'Great Britain',[26] and Robinson has clearly revived Leland's Henrican text to give support to the aggressively imperialist Protestant ideology represented by Grey. For Robinson's purposes, Arthur is the appropriate symbol, and Arthur's foreign conquests are clearly signs of providential approval relevant to the ongoing Protestant enterprise. God's favour towards Israel, his 'elect' (4) nation, is preparation for understanding Arthur's Britain as specially favoured, and it also offers obliquely a justification for the military tactics of Arthur Grey, tactics which ended his office in Ireland:

Whereby as he [God] prospered and protected his holy ones in peace and warres against their enemies, we reade also in the deuine histories from time to time how and by what ordenarie meanes of power, force, and defence, he reached vnto his feeble flocke his mightie arme to the discomforture of the enemie & vtter subuertion both of their power & pollicie, according to his promises aforesaide. Heere then memorable and praiseworthie is the prouidence of this most mightie *God*, who promising helpe vnto the Iewes against the Gentiles, vsed no kinde of

---

[25] In contrast, Richard Grafton's *An Abridgement of the Chronicles of England* (London, 1564) makes very clear that native history is punctuated by a significant hiatus in monarchical lineage; [fo.3.v].

[26] On the title-page to Robinson's translation, Arthur is described as 'King of great *Brittaine*' (1).

speach so much as this, *That he would bend his Bow and dye his shaftes in bloud.*

(4–5)

Robinson notes that 'there were neuer Brittaines wanting of excellent learning and exquisite knowledge to leaue with carefull diligence and credible commendation, the progenie, life, prowesse prosperitie, and triumphant victories of our said auncient Arthure worthely published vnto the worlde' (7). Elizabeth is obviously being urged to adopt the militant poise of this same Arthur, especially in the face of her alarming similarity to the Arthur of the prose *Brut*: 'grete harme was hit þat soche a noble Kyng, and so doughty, hade none childe of his body bigeten'. But Robinson's account here of Arthur, like Kelton's genealogy, is manipulative: the 'progenie' which Robinson slips into his list of Arthur's virtues is one of several places where his work fails to be 'matter of *iust* memory'.

Spenser's choice of Arthur 'as most fitte for the excellency of his person . . . and also furthest from the daunger of enuy, and suspition of present time' ('Letter to Ralegh', 737) appears baffling, or possibly ironic, on closer consideration. Arthur really seems to highlight the great anxieties and inconsistencies of Elizabeth's government and its alleged descent. Arthur's own legitimacy, like Elizabeth's, was questioned, as seen in Malory. And Arthur's Britishness, again like Elizabeth's, is never satisfactorily accounted for in English texts. Kelton's *Chronycle* makes in its full title a false distinction between 'Brittons and Welshemen', the Britons here being the inhabitants of England. Arthur's enemies are the Saxons, and they are never admitted to being the contemporary English. Kelton, who was himself from Shrewsbury and thus only marginally (if that) the Welshman he claims to be,[27] is as misty and gauze-like as Alice's looking-glass when he writes that Tewdwr Mawre, ancestor of Edmund, earl of Richmond and the Tudor dynasty, 'chased the Saxons, Danes and Pictes, from the borders of Wales, with all other foreyn enemyes' ([f.i.v]). Similarly, Richard Grafton writes about Arthur's 'notable battailes against the Saxons' (*Abridgement*, fo. 21[r]). Grafton adds that Arthur 'coulde not clerelye auoide them out of thys land, but y^t

[27] Peter Roberts, 'Tudor Wales, National Identity and the British Inheritance', in Bradshaw and Roberts (eds), *British Consciousness*, 8–42 (15).

they helde their countreys which they were possessed of' (ibid.). Remarkably, Grafton positions his readers in opposition to the Saxons—'them', not 'us'—but also implicates his English readers in the Saxon legacy: they are in '*thys* land'. If the readers, still inhabiting that land, are not Saxons, then it is unclear who is. In the following passage dealing with the reign of Edward II, the prose *Brut* assesses more honestly (if with some exaggeration) the ethnic and political heterogeneity of England/Britain:

þe grete lordes of Engeland were nouȝt alle of o nacioun, but were mellede wiþ oþere nacions, þat is forto seyn, somme Britons, somme Saxones, somme Danois, somme Peghtes, somme Frenchemen, somme Normans, somme Spaignardes, somme Romayns, some Henaudes, some Flemyngus, and of oþere diuerse naciouns, þe whiche nacions acorded nouȝt to the kynde bloode of Engeland.

(220.18–23)

The main reason in Reformation England for ignoring this complexity in favour of Kelton's racially pure British nation was religion: the Old Testament emphasis on the lineage and ethnic homogeneity of God's chosen people powerfully informs the Tudor attraction to the 'British history', as Robinson's epistle to the *Assertion* demonstrates. British identity, God's providential favour, and 'true' religion are intertwined in the argument that Britain was evangelized in the Apostolic era, before St Augustine of Canterbury's mission in 597. Although the pagan Saxons challenged that pure religion, it survived according to Kelton (as well as more authoritative Reformation historians) in Wales:

With vs in Wales, none were opprest
No tirauntes great, with vs did dwelle
There was the place, of peace and rest
Christ and his lawes, for to degest
None durst approche, that to deny
Agayne our faithe, once to reply.
[d.vii.r]

Medieval authorities upheld this view, as seen in the prose *Brut* where St Augustine arrives in Wales to find a Christian Church already well established.[28] Britishness was closely akin

---

[28] The Welsh Christians refuse to join Augustine's new Church of England: 'And þai [the Welsh] saide þat "þai nolde [be odedient] but to þe Erchebisshop of Kerlyoun"; & saide "þai nolde neuer, for no maner þing, bene obedient vnto þe

to Protestantism—or more particularly to the vision of a chosen people, a Hebrew-type tribe wandering in the wilderness for a time and, with the advent of Henry VII and more clearly the reforming Henry VIII, finally reaching or returning to a promised land.[29]

The sixteenth-century debate concerning the historicity of Arthur, exemplified by Polydore Vergil's cool reception of Arthur's reputed foreign conquests and by a number of ensuing texts which either countered Polydore with an absurd insistence upon Arthur's remakable career (Kelton, Leland, Richard Lloyd, John Dee) or else gave a muted aquiescance to his historical existence but without fabulous exploits (Holinshed, Selden), possibly gave Spenser some room in which to manoeuvre. The issue at stake here is not whether *The Faerie Queene* can make a fair case for Arthur's historicity; it is whether Spenser can create from a highly complex literary–historical tradition with strong political associations a dynastic, national, and Protestant epic with its own coherence. The two chronicles in Eumnestes' chamber present the challenges of the historical material and the relevance of these concerns to the moral and thematic concerns of the poem.

(IV) 'BRITON MONIMENTS' AND 'ANTIQUITIE OF FAERIE LOND'

In Memory's chamber, Arthur and Guyon each read a book; the British prince reads '*Briton moniments*' and the elfin knight reads '*Antiquitie* of *Faerie* lond'. Each book relates to its reader, offering them both a chance 'Their countries auncestry to vnderstond' (II.ix.60). The first book relates the traditional 'British history',

---

Englisshe-men"; "ffor þe Englisshe-men," þai saide, "beþ oure aduersaries & oure enemys, and hauen dryuen vs out of oure owen contre; & we beþ Cristen men, and euer haþ bene; & þe Englisshe-men haueþ euermore bene Paynymes, but now late þat þai beþ conuertede." ¶ Seynte Austyne myȝt of ham none oþere answere haue, but saide apertely þat "þai nolde neuer ham meke to him ne to þe peple of Rome."' (98.11–20). Closer to Spenser, Churchyard reiterates this view: 'Saint Augustine could not make the Britaines be obedient to the Archbishop of Canterburie, but yet they only submitted themselues to the Archbiship of Carleon, in Adelbrights tyme that was King of Kent' (*Worthiness of Wales*, 46).

[29] See further Roberts, 'Tudor Wales', in Bradshaw and Roberts (eds), *British Consciousness*, 20 for interesting remarks on Bishop Richard Davies' preface to the Welsh language New Testament of 1567.

the second book presents romance, not in the sense of *Havelok* or indeed the action-world of *The Faerie Queene*, in which the historical world is moving towards perfect justice through providence, but in the sense of the fully achieved condition of narrative closure. The first chronicle is particularized and clearly British, the second presents a semi-abstracted world whose ideal characters and events dimly echo features of English history while remaining fundamentally different. The fact that both chronicles are in Eumnestes' chamber is significant; Spenser begins by claiming that both are true, or 'matter of iust memory'; the faerie chronicle is not read in Phantastes, and that fact invites hope that its world might be reached. In Eumnestes' chamber, the two chronicles, presented side by side, face each other like the image of the mirror employed in this study to describe the similarity and opposition which exists between the real and the ideal. The concern is whether there is a passing through this mirror, whether the scene allows the sense that the historical Britain can through a process of perfection under providential guidance become the ideal Britain represented in the faerie chronicle.

Beginning with the historical chronicle, it is presented as true in the sense of having 'actually happened'. For one, many aspects of its history are 'still there' for us to see:

> That well can witnesse yet vnto this day
> The westerne Hogh, besprincled with the gore
> Of mightie *Goëmot*.
>
> (II.x.10)

> But the sad virgin innocent of all,
> Adowne the rolling riuer she did poure,
> Which of her name now *Seuerne* men do call:
> Such was the end, that to disloyall loue did fall.
>
> (II.x.19)

> So by him *Cæsar* got the victory,
>   Through great bloudshed, and many a sad assay,
> In which him selfe was charged heauily
> Of hardy *Nennius*, whom yet did slay,
> But lost his sword, yet to be seene this day.
>
> (II.x.49)

> Soone after which, three hundred Lordes he slew
> Of British bloud, all sitting at his bord;

Whose dolefull moniments who list to rew,
Th'eternall markes of treason may at *Stonheng* vew.
(II.x.66)[30]

Some of these references are Spenser's additions to his sources,
indicating his deliberate participation in the tradition of things
'still there'; these are not 'antiquities, which no body can know'
(II.Proem.1). On the other hand, knowing these sites does not
promise to give access to an ideal world. The marked feature of
'*Briton moniments*' is the unremittingly realistic depiction of
human history which it offers. Spenser has intensified the violence, disorder, and discontinuity of his sources to present a
British history which offers the strongest sense of the world as
fallen, recalling the emphasis placed in Book I, through the por-
trayal of Redcrosse, on the fallenness of the individual.[31] This
chronicle must be true and the 'matter of iust memory', because
the national experience which it depicts would be undesirable
and unflattering to contemporary readers. This is the side of the
mirror which 'we' are on, a world subject to fortune, time, and
decay. Richard McCabe's insights on Spenser's representation of
Stonehenge are pertinent:

What Spenser has done, is to associate the greatest national 'moniment'
with infamy...Stonehenge is a monument both to honour and to
infamy and the curse of human history is that the two cannot be disent-
angled. The monuments of time bear a disconcerting resemblance to its
ruins.[32]

---

[30] More references in the historical chronicle to origins or things 'still there' are:
III.x.12, 16, 26, 42, 46, 58. The main sources for Spenser's historical chronicle are
Geoffrey of Monmouth, Hardyng, Holinshed, and Stowe. See further: Harper, *Sources
of British Chronicle*; Jerry Leath Mills, 'Spenser and the Numbers of History: A Note
on the British and Elfin Chronicles in *The Faerie Queene*', *PQ* 55 (1976), 281–7.

[31] On Spenser's originality in the handling of his sources and his augmentation of
disaster in the historical chronicle, see: Harper, *Sources of British Chronicle*, 164, 184;
Isabel E. Rathbone, *The Meaning of Spenser's Fairyland* (New York, 1937), 65–154;
Harry Berger, Jr., *The Allegorical Temper* (New Haven, 1957), 89–114; Roche, *Kindly
Flame*, 31–50; Michael O'Connell, 'History and the Poet's Golden World: The Epic
Catalogues in *The Faerie Queene*', *ELR* 4 (1974), 241–67; Joan Warchol Rossi,
'*Britons moniments*: Spenser's Definition of Temperance in History', *ELR* 15
(1985), 42–58 (this article concludes that history and romance are united in Spenser's
vision; my conclusion is precisely the opposite, though I agree with Rossi's strong
linking of the historical chronicle to an understanding of temperance); McCabe,
Pillars of Eternity, 103–9.

[32] McCabe, *Pillars of Eternity*, 109.

Arthur's bones at Glastonbury were similarly double-edged, testimony to his reality but also, because of the numerous wounds
on the skull, proof not only of his death but of the violence with
which his kingship ended. The replacement of Arthur by Artegall
in Merlin's prophecy (III.iii.27), which is the continuation of
'*Briton moniments*', is not surprising, even though it is an admission of Spenser's dilemma. Arthur's direct implication in such a
history as '*Briton moniments*' would make his union with Gloriana inconceivable.[33] And the separateness of that faerie world is
made clear in the contrast which Guyon's chronicle presents to
'*Briton moniments*'.

'*Antiquitie* of *Faerie* lond' represents an experience in which
the sense of providential fulfilment is strong, in which the movement of time is less significant than the sense of stability derived
from the patterned repetition of events. Unlike the bloody upheavals of '*Briton moniments*', here the seamless succession of rulers
reduces the urgency of time:

> His sonne was *Elfinell*, who ouercame
>   The wicked *Gobbelines* in bloudy field:
>   But *Elfant* was of most renowmed fame,
>   Who all of Christall did *Panthea* build:
>   Then *Elfar*, who two brethren gyants kild,
>   The one of which had two heads, th'other three:
>   Then *Elfinor*, who was in Magick skild;
>   He built by art vpon the glassy See
> A bridge of bras, whose sound heauens thunder seem'd to bee.
>
> (II.x.73)

The similarity of names, all beginning *Elf-*, allows these rulers to
merge together into a continuous stream, emphasizing permanence rather than change. In this stanza, furthermore, and
throughout the faerie chronicle, there is a relative absence of
verbs denoting the means of succession. The names of new rulers
are presented without any sense of the action of their arrival: 'But
Elfant...', 'Then *Elfar*...', 'Then *Elfinor*...'. In the historical
chronicle, by contrast, there is an emphasis on the verbal means

---

[33] It is difficult to understand the uninhibited rapture with which Arthur responds
to his nation's history (II.x.69). In the context of what has preceded, his response
seems simplistic. Artegall's relationship to Arthur will be examined in greater detail in
the following chapter.

of succession: 'arose' (II.x.37), 'succeede' (II.x.41), 'Deposed' (II.x.44), 'restord' (II.x.44), 'disthronized' (II.x.44), 'reseized' (II.x.45), 'chosen' (II.x.47), 'dyde' (II.x.53), 'ouerthrew' (II.x.57), 'ouercame' (II.x.58), and so on. The verbs in the historical chronicle lay emphasis on the great energy, struggle, and violence which surrounds the succession to the British throne; the 'ins' and 'outs' expressed by these verbs suggest the rhythms of fortune's wheel, such as Arthur dreamed of in the alliterative *Morte Arthure*. More generally, they emphasize the temporal aspect of history, the occurrence of events by means of actions through time. In the faerie chronicle, however, the paucity of verbs sublimates the sense of change and time. We are given little sense of what happened to previous rulers; each one simply fades away, to be replaced instantly by another, virtually indistinguishable ruler. The sense above all is of a nearly static permanence. Spenser never represented Gloriana's court; but if he had, it might have been similar to the character of the faerie chronicle, with a strong emphasis on being rather than becoming, entity rather than action. Put another way, the world of the faerie chronicle is the world which is achieved at the very end of romances such as *Havelok*; at that point, these romances end because the possibility of narrative development has ceased with the fulfilment of divine providence. Hence the faerie chronicle is characterized more by static permanence than narrative and temporal development and change.

It is clear how the faerie chronicle is not the same as '*Briton moniments*'. What is less obvious, but nevertheless true, is how it *is* the same. As a mirror-opposite, its sameness lies in what A. C. Hamilton calls the 'transparent, historical analogues to the Tudor dynasty.'[34] Elficleos 'is' Henry VII, leaving two sons, Elferon, who 'is' Prince Arthur who 'did vntimely dy' (II.x.75), and Oberon, who 'is' the future Henry VIII. Oberon's heir, Tanaquil, or Gloriana, 'is' Elizabeth. But the mirroring still enforces as great a sense of separation as relation. For example, like Henry VIII Oberon supplied his dead brother's place 'in spousall' (II.x.75). The fact that Henry VIII's experience as a husband was marred by change and violence is necessarily omitted, and that omission is not flattery to the Tudor dynasty but if anything criticism.

---

[34] Hamilton's annotation to II.x.75.

Similarly, Queen Mary, whose restoration of the old religion was, to Catholics, evidence of providential support for their cause, is notably absent.[35] The discrepancy between the actual Tudors and their ideal counterparts is an indication of the failure of the real to match the ideal.[36]

Although the two chronicles are read in one mind—the macrocosmic head of the Castle of Alma—they are never allowed to connect, only mirror each other.[37] The movement of the historical world towards complete providential fulfilment is resisted for the reason of Spenser's profound sense of the fallen nature of British, and more generally human, experience, reflected in the historical chronicles. The gap between '*Briton moniments*' and '*Antiquitie* of *Faerie* lond', or between Arthur conceived as an historical figure and Gloriana, is the subject of the Book: temperance, or more appropriately the original sin against which temperance struggles. '*Briton moniments*' summarizes the abusive excesses of irascible and concupiscent appetites throughout Book II, and the fallen nature of humans is the inhibiting factor which prevents Spenser from allowing a movement of Britain, or the real world, towards an idealized fulfilment. It would be phantastic to present the events of '*Briton moniments*' as possessing the ideal regularity and perfection of the romance world.

Why, then, is '*Antiquitie* of *Faerie* lond' in Eumnestes' chamber? In what sense is the kind of experience which it represents and which the poem as a whole seeks to restore truly remembered? In the *Confessions*, St Augustine writes that human memory, unlike animal memory, has a deep well which contains the memories of things not experienced by the individual personally, namely the memory of the prelapsarian condition of affinity

---

[35] See further: Betteridge, *Tudor Histories*, 120–60.

[36] See further O'Connell, 'History and Poet's Golden World', 80–1.

[37] Harry Berger writes that the two chronicles 'present two different worlds, two utterly irreconcilable views of life, two opposed modes of memory, perception, and consciousness'; Berger, *Allegorical Temper*, 104–5 (see further, 89–114). Roche, *Kindly Flame*, 31–50, O'Connell, 'History and Poet's Golden World', 69–89, Parker, *Inescapable Romance*, 82, Fichter, *Poets Historical*, 183–4, and Andrew Hadfield, *Literature, Politics, and National Identity* (Cambridge, 1994), 194–6 agree with Berger that the British and faerie world are kept separate in Book II. Rathbone, *Meaning of Fairyland*, 125–6 suggests ways in which the two chronicles intersect, though her interpretation fails to take account of the direction in which Spenser's changes have moved the historical chronicle—away from the ideal.

with God.[38] Closer to Spenser, Sidney writes that because humans were made in the image of God, they retain a memory of their prelapsarian perfection. The poet, Sidney argues, is the *anamnesis* who can recall this deeper memory:

give right honour to the heavenly Maker of that maker, who having made man to His own likeness, set him beyond and over all the works of that second nature: which in nothing he showeth so much as in poetry, when with the force of a divine breath he bringeth things forth surpassing her doings—with no small arguments to the credulous of that first accursed fall of Adam, since our erected wit maketh us know what perfection is, and yet our infected will keepeth us from reaching unto it.

(*Defence*, 24.29–25.5)

Calvin, despite a more pessimistic estimation of the human condition, writes that

There is within the human mind, and indeed by natural instinct, an awareness of divinity... To prevent anyone from taking refuge in the pretence of ignorance, God has implanted in all men a certain understanding of his divine majesty. Ever renewing its *memory*, he repeatedly sheds fresh drops.

(*Institutes*, I.iii.1; 43–4; my emphasis)

Platonic and Christian schemes coalesce in the notion that memory, at its deepest level, is the recollection of knowledge which

---

[38] St Augustine reaches this conclusion over an extended argument that can be represented here only in summary. He writes 'By some means or other they [humans who desire happiness] have learnt what it [happiness] is. In some sense they have knowledge of it, and the problem before me is to discover whether or not this knowledge is in the memory. If it is, it means that at some time in the past we have been happy. It may be that we were all once happy individually, or it may be that we were all happy in Adam, the first sinner, in whom we all died and from whom we all descended in a heritage of misery' (226). St Augustine distinguishes the memory of happiness from the personal memory of physical things, such as Carthage (227). St Augustine decides that he cannot find God outside of memory: 'For I have discovered nothing about you except what I have remembered since the time when I first learned about you' (230). 'Truly you [God] do dwell in it [memory], because I remember you ever since I first came to learn of you, and it is there that I find you when I am reminded of you' (231). St Augustine adds, 'For you were not in my memory before I learned of you' (231). By this, I believe he means that he was not consciously aware of God until he learned of him, but God was still present in him, even though he was ignorant of it: 'You were within me, and I was in the world outside myself... You were with me, but I was not with you' (231). See also 224 for St Augustine's praise for the power of memory. References are to: Saint Augustine, *Confessions*, tr. R. S. Pine-Coffin (Harmondsworth, 1961). On relations between the thought of St Augustine and Spenser, see the entry 'Fathers, Latin' by Sean Kane in Hamilton (gen. ed.), *Spenser Encyclopedia*.

humans possessed before souls descended into bodies, or before humans deviated from God's will; both processes, transmigration and the Fall, encourage forgetfulness, reflecting the soul's emergence into time.[39] Native romances which depict the overcoming of this gap, where the known world is providentially guided to completion, may be considered as responding to this deeper level of memory—as indeed Redcrosse did as an individual—but their representation of the historical world achieving that kind of fulfilment can be questioned, as it is in Book II, because of the possibility that it is really constructed out of desire.

Guyon's inability to wash Ruddymane's hands is, as several commentators have suggested, a powerful indication of the fallen condition of human nature, the intractability of original sin.[40] Later, when water is insufficient to quench the fire of Pyrochles' wrath (II.vi.44), the implication is the same. Similarly, when Guyon attacks Furor, the Palmer reminds him that in attempting (fruitlessly) to destroy Furor, he is likely to assimilate fury to his own degradation:

> Which when the Palmer saw, he loudly cryde,
> Not so, O *Guyon*, neuer thinke that so
> That Monster can be maistred or destroyd.
> (II.iv.10)

Just as the chronicles of history and romance do not intersect in Eumnestes' chamber, so in Book II an ideal temperance which is impervious to mutability is not achieved. Maleger's constant revival during his fight with Arthur is analogous to the blood on Ruddymane's hands: both represent the persistence of original sin, an inclination which can be restrained but not elided. If humans possess a non-personal memory of a prelapsarian

---

[39] See also Plotinus, *The Enneads*, tr. Stephen MacKenna, intr. John Dillon (Harmondsworth, 1991), 1.6.2 (p. 47). The Platonic notion of the soul, like the Christian sense of an 'erected wit', is the basis for understanding how humans can remember truths they have not personally experienced. See, for example, *Meno*, 80.d–86.a (pp. 363–71), in *The Collected Dialogues of Plato*, ed. Edith Hamilton and Huntingdon Cairns (Princeton, 1961). The forgetfulness of the soul as it descends into the body, analogous to the Fall albeit of a completely different tradition, is also discussed by Macrobius, *Commentary on the Dream of Scipio*, tr. William Harris Stahl (New York, 1952), XII.9–10 (pp. 135–6).

[40] The theological background to this interpretation of the Ruddymane episode is well illustrated in Alastair Fowler, 'The Image of Mortality: *The Faerie Queene*, II.i-ii', *HLQ* 24 (1961), 91–110 (rpt. in Hamilton (ed.), *Essential Articles*, 139–52).

time, they also inherit a non-personal sin. The final image of the Book confirms the same negative truth. Grille, who had been transformed by Acrasia into a hog, prefers to remain in that shape rather than return to human form:

> Said *Guyon*, See the mind of beastly man,
>   That hath so soone forgot the excellence
>   Of his creation, when he life began,
>   That now he chooseth, with vile difference,
>   To be a beast, and lacke intelligence.
>   To whom the Palmer thus, The donghill kind
>   Delights in filth and foule incontinence:
>   Let *Grill* be *Grill*, and haue his hoggish mind.
>   (II.xii.87)

It is Grille's inability to *remember* 'the excellence / Of his creation', his prelapsarian perfection in the image of God, which leads him to persist in baseness. A more subtle image of humanity's fallen condition occurs during the Bower of Bliss episode. As Guyon and the Palmer penetrate into Acrasia's dwelling, they pass through an entrance 'Archt ouer head with an embracing vine' (II.xii.54). This vine is laden with fruit, including artificial, decorative fruit 'of burnisht gold, / ... Which did themselues emongst the leaues enfold, / As lurking from the vew of couetous guest' (II.xii.55). The vine, acquiring animate force through its 'embracing', the 'burnisht' fruit, and the notion of an object 'lurking' 'emongst the leaues' suggests on the most subliminal level a golden-green Edenic serpent coiled around the tree. Coiling vine and lurking fruit both transfer their characteristics to a third, unseen object, the snake. And the fact that it is unseen increases its insidiousness and its intractability. This is the Fall from paradise, and it is the ineluctable restriction placed on all subsequent human activity, even apparently the Reformed British nation's endeavour to respond to God's call. Ultimately, '*Antiquitie* of *Faerie* lond' must be, like the heavenly Jerusalem seen by Redcrosse, a reference point beyond this world. But Book II is conceptually more difficult than Book I because that Faerie land is so clearly the desired mirror of a political entity, England. In Book V, the divisions between an increasingly complex political entity and its projected mirror-opposite, Faerie land, become severe.

8

'The world ... runne quite out of square': Remembering/Dismembering Native Romance and National Identity in Book V

The analogical relationship between Books II and V is as strong as that between III and IV—perhaps stronger, since III and IV constitute not so much analogical partners as a single discursive narrative unit.[1] Guyon's abrupt appearance in Book V (iii.29) and the role he plays in tempering the wrathful zeal of Artegall's justice (v.iii.36) suggest a thematic relationship between the two Books. One of the most significant connections is the concern both Books have with British history and the attempt to derive national identity through the perception or recollection of history according to a romance, providential narrative. Like Books I and II, Book V needs to be read as part of Spenser's reception of Middle English romance, not only because its linear narrative structure signals a return, after the Ariostan patterns of III and IV, to a characteristically native structure, but also because, like Book II in particular, V is deeply concerned with the roles that memory and phantasy play in the interpretation of national experience. With a heuristic honesty which is usually overlooked, Book V interrogates and ultimately withholds the crossing through the mirror from '*Briton moniments*' to '*Antiquitie of Faerie lond*'. In its denial of a providential support for native history—a point I will argue during the course of this chapter—Book V deepens Spenser's response to the tradition of native romance concerned with mythopoeic representations of national history and identity.

[1] On the analogical structure of *The Faerie Queene*, in which I and VI, II and V, and III and IV represent one version of significant pairings, see: Angus Fletcher, *The Prophetic Moment* (Chicago and London, 1971); James Nohrnberg, *The Analogy of The Faerie Queene* (Princeton, 1976).

The Proems to Books II and V contrast startlingly. Whereas
the earlier Proem promises that the 'happy land of Faery' is
'matter of iust memory' and may be found 'By certaine signes
here set in sundry plance' (II.Proem.1, 4), the Proem to Book V
argues that the world's moral and physical decay has closed off
those passages which might have led to a providential mirror
England:

> . . . through long continuance of his course,
> Me seemes the world is runne quite out of square,
> From the first point of his appointed sourse,
> And being once amisse growes daily wourse and wourse.
>
> (v.Proem.1)

The geometrical metaphor here relates to the sense which the
Proem to Book II gives of the geographical and physical reality
of faerie land. But in the Proem to Book V that physical, spatial
dimension is invoked only to argue for the inaccessibility of 'the
golden age' (v.Proem.2); the world is no longer where it should
be, and its erring remoteness makes the attainment of faerie land
physically—and thus morally—impossible. Whereas in Book II the
moon and planets are potentially accessible new worlds, in the
Proem to Book V the celestial bodies are the very emblems of decay:

> For who so list into the heauens looke,
> And search the courses of the rowling spheares,
> Shall find that from the point, where they first tooke
> Their setting forth, in these few thousand yeares
> They all are wandred much; that plaine appeares.
>
> (v.Proem.5)[2]

In his injunction to look into the heavens and see what 'plaine
appeares', Spenser seems to echo the narrators of Middle English
romances and related texts who invite their readers to examine
the vestigial relics in England deriving from their narrative
worlds. But rather than being 'still there', the planets 'now all
range, and doe at randon roue / Out of their proper places farre
away' (v.Proem,6):

> For that same golden fleecy Ram, which bore
> *Phrixus* and *Helle* from their stepdames feares,

[2] Victor Harris, *All Coherence Gone* (Chicago, 1949) is a useful account of the
scientific dismantling (especially in the seventeenth century, but relevant to this theme
in Book V) of late classical and medieval cosmology.

Hath now forgot, where he was plast of yore,
And shouldred hath the Bull, which fayre *Europa* bore.

And eke the Bull hath with his bow-bent horne
    So hardly butted those two twinnes of *Ioue*,
    That they haue crusht the Crab, and quite him borne
    Into the great *Nemœan* lions groue.
                                              (v.Proem.5–6)

What is remarkable in this passage is not merely its sense of cosmic degradation; the description of the constellations in terms of their mythological narrative worlds, such as the rape of Europa or Phrixus and Helle, also seriously questions the truthfulness and value of poetry. If the positions of the stars no longer validate the events of those narratives—the ram and bull are no longer where they should be for the stories to make sense—then that literature, and all literature, may indeed be nothing but 'painted forgery' (ii.Proem.1).

The emphasis in v.Proem on physical, observable realities and erratic movement, recorded through a process of time—

    ...all this world with them amisse doe moue
    And all his creatures from their course astray,
    Till they arriue at their last ruinous decay.
                                              (v.Proem.6)

    ...[the sun] ne keepes his course more right,
    But is miscaried with the other Spheres.
    For since the terme of fourteene hundred yeres,
    That learned *Ptolomœe* his hight did take,
    He is declyned from that marke of theirs,
    Nigh thirtie minutes to the Southerne lake.
                                              (v.Proem.7)

—provides a key for understanding Book V and its radical difference in relation to providential historical romances such as *Guy of Warwick*: disjunction—things 'runne quite out of square'—is the crucial concept. A passage in *A View of the Present State of Ireland* repeats this idea of disjunction—or a lack of fit between the way things are (history) and the way things ought to be, or at least be becoming (romance)—in a passage reminiscent of the Proem to Book V:

the whole ordinance and institution of that realmes government, was both at first, when it was placed, evill plotted, and also sithence, thorough other over-sights, came *more out of square to that disorder which it is now come unto, like as two indirect lines, the further that they are drawne out, the further they goe asunder.*[3]

Two ideas emerge from this passage and deserve further consideration in relation to Book V; the first concerns memory. Eumnestes' chamber indicated the need for national identity and historical narrative to derive from memory alone, unmingled with Phantastes. In Memory's chamber, the desired relationship between the historical and the idealized accounts of British experience remained unachieved, though its possibility was not absolutely denied. In this passage from the *View*, however, as well as in the Proem to Book V, the obvious functioning of memory— the recollection of recent and even ongoing events, '*daily* wourse and wourse', 'that disorder which it is *now* come unto'—produces an historical narrative which cannot be seen as providentially guided. As history becomes more recent in Book V—in the case of the episodes relating to Ireland and Lord Grey, deriving from Spenser's *personal* memory, not the more distant 'old records from auncient times deriu'd' (II.ix.57)—the poet cannot honestly regard those events in the way that he could in Book I view the English Reformation. Like the erring planets 'from their course astray', the nation's history does not fit the ideal, providential narrative which would give authority, even sanctity, to the nation's experience and ongoing endeavours.

The other point which this passage from the *View* raises and which needs further application to Book V is the developing complexity of what *national* identity means. As England/Britain expands to include Ireland and perhaps participate in an international Protestant league, the history of 'the nation'—viewed providentially or otherwise— becomes more difficult to write.[4]

---

[3] Edmund Spenser, *A View of the State of Ireland*, ed. Andrew Hadfield and Willy Maley (Oxford, 1997), 91; my emphasis.

[4] On the difficulty of British identity in the later stages of Elizabeth's reign, see: Andrew Hadfield, 'From English to British Literature: John Lyly's *Euphues* and Edmund Spenser's *The Faerie Queene*', in Bradshaw and Roberts (eds), *British Consciousness*, 140–58. A considerable body of recent criticism focuses on the political and imaginative treatment of Ireland in Spenser's work, a topic which is relevant to the definition of national identity: Nicholas P. Canny, 'Edmund Spenser and the Development of an Anglo-Irish Identity', *Yearbook of English Studies* 13 (1983),

(1) THE DISJUNCTION OF HISTORY AND ROMANCE

To emphasize and explore the notion of disjunction, Book V draws heavily upon the conventions of romance, recalling in particular the linear narrative favoured in Middle English exemplars. Comparable to Book I or *Lybeaus Desconus*, Book V originates with the plea of a lady, Irena, addressed to Gloriana; 'To whom complayning her afflicted plight, / She her besought of gratious redresse' (v.i.4). Artegall is appointed 'to succour... [this] distressed Dame', imprisoned by the giant Grantorto (v.i.3). That narrative frame provides a set of expectations related to the romance mode: the proper place or course from which the ensuing events and characters may wander in ironic discrepancy. The episode in which Artegall restores to Guyon his appropriated horse further invites readers to expect the idealizing tendencies of the romance mode to govern the whole Book, especially in its later representation of Elizabethan foreign and imperial justice. Guyon claims rightful ownership of the horse, Brigadore, through his knowledge of the creature's hidden birthmark: 'Within his mouth a blacke spot... / Shapt like a horses shoe' (v.iii.32). The ensuing scene is strangely comical; the first unfortunate who attempts to look into Brigadore's mouth is kicked so hard that 'all his ribs... quite in peeces broke'; the next reckless investigator is bitten so hard that he is 'maymed quite, and all his shoulder split' (v.iii.33). When Guyon approaches, however, Brigadore 'follow'd him with gladfull glee / And friskt, and flong aloft, and louted low on knee' (v.iii.34). Recognition scenes such as this—more often involving people than animals, though Odysseus' dog is a notable exception—which depend upon birthmarks, blankets left with abandoned babies, or the piecing together of some sundered token, are so standard in romance that the appearance of one here, fairly early

1–19; Richard A. McCabe, 'The Fate of Irena: Spenser and Political Violence', in Patricia Coughlan (ed.), *Spenser and Ireland* (Cork, 1989), 109–25; Lisa Jardine, 'Encountering Ireland: Gabriel Harvey, Edmund Spenser, and English Colonial Ventures', in Brendan Bradshaw et al. (eds.), *Representing Ireland* (Cambridge, 1993), 60–70; Richard A. McCabe, 'Edmund Spenser, Poet of Exile', *PBA* 80 (1993), 73–1023; Jay Farness, 'Disenchanted Elves: Biography in the Text of *The Faerie Queene* V', in Judith H. Anderson, Donald Cheney, and David A. Richardson (eds), *Spenser's Life and the Subject of Biography* (Amherst, 1996), 18–30.

in the Book, sets up extreme generic expectations.[5] In this recognition scene, things are indeed as they ought to be, as in 'the antique world' where 'simple Truth did rayne, and was of all admyred' (v.Proem.1, 3). At the same time, a ludicrousness in the scene suggests that romance narrative structures will be invoked ironically: their presence will be accompanied by a disconcerting sense, founded upon the accurate use of memory, of how far they are from actual experience—or how actual experience has 'wandred farre' from such idealized, providential structures. Whereas Brigadore is happy to recognize and support Guyon's ownership, characters in Book V such as Malengin will repudiate Gloriana's pretensions to possession.

From the outset, Artegall is a disturbing character. His very conception seems to preclude his being the sort of hero who, like Guy, can weld historical and romance identities, crossing through the mirror to realize a providential narrative of national experience. Artegall may be onomastically 'equal to Arthur', but only in the sense that one-half of a thing divided is equal to the other half; more significantly, both halves are in themselves inadequate. Artegall, who is Arthur's half-brother maternally related (III.iii.27), has come into existence to fill in a difficult gap in the historical theme of *The Faerie Queene*—the breakdown of progeny and rule which the historical Arthur's reign represented.[6] The historical material remains recalcitrant, however. For one, Arthur's father, Uther, was responsible for the unlawful death of Artegall's father, Gorlois—a fact ignored by Spenser though powerfully represented in Thomas Hughes' 1588 adaptation of

---

[5] Pastorella in Book VI is, like Shakespeare's Perdita, a foundling raised by shepherds, but her aristocratic mother recognizes her daughter later in life by Pastorella's rose-shaped mole (VI.xii.3–20).

[6] '*Briton moniments*' ends with the succession of Uther Pendragon (II.x.68), and Merlin's prophecy begins with Artegall (III.iii.27); Arthur is thus omitted from the genealogical tables of British history. Artegall appears in Geoffrey's *Historia* as Artgualchar, earl of Warwick, and in related chronicles. On Artegall's historical and dynastic identity in *The Faerie Queene*, see further: Harper, *Sources of the British Chronicle*, 144; Roche, *Kindly Flame*, 47–50; Fichter, *Poets Historical*, 176 and f. 20. Ad Putter, 'Finding Time for Romance: Mediaeval Arthurian Literary History', *MÆ* 63 (1994), 1–18 investigates how various writers exploited temporal gaps in Geoffrey's history to insert romance adventures which were independent of chronology. *The Faerie Queene* could be added to the medieval texts Putter considers; in writing about Arthur's principality, a period for which no records exist, Spenser quite simply 'buys time'.

the Arthurian story to the form of the Senecan revenge tragedy.[7] Furthermore, it is clear from Merlin's prophecy (III.iii.27–9) that Artegall never actually becomes king. His unnamed son, however, 'from the head / Of his coosin *Constantius* without dread / Shall take the crowne, that was his fathers right' (III.iii.29)—an act which sounds more like violent acquisition than succession upon the natural death of Constantine. In Geoffrey of Monmouth, Arthur leaves his crown to Constantine, Cador's son.[8] In Merlin's prophecy, Constantine's reign now appears to be illegitimate, or at the cost of Artegall's right; in the context of the well-known historical materials, Artegall's son appears to be at war with Arthur's wishes. The relationship between Arthur and Artegall, viewed in the context of 'antique Registers' (II.ix.59) of British history, has greater potential to be acrimonious than fraternal.[9]

If Spenser's treatment of Arthur avoids the flagrant contempt for memory embodied in Kelton's genealogy, he has still not resolved the essentially problematic nature of Arthur as a national hero. Between Uther and Constantine remains one of the 'canker holes' marring some of Eumnestes' documents (II.ix.57). The very fact that Spenser has had to split Arthur into two figures—one, Artegall, to take his awkward place in history and the other, Prince Arthur, to be a symbolic and idealized figure in pursuit of Gloriana—is emblematic of the disjunction between history and romance which especially widens in Book V. The idealized Artegall whom Britomart first sees in Merlin's mirror (III.ii.24–5) is not matched by the protagonist of Book V, and the discrepancy is not surprising since Britomart looks into the mirror with vanity and desire: 'Her selfe a while therein she vewd in vaine' and wondered 'Whom fortune for her husband would allot' (III.ii.22, 23). Like MacDonald's mirror, this mirror seems to reflect the imaginative or phantastic aspirations of the viewer.

---

[7] [Thomas Hughes et al.], *The Misfortunes of Arthur*, ed. Brian Jay Corrigan (New York and London, 1992). After introductory speeches and a dumbshow, the play opens with the ghost of Gorlois promising revenge 'On ruthlesse *Brytaines* and *Pendragons* race' (I.i.26).

[8] Spenser states that Cador is Artegall's brother (III.iii.27).

[9] Interestingly, in Richard Grafton's *Abridgement of the Chronicles of England*, Constantine's rule is challenged by the two sons of Mordred, 'for they claimed the land by the righte of their father' (fo. 22[r]).

If this idealized reflection is really anyone, then it is Arthur, and Arthur only becomes free to move into that mirror-world, which is the world of Gloriana, with the shedding of his historical identity. Arthur will not, after all, be Elizabeth's ancestor; Britomart's dream in Isis' church clearly indicates that Artegall is the forebearer of Elizabeth (v.vii.15–16, 21–3). This is a startling conclusion, considering the Tudor propagandistic investment in the figure of Arthur as an ancestor. However, the doubts concerning his historicity raised by Polydore Vergil, among others, as well as the recalcitrance of the Arthurian material itself, have made inevitable Spenser's positioning of Artegall, rather than Arthur, as the dynastic head of the Tudors. This change has two critical implications. One is that Elizabeth's ancestor is an historical figure who, as will be seen in more detail, is imperfect, human, inconsistent—that is, firmly on *our* side of the mirror, which is the fallen world; and so too Elizabeth remains trapped in that historical, mutable world. The other point is that Arthur's required shedding of historicity means that he cannot be a figure of 'iust memory'. We are forced to recognize him as a phantastic creation, and the specifically nationalistic vision of crossing through the mirror from '*Briton moniments*' to '*Antiquitie* of *Faerie* lond' is exposed, like Alice's crossing, as the bastard of desire. With the division of Artegall and Arthur, we are back to Malory's ambiguous double ending for the king—both *quondam* and *futurus*, Glastonbury and Avalon. Spenser's response reflects a more drastic separation of history from romance. In Book V, looking for verifiable providential patterns within the enclosed narrative of national historical discourse becomes problematic in a way that was only adumbrated in Malory and did not really exist in other Middle English romances. The tensions within Book V now need closer examination in the context of that earlier romance-historical tradition.

(II) MITIGATED JUSTICE IN BOOK V

The historical Arthurian matter which Artegall assumes is Arthur's extensive foreign conquests. Geoffrey of Monmouth's *Historia*, the prose *Brut*, Hardyng's *Chronicle*, and Malory's 'Tale of the Emperor Lucius' relate Arthur's victories over various parts of Europe, and Artegall's battles in v.viii–xii build upon this image of the British king.[10] In those earlier texts, as in a similar romance focusing on foreign conquests, *Richard Coeur de Lion*, the protagonists' victories could be taken as evidence of providential support for English/British and/or Christian expansion. In the *View*, Irenius invokes Arthur's conquest of Ireland, if not as evidence of providential support for England's presence in Ireland, then at least for the authority which derives from historical precedent: 'Finally it appeareth by good record yet extant, that King Arthur, and before him Gurgunt, had all that iland under their allegiance and subjection' (52). Irenius adds that he could list many 'names of places, persons, and speeches' (52)—in effect, things 'still there'—which would attest to the historical reality of Arthur's conquest of Ireland. Similarly, John Dee argues in *General and Rare Memorials* (1577) for the historical reality of Arthur's foreign conquests in order to bolster England's political clout internationally.[11]

That same military Arthur is the starting point for Artegall in Book V, though the interest in Book V, reflecting Spenser's more thoughtful engagement with the received materials, lies in the disjunction which exists between Artegall and his context. Put simply, Artegall gives the impression of being a character who has wandered into the wrong kind of story, unlike say the Arthur of Malory's 'Tale of Emperor Lucius'. Like Don Quixote, Artegall's own sense of providential support and chivalric authority are continuously undermined by a landscape which denies idealized romance fictions; both knights are foreigners in their contexts. Spenser, like Cervantes, draws deeply upon the conventions and narrative structures of medieval romance in order to portray Artegall in terms analogous to the heavenly bodies in the Proem—'wandered farre from where it first was pight' (4), 'wandred much' (5), 'forgot, where he was plast of yore' (5), 'Out of their proper places farre away' (6), 'ne keepes his course more

---

[10] Of course, Spenser's Prince Arthur also joins Artegall in these exploits, though without suffering the moral taint which will be seen to attach itself to Artegall. Arthur still participates in the poem's historical narrative in Book V, but he is disengaged from the political implications of that endeavour; he does not suffer from Envie and Detraction, perhaps because he has been written out of the genealogical narrative.

[11] See further: Roberts, 'Tudor Wales', in Bradshaw and Roberts (eds), *British Consciousness*, 29–33.

right' (7), 'miscaried with the other Spheres' (7). In the right sort of narrative world, both Artegall and Don Quixote would be impressive. But Artegall's disjunctive relationship with his context intensifies as these environs become more insistently historical and matter of recent memory. Consequently, we are led to conclude that the 'right sort of narrative world' can only be imaginative or phantastic rather than historical.

A few episodes early in Book V build upon the romance traditions established in previous Books in order to portray Artegall as the knight 'runne quite out of square'. For example, Artegall retreats ignominiously from Munera's castle when he is denied entry, 'with reprochfull blasphemy defide' and 'Beaten with stones downe from the battilment' (v.ii.20). Under a hail of stones, he is not given the chance for a chivalric response. His order to 'his seruant *Talus* to inuent / Which way he enter might, without endangerment' (v.ii.20) suggests already that Artegall is affected by, though without necessarily adapting to, his surroundings; no knight in Malory worthy of the name would seek to avoid 'endangerment', particularly while sending a 'seruant' to face that danger. The following line— 'Eftsoones his Page drew to the Castle gate' (v.ii.21)— draws upon romance idiom to emphasize Artegall's failure and misplacement; 'Eftsoones' has become by this point a signal-word for the poem's chivalric, romance origins, but the word 'Page' (rather than 'knight') is here incongruous. Nicholas Canny's observations concerning the *View* are also enacted here in Artegall's betrayal of those principles— justice and chivalry—from which he derives his authority. Canny sees in the *View* the argument 'that any civil people who settled in such a society [i.e., 'which had fallen totally from the ways of civility'] and who sought to achieve social amelioration through persuasive means would inevitably become absorbed into the corruption of their host community'.[12]

Several Middle English romances, specifically those in which an English hero travels overseas and into pagan lands, provide contrasting models for the colonial experience in Book V. Because Artegall is a knight on an archetypal chivalric quest, the memories of similar crusading, voyaging, or exiled knights, such as

[12] Nicholas Canny, 'Introduction: Spenser and the Reform of Ireland', in Coughlan (ed.), *Spenser and Ireland*, 9–24 (20).

Bevis and Guy, must come into play. All of these knights find themselves in pagan lands, and the response of the medieval characters is unambiguously combative. Bevis will not convert to Islam, we recall, 'For al þe seluer ne al þe golde, / Þat is vnder heuene liзt'; nor will he marry the Sultan's daughter, Josian, until she converts to Christianity. Furthermore, his attack on the pagan knights who mock his ignorance of Christmas Day demonstrates Bevis' absolute resistance of assimilation into the 'foreign' host society. The conversion of Josian to Christianity represents well what Canny has detected in the *View*, the outsider's compulsion 'to achieve social [or religious] amelioration [as the outsider perceives it] through persuasive means'; what *Bevis* and other Middle English romances give no insight to, however, is the permeability of the boundaries separating both sides in this opposition. Despite the negative effects which pagan or wild environments have on displaced youths at an early stage, their innate tendency to overcome those environments is clear. The hero in no sense remains permanently or deeply affected by his exile, and the entire direction of the story is away from the 'corruption of the host community', as Canny phrases it.

Artegall and Book V present exactly the opposite process, a reversal of the 'displaced youth' and by implication an antithesis to Book I. Artegall starts from the position of being one of Gloriana's knights—indeed, the projected ancestor of Elizabeth—and he journeys outwards from that centre into 'furthest Nations' (v.Proem.11). He slowly forgets, rather than remembers, his identity as he is absorbed into a foreign landscape. Another early episode, following the destruction of the 'Communist Giant', indicates the reversal of the displaced youth story in Artegall—a movement towards wildness and rusticity, in which he is paradoxically both out of place and overtaken by place. A 'lawlesse multitude' sets out to attack the knight:

> He much was troubled, ne wist what to doo.
> For loth he was his noble hands t'embrew
> In the base blood of such a rascall crew.
>
> (v.ii.52)

Artegall is unable to deal with surroundings which do not fit the conditions of the chivalric world. It may be appropriate in relation to chivalry that a knight should not attack 'base blood', but how can a figure representing political justice shirk from a 'lawlesse multitude'? Talus brutally closes the gap between Artegall and his surroundings, and the Iron Man's extreme violence furthers the sense of disjunction between romance and historical modes in Book V and Artegall's moral contamination.

Book V continues to invoke the romance paradigm of foreign conquest in order to explore the tensions which arise when that romance ethos is enacted in an historical world, such as '*Briton moniments*', where providential support is difficult to discern and invoked equally by competing sides. Eudoxus, the somewhat naive English persona in Spenser's *View*, sees 'in this mingling of nations' in Ireland and Europe generally 'a wonderfull providence and purpose of Almighty God, that stirred up the people in the furthest parts of the world, to seeke out their regions so remote from them, and by that meanes both to restore their decayed habitations, and to make himselfe knowne to the Heathen' (53). This attitude is well enacted in a romance such as *Richard Coeur de Lion*, where the paganism of the people whose countries Richard invades makes them the enemies of God; grotesquely, their only value in creation is as food for the Christian crusaders. Militant invasion and expansion are represented in Middle English romance as justified and even divinely supported when hostility is directed towards the heathen, and Eudoxus' comment seems to extend that prejudice into the sixteenth century. In the *View*, Catholic Irish are like the saracens in the medieval 'crusade' romances, and they may be opposed in their own land with the authority of divine will.[13] In distinction from the *View*, however, Book V refuses to present that sort of simple opposition without tension. Instead, this Book constantly undermines this providential reading of history, particularly in relation to British identity and the nation's ability to assimilate foreign territories without loss or disfigurement of that identity. In the episode of the Communist Giant, for example, providence is a far more problematic concept than Eudoxus allows. Artegall's defence of the distribution of the world's riches is based on God's providence and omnipotence:

---

[13] See further: McCabe, 'Fate of Irena', in Coughlan (ed.), *Spenser and Ireland*, 112.

He maketh Kings to sit in souerainty;
He maketh subiects to their powre obay;
He pulleth downe, he setteth vp on hy;
He giues to this, from that he takes away.
For all we haue is his: what he list doe, he may.

What euer thing is done, by him is donne,
Ne any may his mighty will withstand.

(v.ii.41–2)

Guy of Warwick would concur with this view, but Artegall's argument is undermined by the circumstances of the world through which he moves. The knight's statement to the Giant that all the planets 'in their courses guide' and 'euery one doe know their certaine bound' (v.ii.35–6) is unconvincing in the context of the Book's Proem. In contrast, the Giant's awareness of 'how badly all things present bee, / And each estate quite out of order goth' (v.ii.37) receives the support of the Proem and the events of Book V as they continue to unfold. Talus' brutal and abrupt dispatching of the Giant feels like an wholly inadequate response to a literally big problem.[14]

Artegall derives in part from the conquesting Arthur of the historical tradition, and he also draws upon the experience of Lord Arthur Grey, Lord Deputy of Ireland and Spenser's former employer.[15] However, Grey, as drawn in the *View*, differs significantly from Artegall. However much circumstances in Ireland or indeed in the English court undermined his authority, Grey is praised for remaining faithful to his beliefs and principles:

the realme was left like a ship in a storm, admidst all the raging surges, unruled, and undirected of any: for they to whom she was committed, either fainted in their labour, or forsooke their charge. But hee (like a most wise pilote,) kept her course carefully, and held her most strongly even against those roaring billowes, that he safely brought her out of all.

(28)

---

[14] O'Connell, *Mirror and Veil*, 136–9 offers a contrary interpretation: he sees Artegall's defence and Talus' execution of the law as a convincing counter to the pessimism of the Proem.

[15] On Grey in relationship to Spenser, see Ciaran Brady, 'Grey, Arthur', in Hamilton (gen. ed.), *Spenser Encyclopedia*; Jean R. Brink, '"All his mind on honour fixed": The Preferment of Edmund Spenser', in Anderson, Cheney, and Richardson (eds), *Spenser's Life*, 45–64; Richard Rambuss, 'Spenser's Lives, Spenser's Careers', in ibid., 1–17.

Although the metaphor employed here is different, the passage is comparable to the depiction of the erring constellations of v.Proem; Grey is praised for not wandering, unlike the heavenly bodies, from his proper course. Artegall, however, does deviate from the fixed line of his quest, not only in his subjugation to Radigund but more subtly in his degrading assimilation of the guile and counterfeit which throughout Book V stand as the antithesis of justice. In the *View*, Irenius notes that the Old English, or the Anglo-Norman settlers of Ireland, 'are degenerated and growne almost mere Irish, yea, and more malitious to the English then the Irish themselves'; Eudoxus is amazed 'that an Englishman, brought up in such sweet civility as England affords, should find such likeing in that barbarous rudenes, that he should forget his owne nature, and forgoe his owne nation!' (54).[16] Artegall's tendency towards guile represents not only this 'degenerate' cultural assimilation; it also undermines the authority of the justice which he represents, redefining that justice as relative rather than absolute.

The natural antithesis between justice and guile pervades Book V. Isis places a foot on a crocodile to indicate her mastery over 'forged guile' (v.vii.7); the historical allegory of Mary Queen of Scots is apposite in Book V because she is an emblem of guile, and thus as Duessa brought to justice; and guile is well represented by Pollente and Dolon, with their delight in trapdoors. The opening episode of Book V, the encounter with Sanglier, foreshadows Artegall's problematic adoption of guile in his role as justice. In an effort to expose Sanglier's falsehood, Artegall 'cast about by sleight the truth thereout to straine' (v.i.24). Pollente similarly 'by sleight' (v.ii. 7) defeats his enemies, and it is difficult to see how the same means can produce two morally different ends, one absolute good and one absolute bad. Romances depicting the struggles of Christians against pagans depend upon and enforce a hard-edged distinction of right and wrong. However Irenius' observation that the Old English in Ireland are 'growne almost mere Irish' confounds that binary opposition in the complexities of colonial experience. A moral relativism which did not exist in

---

[16] Cf. *View*, 36: English wards raised by Irish lords are 'brought up lewdly, and Irish-like'. In these passages, the *View* contradicts the nature-over-nurture theme of the romances of orphaned youths, assimilated into Book I and represented more literally in Pastorella in Book VI.

Book I or in the earlier romance texts is now intruding into the increasingly historical, because more accurately remembered, world of Book V. The description of how Artegall employs 'sleight' allows the reader an uneasy reaction: 'straine' in particular is ambiguous, and it could have the sense of 'forcing', and therefore impairing, the object 'truth'.

In the context of the episode, Artegall's response to Sanglier seems ultimately just, but his employment of guile, or sleight, becomes more ambiguous when Artegall and Arthur defeat Adicia and the Souldan. To deceive Adicia, Artegall decides to disguise himself 'in th'armour of a Pagan knight' (v.viii.26) and approach the enemy castle with Samient as a mock prisoner. Artegall and Arthur are 'thinking best by counterfet disguise / To their deseigne to make the easier way' (v.viii.25). Counterfeiting, seeking expedient solutions, and in the process adopting specifically pagan armour are at least an affront to chivalry, as Malory and others have defined it, and the absolute authority which Artegall assumes for his representation of justice must suffer as he becomes assimilated into an anti-romance landscape of relatives. In a very Malorian moment, he upbraids Burbon for abandoning his shield—'That is the greatest shame and foulest scorne, / Which vnto any knight behappen may / To loose the badge, that should his deedes display' (v.xi.52)—but is fully prepared, like Duessa, to conceal himself behind the false show of another knight's armour. Burbon's pragmatic relativism—'yet when time doth serue, / My former shield I may resume againe' (v.xi.56)—may be excessively optimistic given the contingency of this world.

Artegall continues to fall short as an emblematic figure of justice through his assimilation of native, here specifically Irish, guile.[17] At the same time, he embodies stiffly the assumptions and self-righteousness of a knight in the romance world. He hypocritically criticizes Terpine, for example, for running 'so fondly far astray, / As for to lead your selfe vnto your owne decay' (v.iv.26); Artegall's assumption here that there is simply one way forward is

[17] My interpretation of the Irish episodes and Book V in general as heuristically problematic differs from Vincent P. Carey and Claire L. Carroll, 'Factions and Fictions: Spenser's Reflections of and on Elizabethan Politics', in Anderson, Cheney, and Richardson (eds), *Spenser's Life*, 31–44; Carey and Carroll see Spenser's interpretation of Irish politics as 'idealized rewriting' and 'gilded history' (39).

challenged not only by the circumstances of the narrative world
of Book V but also by his own accommodation of expedient
alternatives. In another scene, as a prisoner of Radigund, Artegall
falsely reciprocates the affection of the go-between, Clarinda,
choosing 'faire words, fit for the time and place' (v.v.55); like
Burbon, who will wait until 'time doth serue' before he resumes
his shield, Artegall shapes his morality according to the temporal
experience in which he is bound. We can recall in contrast, how
Bevis, when imprisoned in Damascus, would not accommodate
his speech to achieve expedient ends; his sense of the unity of
language and truth, regardless of time and circumstances, was
rewarded by a providential, miraculous release. In the radically
different landscape of Book V, Malengin above all represents the
element of guile which exploits the randomness and disjunctive-
ness of the universe, as noted in the Proem. At least in relation to
national identity, he implicitly questions the providential order-
ing of the world. Malengin

> ... so crafty was to forge and face
> So light of hand, and nymble of his pace,
> So smooth of tongue, and subtile in his tale,
> That could deceiue one looking in his face.
>
> (v.ix.5)

Malengin 'in slights and iugling feates did flow, / And of legier-
demayne the mysteries did know' (v.ix.13). His home, appropriately, is an untraceable labyrinth:

> And all within, it full of wyndings is,
> And hidden wayes, that scarse an hound by smell
> Can follow out those false footsteps of his,
> Ne none can backe returne, that once are gone amis.
>
> (v.ix.6)

Malengin's elusiveness echoes Irenius' description of the Irish—'a
flying enemie, hiding himselfe in woodes and bogges, from
whence he will not drawe forth...Therefore to seeke him out
that still flitteth, and follow him that can hardly bee found, were
vaine and bootlesse' (96).[18]

---

[18] Both passages tellingly employ terms from hunting: the 'hound' and 'drawe forth'.

Arthur and Artegall are curiously intrigued by the description of Malengin's home—'their hearts gan earne, / To vnderstand that villeins dwelling place' (v.ix.7)—and their interest in its indirections may suggest their own deviant proclivities. Samient, who is guiding them to Mercilla, notes that if Malengin's dwelling would not 'let your pace / Towards my Ladies presence by you ment' (v.ix.7), she would guide them there. The knights then strangely insist upon this detour, wandering from their direct line: 'For neither will one foot, till we that carle haue hent' (v.ix.7). Artegall and Arthur once again use guile to 'ensnarle' (v.ix.9) Guile, or Malengin; in an action which goes against the conventions of chivalry as represented in Middle English romance texts such as *Guy* or *Le Morte Darthur*, they send Samient forward as bait. Samient's name, meaning 'bringing together', seems ironically appropriate in that the situation conflates the values of the knights and of Malengin, challenging the borders which ought to exist between justice and guile. Artegall and Arthur are no match for Malengin's protean evasions, and his guile is about to engulf theirs when Talus determines another brutal and dissatisfying ending:

> ... he with his yron flayle
> Gan driue at him, with so huge might and maine,
> That all his bones, as small as sandy grayle
> He broke, and did his bowels disentrayle;
> Crying in vaine for helpe, when helpe was past.
>   (v.ix.19)

O'Connell's sense that the 'final capture and destruction [of Malengin] by Talus represents Spenser's fondest wish for his adopted homeland'[19] seems to overlook the ambiguity of Artegall, particularly the disjunction between his knightly posturing and his assimilation of guile, and also the unease with which Malengin's death is presented. Its extreme violence, set against the victim's cry for help (a pathetic gesture not usually given to the villains and saracens of romance) results in a disturbing scene. The transition between st. 19 and 20 is particularly uneasy:

> There they him left a carrion outcast;
> For beasts and foules to feede vpon for their repast.

---

[19] 'The Faerie Queene V', in Hamilton (gen. ed.), *Spenser Encyclopedia*.

> Thence forth they passed with that gentle Mayd,
> To see her Ladie...
>
> (v.ix.19–20)

Between these two stanzas is a gap across which the preceding brutality and the subsequent gentility are not bridged.

(III) BOOK V AND ELIZABETH

Book V is more poetically interesting than much criticism has acknowledged precisely because it allows such tensions to exist, holding the force of irrepressible memories of historical experience. Suitably, Astraea, the goddess of justice who has raised Artegall, is as deeply ambivalent as her protégé. In a reversal of the established link between Elizabeth's accession and Virgil's prophecy of the return of Astraea in his fourth Eclogue, Astraea in Book V has abandoned the earth because of its sinfulness: 'she hath now an euerlasting place, / Mongst those twelue signes, which nightly we doe see' (v.i.11). Her failure to face and combat sin is strange, and possibly critical of Elizabeth's refusal to commit England to a militant international Protestant agenda. Astraea's action is particularly dubious since she now resides 'Mongst those twelue signes' which, the Proem has demonstrated, are 'from their course astray, / Till they arriue at their last, ruinous decay' (V.Proem.6); she is unlikely there to procure an 'euerlasting place', and the certain decay of Astraea must mirror the debilitation and death of Elizabeth herself.

Everything about Astraea continues to be ironic in Book V: she bribes the child Artegall 'with gifts' to join her for rearing (v.i.6); and she steals for him a sword 'gotten by her slight' (v.i.9)/ Other female figures in the Book similarly offer ambiguous or obliquely critical imaginative responses to Elizabeth, and these images dismantle the romance mode in the Book and prevent the work from representing recent British political and military activity as providentially sustained and hence absolutely just. Mercilla's court, a representation of the Elizabethan centre, is a focal point for the anxiety of the historical, anti-romance landscape of Book V. Artegall and Arthur approach Mercilla through 'a large wyde roome, / All full of people making troublous din' (v.ix.23). The subtle tension in this scene grows with the sight of the brutally restrained Bon Font, an image which undercuts the ostensible definition of Mercilla's name. What is most worrying in the case of Bon Font is the unaccountability of the repressive, authoritarian regime which has imposed his harsh punishment: his crime is written down 'In cyphers strange, that few could rightly read' (v.ix.26).[20] Mercilla displays 'piteous ruth' (v.x.50) for Duessa, and her empathy may suggest a shared duplicity; in the golden age 'simple Truth did rayne' (V.Proem.3), but the throne is now possessed by an ambivalent figure who 'Would haue... [her] passion hid' (v.ix.50). Her tears of pity fall 'in stead' of 'iust vengeance', but with the same outcome (v.ix.50); the tears do not replace a condemnatory judgement, they merely mask that judgement in a form designed to appear sympathetic.

Duessa in Book V is of course chiefly reminiscent of Mary Queen of Scots, but standing in front of Mercilla/Elizabeth she is also appropriately a double or mirror-image for the queen's own dividedness.[21] Britomart, in contrast, displays the behaviour which Elizabeth is encouraged to offer to her adventuring knights—strong, effective support. When Artegall is captured by Radigund, Britomart, like the active Una of Book I, 'rode vppon her ready way, / To seeke her Knight' (v.vi.18); after defeating Radigund, she changed 'all that forme of common weale' among the Amazons and 'did true Iustice deale' (v.vii.42). But if Britomart demonstrates how Elizabeth should govern, then Radigund may be an oblique, critical representation of the queen as she emasculates and frustrates her courtiers, civil servants, and warriors.[22] Radigund 'doth subdue' all knights 'by force or guile'; 'she doth them of warlike armes despoile, / And cloth in womens weedes'; she feeds them on scant diet 'Them to disable from reuenge aduenturing' (v.iv.31). Significantly, the

[20] James VI famously objected to the representation of his mother, Mary Stuart, as Duessa in v.ix, expressing the hope that 'Edward [sic] Spencer for his faulte, may be dewly tryed and punished'. The appearance of Bon Font in the same Canto suggests Spenser's awareness of the dangerous nature of the material. James' complaint to Lord Burghley is cited in Frederic Ives Carpenter, *A Reference Guide to Edmund Spenser* (Chicago, 1923), 41–2. On the Bon Font episode, see: Jonathan Goldberg, *James I and the Politics of Literature* (Baltimore and London, 1983), 1–17; Farness, 'Disenchanted Elves', in Anderson, Cheney, and Richardson (eds), *Spenser's Life*, 27.

[21] See further: Richard A. McCabe, 'The Masks of Duessa: Spenser, Mary Queen of Scots, and James VI', *ELR* 17 (1987), 224–42.

[22] Cf. O'Connell, *'The Faerie Queene* V', in Hamilton (gen. ed.), *Spenser Encyclopedia*, who sees Radigund as a representation of Mary Stuart.

description of Radigund just prior to her fight with Artegall carefully echoes the earlier description of Belphoebe, one of the more explicit representations of Elizabeth in the poem.[23] Radigund's subjugation of Artegall, which includes a mock dubbing ceremony 'In signe of true subiection to her powre' (v.v.18) and is signalled by the breaking of his sword, offers a richly imaginative reworking of Elizabeth's emasculating recall of Arthur Grey. The implication of this allegory is that Elizabeth in her historical actions frustrates the reading of British history as romance. As Artegall's descendant rather than Arthur's, Elizabeth embodies the temporal change and complexity of the unidealized historical world.

Book V is contained within the world of '*Briton moniments*'—the world of violent verbal effects, of upheaval and failed justice. The constant, verbless world of '*Antiquitie* of *Faerie* lond' is nowhere in sight, and if it still exists as a reality in memory then its presence has become sublimated under recent and raw memories reflecting historical change and confusion. Artegall's battle with Grantorto epitomizes this Book's movement away from the providential historical-romance, exemplified by Guy of Warwick's providentially supported battle against the Danish giant outside Winchester, towards the historical experience of mitigation and relativism. The distinction which exists between Redcrosse and the dragon is not so clearly demarcated in the battle between 'Justice' and 'Great Wrong'. The brevity of the contest and the paucity of description represent, for a start, significantly lost or neglected opportunities to stress absolute moral differences between the two combatants. And Artegall's ducking his head in battle—'No shame to stoupe, ones head more high to reare, / And much to gaine, a litle for to yield' (v.xii.19)— recalls the expediency of Burbon, who abandons his shield with the intent of resuming it 'when time doth serue'. Indeed, Artegall

---

[23] Radigund is 'All in a Camis light of purple silke' (v.v.2), and Belphoebe wears 'a silken Camus lylly whight' (ii.iii.26); Radigund's dress is 'Trayled with ribbands diuersly distraught', and Belphoebe's is similarly 'Purfled vpon with many a folded plight, / ... besprinckled ... throughout / With golden aygulets'; Radigund's skirt 'was short tucked for light motion / Vp to her ham', and Belphoebe's skirt 'Below her ham ... did somewhat traine' (ii.iii.27); both women wear 'buskins' (ii.iii.27;v.v.3); Belphoebe's buskins are 'bard with golden bendes' and Radigund's 'Basted with bends of gold'.

also deliberately abandons his shield when Grantorto's axe becomes embedded in it (v.xii.22). Such pragmatism may in fact be necessary and efficient, but its cost must be the loss of any sense of absolute, as opposed to personal or relative, right. Artegall's shield, embedded with an axe, abandoned in the course of defending Irena's 'right', is an appropriate symbol for the cultural and moral collision examined in Book V. His damaged badge provides the strongest contrast with Arthur's providential shield of grace, 'perfect pure and cleene /...Hewen out of Adamant rocke.../ That point of speare it neuer percen could, / Ne dint of direfull sword diuide the substance would' (i.vii.33). That shield, we remember, 'may be seene' in 'Faerie lond' (i.vii.36); and, sadly, Artegall's equally symbolic shield is 'still there' throughout the world. There can finally be no crossing through the mirror in relation to the British nation's history; Arthur will become the intangible and unhistorical phantasm of Avalon or Cleopolis, and Artegall, pursued by Envie and Detraction, will yield the wounded skull at Glastonbury.

Conclusion

The liking of this vnlawfull lust, whereto this worthie was inclind,
Depriued him by iudgment iust, from life and kingdome (as I find)
And threw him downe most sodainlie, amid his fame and victorie.
Whereby Gods plague and punishment vpon adulterers is seen . . .
For Mordred his fatall fo, he did beget incestuously,
Vnto his vtter ouerthrow, on his owne sister wickedly:
And thus the father was forlorne, through his sons force in incest borne.[1]

Richard Lloyd's condemnatory assessment in 1584 of Arthur,
matched a few years later in Thomas Hughes' play *The Misfortunes of Arthur*, written for performance before the queen, indicates well the obstacles involved in viewing the historical Arthur as
a national hero and genealogical head. In these two works, without an Artegall to assume his historical role, Arthur himself is
haunted by Envie and Detraction, thrown 'downe most sodainlie,
amid his fame and victorie'. The Tudor dynasty, susceptible to
charges of incest and bastardry, should have been particularly
sensitive to the latent parallels. Henry 'supplies, in spousal' the
place of his brother Arthur, but the fact that that 'emptie place'
had been previously occupied was a source of moral anxiety for
many; and if Henry had Mordred qualities, so too did Elizabeth,
who in Catholic propaganda was represented as not only illegitimate but also the product of a second incestuous match.[2] The
relationships between history and romance, or narrative shaped
in accordance with a sense of God's purpose and justice, are
fraught with difficulty. Because this sort of historical-romance
discourse is invariably political and most often concerned with
some aspect of defining a nation, it seems particularly worthwhile

---

[1] Lloyd, *Nine Worthies* [f.i.v].

[2] The 1536 Succession Act effectively declared Elizabeth illegitimate: J. E. Neale,
Queen Elizabeth I (Harmondsworth, 1960), 14. Nicholas Sanders, an English recusant, depicted Elizabeth as the product of an incestuous union in which Anne Boleyn
was the offspring of an earlier affair between Henry VIII and the wife of Thomas
Boleyn: James Emerson Phillips, *Images of a Queen* (Berkeley and Los Angeles, 1964),
109–10, 172–7.

to trace the development of some of its key themes in native texts over a considerable span of literary and historical time. I have tried to demonstrate in this study a literary-historical tradition with its own coherence, extending from the thirteenth century to the sixteenth. Middle English romance was for Spenser much more than a storehouse of narratives and language. It was a substantial literary and cultural tradition which offered fascinating representations of historical experience—belonging both to individuals and to the nation—in relation to the idealizing influences of providence or wish-fulfilment. Malory responded powerfully to the native tradition's interest in the romance mode as a mirror for England. In his handling, memory—in the shape of both received historical accounts of Arthur and, indicated in the famous rebuke to 'ye all Englysshemen', the recollection of recent and contemporary strife—darkens the close of Arthur's reign. The ambiguity which surrounds Arthur's death allows a faint glimmer of hope that from this historical world of loss a providential rescue may come; but that hope becomes meaningless if another, unexamined area of complexity—Arthur's Britishness, as opposed to Englishness, and thus what in political terms his return must mean—is opened up.

Spenser's reception of the rich and complex imaginative, historical, and political traditions involved in Middle English romance is an aspect of *The Faerie Queene* which has been grossly neglected. What those traditions offered, what opportunities and challenges they posed for a Protestant and politically oriented Elizabethan poet, and how those materials were worked by Spenser into his own heuristic process are topics which, I hope this study has persuaded, deserve more careful examination. Many areas and topics relating to Spenser's interaction with Middle English romance remain untouched, such as his completion in Book IV of Chaucer's *Squire's Tale*. This monograph has dealt only with Books I, II, and V because they arguably present a coherent narrative of response to native romance which does not necessitate detailed consideration of the convergent influences of Ariosto and Tasso; opening the door to Italianate romance, necessary in consideration of the other Books, would have resulted in a much larger, and possibly more diffuse, study. The general neglect of interest in Spenser's use of native romance hopefully justifies a focused and single-minded book such as this.

Spenser's adaptation of romances of displaced youths and slandered women into the Protestant allegory of Book I is an astonishing act of literary reception. As a memory of earlier texts, Book I casts those native romances as prophetic. The native romances, lately suffering from the censure of Elizabethan moralists and literary wits, are suddenly in Spenser's text remembered as legitimately conceived; like *The Shepheardes Calender* or Pastorella, they are by some token recognized and embraced by their true parents, Elizabethan Protestant readers. Like Shakespeare's Perdita, a romance such as *Bevis* is in Book I restored to unquestionable legitimacy.

The use of the romance mode as a mirror for providential national history follows naturally from Book I as well as from the numerous native romances which explored this perspective. What again makes Spenser's particular act of memory so engaging is his intellectual refusal to settle for phantastic, propagandistic solutions. Spenser does not deny providence, but he does reject over the course of Books II and V the easy yoking of providence to a sense of nationhood. Memory of the historical experience of a large, complex nation, or really nations, produces a complicated and erratic session of events with no obviously discernible providential structure; as Lady Philosophy says to Boethius, 'It is because you men are in no position to contemplate this order that everything seems confused and upset' (IV.vi; p. 137). A 'position' which *will* allow the Christian individual to understand the role of providence in creation must be one which looks beyond or stands outside of the self-contained political discourse of nationhood. The need to extend the providential narrative beyond this world was clear in Book I, where the teleological emphasis given to the 'Fair Unknown' story and the view of the heavenly Jerusalem allowed for a God-given defeat of the dragon. In contrast, Books II and V express greater anxiety about the nature and presence of providence because their narratives are contained within a troubled concept of British and English identity. The pressure of time ensures that neither Elizabeth nor Arthur can be both the once and the future king, if they are truly or justly remembered. *The Mutabilitie Cantos* ends with a return to the teleological perspective of Contemplation's mount; the poet asks for 'that Sabaoths *sight*' 'when no more *Change* shall be' (VII.viii.2; first emphasis mine), knowing that the things to be seen in this world, the things which are 'still there', cannot provide the same window onto eternity. The poet finally looks not backwards, to 'matter of iust memory', but forwards, 'when iust time expired should appeare' (1.ix.14). Arthur's hope here for Gloriana is an adumbration of that future rather than historical event, but the Apocalypse is a future which brings the past into itself, full circle, as it marks the end of time and the return of creation to creator. Until that 'beyond-time', which we are invited to remember and anticipate, we remain in the discourse of history, however much we fashion it through Phantastes into romance:

And thus doe all humaine affairs ebbe and flowe, soe that nothinge is so certaine as incertayntee it selfe, and continuall chaunge ether into better or into worse.[3]

[3] Polydore Vergil, *English History*, ed. Ellis, 307.

Bibliography

(A) FACSIMILES

*The Auchinleck Manuscript: National Library of Scotland Advocates'
MS 19.2.1*, intr. Derek Pearsall and I. C. Cunningham. London,
1977.
Bale John. *The Image of Bothe Churches*. The English Experience 498.
Amsterdam and New York, 1973.
Cambridge University Library MS Ff.2.38, intr. Frances McSparran and
P. R. Robinson. London, 1979.
*The Ellesmere Manuscript of Chaucer's Canterbury Tales: A Working
Facsimile*, intr. Ralph Hanna. Cambridge, 1989.
The Findern Manuscript: Cambridge University Library MS Ff.1.6, intr.
Richard Beadle and A. E. B. Owen. London, 1977.
The Geneva Bible: A Facsimile of the 1560 Edition, intr. Lloyd E. Berry.
Madison, 1969.
Facsimile of British Museum MS. Harley 2253, intr. N. R. Ker. EETS
255. London, 1965.
*Sir Thomas Malory: Le Morte D'Arthur, Printed by William Caxton in
1485*, intr. Paul Needham. London, 1976.
The Thornton Manuscript (Lincoln Cathedral MS 91), intr. D. S. Brewer
and A. E. B. Owen. London, 1975.
*The Great Tournament Roll of Westminster: A Collotype Reproduction
of the Manuscript*, intr. Sydney Anglo, forward by Sir Anthony
Wagner. 2 vols. Oxford, 1968.
The Winchester Malory: A Facsimile, intr. N. R. Ker. EETS SS 4. London, 1976.

(B) PRIMARY SOURCES

Adam of Domerham. *Historia de rebus gestis Glastoniensibus*, ed. T.
Hearne. 2 vols. Oxford, 1727.
The Buik of Alexander, ed. R. L. Graeme Ritchie. STS 12, 17, 21, 25.
Edinburgh, 1921, 1925, 1927, 1929.
Kyng Alisaunder, ed. G. V. Smithers. EETS 227, 237. London, 1952.
Alexander and Dindimus, ed. Walter W. Skeat. EETS ES 31. London,
1878.
Amis and Amiloun, ed. MacEdward Leach. EETS 203. London, 1937.

An Anonymous Short English Metrical Chronicle, ed. Ewald Zettl. EETS 196. London, 1935.

Arber, Edward, ed. *A Transcript of the Registers of the Company of Stationers of London, 1554–1640.* 5 vols. London, 1875–94.

Ariosto, Ludovico. *Orlando Furioso*, tr. Guido Waldman. London, 1974.

Aristotle. *Nicomachean Ethics*, tr. Terence Irwin. Indianapolis, 1985.

Arthur: A Short Sketch of his Life in English Verse, ed. Frederick J. Furnivall. EETS 2. London, 1864.

Of Arthour and of Merlin, ed. O. D. Macrae-Gibson. EETS 268, 279. London, 1973, 1979.

Ascham, Roger. *English Works*, ed. William Aldis Wright. Cambridge, 1904.

Athelstan: A Middle English Romance, ed. A. McI. Trounce. EETS 224. London, 1951.

Augustine, St. *Confessions*, tr. R. S. Pine-Coffin. Harmondsworth, 1961.

—— *Concerning the City of God against the Pagans*, tr. Henry Bettenson, intr. John O'Meara. Harmondsworth, 1984.

Bale, John. *Scriptorum Illustrium Maioris Brytannie... Catalogus.* Basle, 1557–9.

Barclay, Alexander. *The Life of St George*, ed. William Nelson. EETS 230. London, 1955.

[Beauchamp]. *Pageant of the Birth, Life, and Death of Richard Beauchamp Earl of Warwick K. G. 1389–1439*, ed. Viscount Dillon and W. H. St John Hope. London, 1914.

—— *The Beauchamp Cartulary: Charters 1100–1268*, ed. Emma Mason. Lincoln, 1980.

Benoit de Sainte-Maure. *Le roman de Troie*, ed. Léopold Constans. SATF, 6 vols. Paris, 1904–12.

[Berners]. Bourchier, Sir John (Lord Berners). *The Boke of Duke Huon of Burdeux*, ed. S. L. Lee. EETS ES 40, 41, 43, 50. London, 1882, 1883, 1884, 1887.

—— *The History of the Valiant Knight Arthur of Little Britain*, ed. E. V. Utterson. London, 1814.

—— 'A Textual Edition on Modern Principles of *Arthur of Little Britain*, A Romance of the Sixteenth Century Translated by John Bourchier, Lord Berners', ed. George Emile Mitchell. Ph.D. thesis. University of Notre Dame, 1969.

—— [See also under Froissart, Jean.]

[*Bevis*]. *Syr Beuis of Hampton.* London, [c. 1585].

—— *The Romance of Sir Beues of Hampton*, ed. Eugene Kölbing. EETS ES 46, 48, 65. London, 1885, 1886, 1894.

—— '*Sir Beves of Hampton*: Study and Edition', ed. Jennifer Fellows. 5 vols. Ph. D. thesis. University of Cambridge, 1980.

Biblia sacra iuxta vulgatam versionem, gen. ed. Robertus Weber. 3rd edn. amended Bonifatius Fischer. Stuttgart, 1983.

Boethius. *The Consolation of Philosophy*, tr. V. E. Watts. Harmondsworth, 1969.

Le Bone Florence of Rome, ed. Carol Falvo Heffernan. Manchester, 1976.

[*Book of Homilies*]. *Certain Sermons or Homilies (1547) and a Homily Against Disobedience and Wilful Rebellion (1570)*, ed. Ronald B. Bond. Toronto, 1987.

The Brut, or the Chronicles of England, ed. Friedrich W. D. Brie. EETS 131, 136. London, 1906, 1908.

Burton, Robert. *The Anatomy of Melancholy*, ed. Floyd Dell and Paul Jordan-Smith. New York, 1955.

Calvin, John. *Institutes of the Christian Religion*, ed. John T. McNeill, tr. Ford Lewis Battles. LCC 20, 21. Philadelphia, 1960.

Caradoc of Llancarvan. *Life of St Gildas*, in *Gildae De excidio Britanniae*, ed. Hugh Williams. 2 vols. London, 1899–1901, II, 395–413.

Carroll, Lewis. *Alice's Adventures in Wonderland & Through the Looking-Glass, and What Alice Found There*. London, 1978.

Caxton, William. *Caxton's Book of Curtesye*, ed. Frederick J. Furnivall. EETS ES 3. London, 1868.

—— *The Lyf of the Noble and Crysten Prynce, Charles the Grete*, ed. Sidney J. H. Herrtage. EETS ES 36, 37. London, 1870, 1871.

—— *The Right Plesaunt and Goodly Historie of the Foure Sonnes of Aymon*, ed. Octavia Richardson. EETS ES 44, 45. London, 1884, 1885.

—— *Caxton's Eneydos*, ed. W. T. Culley and F. J. Furnivall. EETS ES 57. London, 1890.

—— *Caxton's Blanchardyn and Eglantine*, ed. Leon Kellner. EETS ES 58. London, 1890.

—— *Godeffroy of Boloyne, or The Siege and Conqueste of Jerusalem*, ed. Mary Noyes Colvin. EETS ES 64. London, 1893.

—— *The Recuyell of the Historyes of Troye*, ed. H. Oskar Sommer. 2 vols. London, 1894.

—— *The History of Jason*, ed. John Munro. EETS ES 111. London, 1913.

—— *Paris and Vienne*, ed. MacEdward Leach. EETS 234. London, 1957.

—— *The Book of the Knight of the Tower*, ed. M. Y. Offord. EETS SS 2. London, 1971.

—— [See also under Christine de Pisan, Jacobus de Voragine, and Llull, Ramon.]

[Cervantes]. Miguel de Cervantes Saavedra. *The Adventures of Don Quixote*, tr. J. M. Cohen. Harmondsworth, 1950.

Chaucer, Geoffrey. *The Riverside Chaucer*, gen. ed. Larry D. Benson. 3rd. edn. Boston, 1987.

Chrétien de Troyes. *Arthurian Romances*, tr. D. D. R. Owen. London, 1987.

Christine de Pisan. *The Book of Fayttes of Armes and of Chyvalrye*, tr. William Caxton, ed. Alfred T. P. Byles. EETS 189. London, 1932.

Churchyard, Thomas. *The Worthiness of Wales*. Spenser Society 20. New York, 1876.

Cursor Mundi, ed. Richard Morris. EETS 57, 59, 62, 66, 68, 99, 101. London, 1874, 1875, 1876, 1877, 1878, 1892, 1893.

Dares Phrygius. *De excidio Troiae historiae*, ed. Ferdinand Meister. Leipzig, 1873.

—— *The Trojan War: The Chronicles of Dictys of Crete and Dares the Phrygian*, tr. R. M. Frazer, Jr. Bloomington and London, 1966.

[*Degare*]. *Syr Degore*. London, 1560.

[*Degrevant*]. *The Romance of Sir Degrevant*, ed. L. F. Casson. EETS 221. London, 1949.

[*Destruction of Troy*]. *The 'Gest Hystoriale' of the Destruction of Troy*, ed. Geo. A. Panton and David Donaldson. EETS 39, 56. London, 1869, 1874.

Drayton, Michael. *The Works of Michael Drayton*, ed. J. William Hebel et al. 5 vols. Oxford, 1961.

Dugdale, William. *Antiquities of Warwickshire*. London, 1656.

Dunbar, William. *The Poems of William Dunbar*, ed. James Kinsley. Oxford, 1979.

[*Eglamour*]. *Sir Eglamour of Artois*, ed. Frances E. Richardson. EETS 256. London, 1965.

Fellows, Jennifer, ed. *Of Love and Chivalry: An Anthology of Middle English Romance*. London, 1993.

Floris and Blauncheflur: A Middle English Romance, ed. F. C. de Vries. Groningen, 1966.

Foxe, John. *The Acts and Monuments of John Foxe*, ed. George Townsend. 8 vols. London, 1843–1849.

French, Walter Hoyt and Charles Brockway Hale, eds *Middle English Metrical Romances*. 2 vols. New York, 1964.

Froissart, Jean. *The Chronicle of Froissart Translated out of French by Sir John Bourchier Lord Berners*. Tudor Translations 27–32. 6 vols. London, 1901–03.

Generydes: A Romance in Seven-Line Stanzas, ed. W. Aldis Wright. EETS 55, 70. London, 1873, 1878.

Geoffrey of Monmouth. *The Historia regum Britannie* [sic] *of Geoffrey of Monmouth*, ed. Neil Wright. Cambridge, 1985.

—— *The History of the Kings of Britain*, tr. Lewis Thorpe. Harmondsworth, 1966.

—— *Life of Merlin: Vita Merlini*, ed. and trans. Basil Clarke. Cardiff, 1973.

[Gerald of Wales]. *Giraldi Cambrensis Opera*, ed. J. S. Brewer, J. F. Dimock, and George F. Warner. RS 21. 8 vols. London, 1861–91.

[*Gesta Romanorum*]. *The Early English Version of the Gesta Romanorum*, ed. S. J. H. Herrtage. EETS ES 33. London, 1879.

Grafton, Richard. *An Abridgement of the Chronicles of England*. London, 1564.

Gower, John. *The English Works of John Gower*, ed. G. C. Macaulay. EETS ES 81, 82. London, 1900, 1901.

Gui de Warewic, ed. Alfred Ewert. Paris, 1932, 1933.

[*Guy*]. *The Romance of Guy of Warwick: The Second or 15th-Century Version*, ed. Julius Zupitza. EETS ES 25, 26. London, 1875, 1876.

—— *The Romance of Guy of Warwick: Edited from the Auchinleck MS. in the Advocates' Library, Edinburgh and from MS. 107 in Caius College, Cambridge*, ed. Julius Zupitza. EETS, ES 42, 49, 59. London, 1883, 1887, 1891.

—— *Guy of Warwick*, ed. G. Schleich. Palaestra 139. Leipzig, 1923.

Hardyng, John. *The Chronicle of John Hardyng… Together with the Continuation by Richard Grafton*, ed. Henry Ellis. London, 1812.

Havelok, ed. G. V. Smithers. Oxford, 1987.

[*Haveloc*]. *Le Lai d'Haveloc and Gaimar's Haveloc Episode*, ed. Alexander Bell. Manchester, 1925.

Henslowe, Philip. *Henslowe's Diary*, ed. W. W. Greg. 2 vols. London, 1904–8.

[*Horn*]. *King Horn: An Edition Based on Cambridge University Library MS Gg.4.27(2)*, ed. Rosamund Allen. New York and London, 1984.

Horn Childe and Maiden Rimnild, ed. Maldwyn Mills. Heidelberg, 1988.

[Hughes, Thomas et al.]. *The Misfortunes of Arthur*, ed. Brian Jay Corrigan. New York and London, 1992.

Hurd, Richard. *Letters on Chivalry and Romance*, ed. Hoyt Trowbridge. Los Angeles, 1963.

Ipomedon in drei englischen Bearbeitungen, ed. Eugen Kölbing. Breslau, 1889.

[*Isumbras*]. *Sir Ysumbras*, ed. J. Zupitza and G. Schleick. Palaestra 15. Berlin, 1901.

Ywain and Gawain, ed. Albert B. Friedman and Norman T. Harrington. EETS 254. London, 1964.

Ywain and Gawain, Sir Percyvell of Gales, The Anturs of Arther, ed. Maldwyn Mills. London and Rutland, Vermont, 1992.

Jacobus de Voragine. *Legenda aurea, vulgo historia Lombardica dicta*, ed. T. Graesse. 2nd. edn. Leipzig, 1850.

—— *The Golden Legend, or Lives of Saints*, tr. William Caxton, ed. F. S. Ellis. 7 vols. London, 1900.

James, Henry. *The Art of the Novel: Critical Prefaces*, intr. Richard P. Blackmur. New York and London, 1934.

John of Glastonbury. *The Chronicle of Glastonbury Abbey: An Edition, Translation and Study of John of Glastonbury's Cronica sive antiquitates Glastoniensis ecclesie*, ed. James P. Carley and tr. David Townsend. Woodbridge, 1985.

Johnson, Richard. *The Most Famous History of the Seauen Champions of Christendome*, London, 1596.

Jonson, Ben. *Ben Jonson's Literary Criticism*, ed. James D. Redwine, Jr. Lincoln, Nebraska, 1970.

Joseph of Arimathie: Otherwise Called the Romance of the Seint Graal, or Holy Grail, ed. Walter W. Skeat. EETS 44. London, 1871.

The Kalender of Shepherdes, ed. H. Oskar Sommer. 3 vols. London, 1892.

The Kalender & Compost of Shepherds, ed. G. C. Heseltine. London, 1930.

Kelton, Arthur. *A Chronycle with a Genealogie Declarying that the Brittons and Welshemen Are Lineallye Dyscended from Brute...* London, 1547.

Laȝamon. *Brut*, ed. G. L. Brook and R. F. Leslie. EETS 250, 277. London, 1963, 1973.

[*Lai le Freine*]. 'The Middle English *Lai le Freine*', ed. Margaret Wattie. *Smith College Studies in Modern Languages*, vol. 10, no. 3 (1929), *passim*.

Lancelot do Lac: The Non-Cyclic Old French Prose Romance, ed. Elspeth Kennedy. 2 vols. Oxford, 1980.

Lancelot: roman en prose du XIIIe siècle, ed. Alexandre Micha. TLF 247, 249, 262, 278, 283, 286, 288, 307, 315. Paris and Geneva, 1978, 1979, 1980, 1982, 1983.

Langland, William. *The Vision of Piers Plowman: A Complete Edition of the B-Text*, ed. A. V. C. Schmidt. London and Melbourne, 1987.

['Langtoft, Peter']. *Peter Langtoft's Chronicle*, ed. Thomas Hearne. 2 vols. London, 1810. (In fact, this is an edition of the second part of Robert Mannyng's *Chronicle*.)

The Laud Troy Book, ed. J. Ernst Wülfing. EETS 121, 122. London, 1902, 1904.

Leland, John. *The Assertion of King Arthure*, tr. Richard Robinson, in Middleton, *Famous History of Chinon*, ed. Mead (1925), separately paginated.

—— *Leland's Itinerary in England and Wales*, ed. Lucy Toulmin Smith, foreward Thomas Kendrick. 5 vols. Carbondale, 1964.

Llull, Ramon. *The Book of the Ordre of Chyvalry*, tr. William Caxton, ed. Alfred T. P. Byles. EETS 168. London, 1926.

Lovelich, Henry. *Merlin: A Middle-English Metrical Version of a French Romance*, ed. Ernst A. Kock. EETS ES 93, 112, OS 185. London, 1904, 1913, 1932.

—— *The History of the Holy Grail*, ed. Frederick J. Furnivall. EETS ES 20, 24, 28, 30. London, 1874, 1875, 1877, 1878.

[Lupold von Wedel]. 'Journey Through England and Scotland Made by Lupold von Wedel in the Years 1584–1585'. *TRHS* n.s. 9 (1895), 258–9.

Lybeaus Desconus, ed. M. Mills. EETS 261. London, 1969.

Lydgate, John. *Lydgate's Troy Book*, ed. Henry Bergen. EETS ES 97, 103, 106, 126. London, 1906, 1908, 1910, 1935.

—————— *Lydgate's Siege of Thebes*, ed. Axel Erdmann and Eilert Ekwall. EETS ES 108, 125. London, 1911, 1930.

—— *The Minor Poems of John Lydgate*, ed. Henry Noble MacCracken. EETS ES 107, OS 192. Oxford, 1911, 1934.

MacDonald, George. *Phantastes: A Faerie Romance for Men and Women*. London, 1858.

Macrobius. *Commentary on the Dream of Scipio*, tr. William Harris Stahl. New York, 1952.

Malory, Sir Thomas. *The Morte Darthur: Parts Seven and Eight*, ed. D. S. Brewer. London, 1968.

—— *King Arthur and his Knights*, ed. Eugène Vinaver. London, 1968.

—— *The Works of Sir Thomas Malory*, ed. Eugène Vinaver, rev. P. J. C. Field. 3rd edn. 3 vols. Oxford, 1990.

Mannyng, Robert. *The Story of England by Robert Manning of Brunne, A.D. 1338*, ed. Frederick J. Furnivall. RS. 2 vols. London, 1887.

—— [See also 'Langtoft, Peter'.]

Marie de France. *Les Lais de Marie de France*, ed. Jean Rychner. CFMA 93. Paris, 1983.

Melusine, ed. A. K. Donald. EETS ES 68. London, 1895.

Merlin, or The Early History of King Arthur: A Prose Romance, ed. Henry B. Wheatley, intr. William Edward Mead. EETS 10 21, 36, 112. London, 1865, 1866, 1869, 1899.

Merlin, ed. Alexandre Micha. TLF 281. Geneva, 1967.

Metham, John. *The Works of John Metham, Including the Romance of Amoryus and Cleopes*, ed. Hardin Craig. EETS 132. London, 1916.
Middleton, Christopher. *The Famous History of Chinon of England*, ed. William Edward Mead. EETS 165. London, 1925.
Mills, Maldwyn, ed. *Six Middle English Romances*. London and Melbourne, 1973.
Minot, Laurence. *The Poems of Laurence Minot 1333–1352*, ed. Thomas Beaumont James and John Simons. Exeter, 1989.
The Mirror for Magistrates, ed. Lily B. Campbell. Cambridge, 1938.
Montemayor, George of. *A Critical Edition of Yong's Translation of George of Montemayor's Diana and Gil Polo's Enamoured Diana*, ed. Judith M. Kennedy. Oxford, 1968.
La Mort le roi Artu: roman du XIIIe siècle, ed. Jean Frappier. TLF 58. 3rd edn. Geneva and Paris, 1964.
Morte Arthure, ed. Edmund Brock. EETS 8. 2nd edn. London, 1871.
Le Morte Arthur, ed. J. Douglas Bruce. EETS ES 88. London, 1903, rpt. 1959.
Nashe, Thomas. *The Works of Thomas Nashe*, ed. Ronald B. McKerrow, rev. F. P. Wilson. 2nd edn. 5 vols. Oxford, 1958.
Nichols, John, ed. *The Progresses and Public Processions of Queen Elizabeth*. 3 vols. London, 1823.
[*Orfeo*]. *Sir Orfeo*, ed. A. J. Bliss. 2nd edn. Oxford, 1966.
Partonope of Blois, ed. A. Trampe Bödtker. EETS ES 109. London, 1912.
[*Perlesvaus*]. *The High Book of the Grail: A Translation of the Thirteenth-Century Romance of Perlesvaus*, tr. Nigel Bryant. Cambridge, 1978.
The Piers Plowman Tradition: A Critical Edition of Pierce the Ploughman's Crede, Richard the Redeless, Mum and the Sothsegger and the Crowned King, ed. Helen Barr. London and Rutland, Vermont, 1993.
Plato. *The Collected Dialogues of Plato, Including the Letters*, ed. Edith Hamilton and Huntingdon Cairns. Princeton, 1961.
Plotinus. *The Enneads*, tr. Stephen MacKenna, intr. John Dillon. Harmondsworth, 1991.
[*Ponthus*]. *King Ponthus and the Fair Sidone*, ed. Frank Jewett Mather. Baltimore, 1897.
Puttenham, George. *The Art of English Poesie*, ed. Gladys Doidge Willcock and Alice Walker. Cambridge, 1936.
La Queste del Saint Graal: roman du XIIIe siècle, ed. Albert Pauphilet. CFMA 33. Paris, 1967.
Reardon, B. P., ed. *Collected Ancient Greek Novels*. Berkeley and London, 1989.

Renaut de Beaujeu. *Le Bel Inconnu*, ed. G. Perrie Williams. CFMA 38. Paris, 1967.

[*Richard Coeur de Lion*]. *Der mittelenglische Versroman über Richard Löwenherz*, ed. Karl Brunner. Wiener Beiträge zur englischen Philologie 42. Vienna and Leipzig, 1913.

Robert de Boron. *Merlin: roman de XIIIe siècle*, ed. Alexandre Micha. TLF 281. Geneva, 1979.

—— *Le roman de l'estoire dou graal*, ed. William A. Nitze. CFMA 57. Paris, 1983.

Robbins, Rossell H., ed. *Historical Poems of the XIVth and XVth Centuries*. New York, 1959.

Rous, John. *The Rous Roll*, ed. Charles Ross. Gloucester, 1980.

Sands, Donald B., ed. *Middle English Verse Romances*. Exeter, 1986.

Schmidt, A. V. C. and Nicolas Jacobs, eds *Medieval English Romances*. London, 1980.

The Seege or Batayle of Troye, ed. Mary Elizabeth Barnicle. EETS 172. London, 1927.

Shakespeare, William. *The Complete Works*, gen. ed. Stanley Wells and Gary Taylor. Oxford, 1988.

Sidney, Sir Philip. *A Defence of Poetry*, ed. Jan Van Dorsten. Oxford, 1973.

—— *The Countess of Pembroke's Arcadia*, ed. Maurice Evans. Harmondsworth, 1977.

—— *The Countess of Pembroke's Arcadia (The Old Arcadia)*, ed. Katherine Duncan-Jones. Oxford and New York, 1994.

Skelton, John. *The Complete English Poems*, ed. John Scattergood. Harmondsworth, 1983.

The South English Legendary, ed. Charlotte D'Evelyn and Anna J. Mill. EETS 235, 236, 244. London, 1956, 1959.

The Sowdone of Babylone, ed. Emil Hausknecht. EETS ES 38. London, 1881.

Spenser, Edmund. *The Faerie Queene*, ed. A. C. Hamilton. London and New York, 1977.

—— *The Yale Edition of the Shorter Poems of Edmund Spenser*, ed. William A. Oram et al. New Haven and London, 1989.

—— *A View of the State of Ireland*, ed. Andrew Hadfield and Willy Maley. Oxford, 1997.

S[tow], I[ohn]. *Certaine Worthye Manuscript Poems of Great Antiquitie*. London, 1597.

[Tasso, Torquato]. *Godfrey of Bulloigne: A Critical Edition of Edward Fairfax's Translation of Tasso's Gerusalemme Liberata, together with Fairfax's Original Poems*, ed. Kathleen M. Lea and T. M. Gang. Oxford, 1981.

The Three Kings' Sons, ed. F. J. Furnivall. EETS ES 67. London, 1895.

Torent of Portyngale, ed. E. Adam. EETS ES 51. London, 1887.

[*Tristrem*]. *Sir Tristrem*, ed. George P. McNeill. STS 8. Edinburgh and London, 1886.

Vergil, Polydore. *Polydore Vergil's English History*, Vol. 1, ed. Henry Ellis. CS 36. London, 1846.

Virgil. *Eclogues, Georgics, Aeneid, The Minor Poems*, ed. and tr. H. Ruston Fairclough. Loeb. 2 vols. 2nd edn. Cambridge, Mass., and London, 1934, 1935.

The Vulgate Version of the Arthurian Romances, ed. H. Oskar Sommer. 8 vols. Washington, D.C., 1908–16.

Wace. *Le roman de Brut de Wace*, ed. Ivor Arnold. SATF. 2 vols. Paris, 1938, 1940.

The Wars of Alexander, ed. Hoyt N. Duggan and Thorlac Turville-Petre. EETS SS 10. Oxford, 1989.

Watson, Henry. *Valentine and Orson*, ed. Arthur Dickson. EETS 204. London, 1937.

Weber, Henry, ed. *Metrical Romances of the Thirteenth, Fourteenth, and Fifteenth Centuries*. 2 vols. Edinburgh, 1810.

William of Malmesbury. *De gestis regum Anglorum*, ed. William Stubbs. RS 90. London, 1887, 1889.

—— *The Early History of Glastonbury: An Edition, Translation and Study of William of Malmesbury's De antiquitate Glastonie ecclesie*, ed. and trans. John Scott. Woodbridge, 1981.

[*William of Palerne*]. *The Romance of William of Palerne*, ed. Walter W. Skeat. EETS ES 1. London, 1867.

Worcester, William. *Itineraries*, ed. J. H. Harvey. Oxford, 1969.

Wright, T., ed. *Political Poems and Songs*. RS 14. London, 1859–61.

(C) SECONDARY SOURCES

Abrams, Lesley and James P. Carley, eds. *The Archaeology and History of Glastonbury Abbey: Essays in Honour of the Ninetieth Birthday of C. A. Ralegh Radford*. Woodbridge, 1991.

Ackerman, Robert W. 'Henry Lovelich's *Merlin*'. *PMLA* 67 (1952), 473–84.

Adams, Robert P. '"Bold Bawdry and Open Manslaughter": The English New Humanist Attack on Medieval Romance'. *HLQ* 23 (1959–60), 33–48.

Alpers, Paul J. *The Poetry of The Faerie Queene*. Princeton, 1967.

—— ed. *Elizabethan Poetry: Modern Essays in Criticism*. Oxford, 1967.

Alsop, J. D. and Wesley M. Stevens. 'William Lambarde and Elizabethan Polity'. *Studies in Medieval and Renaissance History* n.s. 8 (1986), 231–65.

Anderson, Judith H. *The Growth of a Personal Voice*. New Haven, 1976.

—— Donald Cheney, and David A. Richardson, eds. *Spenser's Life and the Subject of Biography*. Amherst, 1996.

Anglo, Sydney. *Spectacle, Pageantry, and Early Tudor Policy*. Oxford, 1969.

Archibald, Elizabeth. 'Beginnings: *The Tale of King Arthur* and *King Arthur and the Emperor Lucius*', in Archibald and Edwards, eds *Companion to Malory*, 133–51.

—— and A. S. G. Edwards, eds *A Companion to Malory*. Cambridge, 1996.

Aston, Margaret. 'English Ruins and English History: The Dissolution and the Sense of the Past'. *JWCI* 36 (1973), 231–55.

Atchity, Kenneth John, ed. *Eterne in Mutabilitie: The Unity of The Faerie Queene*. Hamden, Conn., 1972.

Atkinson, Stephen C. B. 'Malory's Lancelot and the *Queste of the Grail*', in Spisak, ed., *Studies in Malory*, 129–52.

Auerbach, Eric. *Mimesis: The Representation of Reality in Western Literature*, tr. Willard R. Trask. Princeton, 1953.

Barnes, Geraldine. *Counsel and Strategy in Middle English Romance*. Cambridge, 1993.

Barron, W. R. J. 'Arthurian Romance: Traces of an English Tradition'. *English Studies* 61 (1980), 2–23.

—— *English Medieval Romance*. Harlow, 1987.

Baswell, Christoper and William Sharpe, eds. *The Passing of Arthur: New Essays in the Arthurian Tradition*. New York and London, 1988.

Baugh, Albert C. 'The Middle English Romance: Some Questions of Creation, Presentation, and Preservation'. *Speculum* 42 (1967), 1–31.

Bennett, H. S. 'The Production and Dissemination of Vernacular Manuscripts in the Fifteenth Century'. *Library*, 5th ser. vol. 1 (1946–7), 167–75.

—— *English Books & Readers 1558 to 1603*. Cambridge, 1965.

—— *English Books & Readers 1475–1557*. 2nd. edn. Cambridge, 1969.

Bennett, J. A. W., ed. *Essays on Malory*. Oxford, 1963.

—— *Middle English Literature*, ed. and completed Douglas Gray. Oxford, 1986.

Bennett, Josephine Waters. *The Evolution of 'The Faerie Queene'*. Chicago, 1942.

Benson, C. David. 'The Ending of the *Morte Darthur*', in Archibald and Edwards, eds, *Companion to Malory*, 221–38.

Benson, Larry D. *Malory's Morte Darthur*. Cambridge, Mass., and London, 1976.

—— and John Leyerle, eds. *Chivalric Literature: Essays on Relations Between Literature and Life in the Later Middle Ages*. Studies in Medieval Culture 14. Kalamazoo, 1980.

Berger, Harry, Jr. *The Allegorical Temper: Vision and Reality in Book II of Spenser's Faerie Queene*. New Haven, 1957.

Bergeron, David M. *English Civic Pageantry 1558–1642*. London, 1971.

Betteridge, Thomas. *Tudor Histories of the English Reformations, 1530–83*. Aldershot, 1999.

Blake, N. F. 'William Caxton: his Choice of Texts'. *Anglia* 83 (1965), 289–307.

—— 'Caxton and Courtly Style'. *Essays & Studies* n.s. 21 (1968), 29–45.

—— 'Wynkyn de Worde: The Later Years'. *G-J* (1972), 128–38.

—— 'Caxton Prepares his Edition of the *Morte Darthur*'. *Journal of Librarianship* 8 (1976), 272–85.

Blanchfield, Lynne S. 'The Romances in MS Ashmole 61: An Idiosyncratic Scribe', in Mills, Fellows, and Meale, eds, *Romance in Medieval England*, 65–87.

—— 'Rate Revisited: The Compilation of the Narrative Works in MS Ashmole 61', in Fellows et al., eds, *Romance Reading*, 208–22.

Bliss, A. J. 'Notes on the Auchinleck MS'. *Speculum* 26 (1951), 652–8.

Boffey, Julia and John J. Thompson. 'Anthologies and Miscellanies: Production and Choice of Texts', in Griffithes and Pearsall, eds, *Book Production and Publishing*, 279–315.

Bone, Gavin. 'Extant Manuscripts Printed from by W. de Worde with Notes on their Owner, Roger Thorney'. *Library* 4th ser. 12 (1931–32), 284–306.

Bornstein, Diane. 'William Caxton's Chivalric Romances and the Burgundian Renaissance in England'. *English Studies* 57 (1976), 1–10.

Bradstock, Margaret. '*Sir Gowther*: Secular Hagiography or Hagiographical Romance or Neither?'. *Australasian University Modern Language Association* 59 (1983), 26–47.

Braswell, Laurel. '*Sir Isumbras* and the Legend of Saint Eustace'. *Medieval Studies* 27 (1965), 128–51.

Brewer, D. S. '"the hoole book"', in Bennett, ed., *Essays on Malory*, 41–63.

—— 'The Paradox of the Archaic and the Modern in *Laȝamon's Brut*', in Malcolm Godden, Douglas Gray, and Terry Hoad, eds, *Anglo-Saxon to Early Middle English: Studies Presented to E. G. Stanley*. Oxford, 1984, 188–205.

—— 'Malory: The Traditional Writer and the Archaic Mind', in *Arthurian Literature I*, ed. Richard Barber. Cambridge, 1981, 94–120.

Brink, Jean R. '"All his minde on honour fixed": The Preferment of Edmund Spenser', in Anderson, Cheney, and Richardson, eds, *Spenser's Life*, 45–64.

Brunner, Karl. 'Middle English Metrical Romances and Their Audience', in MacEdward Leach, ed., *Studies in Medieval Literature in Honor of Professor Albert Croll Baugh*. Philadelphia, 1961.

Bühler, C. F. *The Fifteenth-Century Book: The Scribes, the Printers, the Decorators*. Philadelphia, 1960.

Bullock-Davies, Constance. '"*Exspectare Arturum*": Arthur and the Messianic Hope'. *Bulletin of the Board of Celtic Studies* 29 (1982), 432–40.

Burgess, Glyn S. *The Lais of Marie de France: Text and Context*. Manchester, 1987.

Burrow, Colin. *Epic Romance: Homer to Milton*. Oxford, 1993.

—— *Edmund Spenser*. Plymouth, 1996.

Burrow, John A. '*Sir Thopas* in the Sixteenth Century', in Douglas Gray and E. G. Stanley, eds, *Middle English Studies Presented to Norman Davis*. Oxford, 1983, 69–91.

Buxton, John. *Sir Philip Sidney and the English Renaissance*. 2nd edn. London and New York, 1964.

Canny, Nicholas P. 'Edmund Spenser and the Development of an Anglo-Irish Identity'. *Yearbook of English Studies* 13 (1983), 1–19.

—— 'Introduction: Spenser and the Reform of Ireland', in Coughlan, ed., *Spenser and Ireland*, 9–24.

Carey, Vincent P. and Clare L. Carroll. 'Factions and Fictions: Spenser's Reflections of and on Elizabethan Politics', in Anderson, Cheney, and Richardson, eds, *Spenser's Life*, 31–44.

Carley, James P. 'Polydore Vergil and John Leland on King Arthur: The Battle of the Books'. *Interpretations* 15 (1984), 86–100.

—— 'The Manuscript Remains of John Leland, "The King's Antiquary"'. *TEXT* 2 (1985), 111–20.

Carlson, David R. 'The Writings and Manuscript Collections of the Elizabethan, Alchemist, Antiquary, and Herald Francis Thynne'. *HLQ* 52 (1989), 203–72.

Carpenter, Frederic Ives. *A Reference Guide to Edmund Spenser*. Chicago, 1923.

Carruthers, Mary J. *The Book of Memory: A Study of Memory in Medieval Culture*. Cambridge Studies in Medieval Literature 10. Cambridge, 1990.

Cate, Wirt Armistead. 'The Problem and Origin of the Griselda Story'. *SP* 29 (1932), 389–405.

Childress, Diana T. 'Between Romance and Legend: "Secular Hagiography" in Middle English Literature'. *PQ* 57 (1978), 311–22.

Collinson, Patrick. 'Biblical Rhetoric: the English Nation and National Sentiment in the Prophetic Mode', in Claire McEachern and Debora Shuger, eds *Religion and Culture in Renaissance England*. Cambridge, 1997, 15–45.

—— 'Truth, Lies and Fiction in Sixteenth-Century Protestant Historiography', in Donald R. Kelley and David Harris Sacks, eds, *The Historical Imagination in Early Modern Britain*. Cambridge, 1997, 37–68.

Cooper, Helen. *Pastoral: Medieval into Renaissance*. Ipswich, 1977.

—— *The Structure of The Canterbury Tales*. London, 1983.

—— *Oxford Guides to Chaucer: The Canterbury Tales*. Oxford, 1989.

—— 'Romance after 1400', in David Wallace, ed., *The Cambridge History of Medieval English Literature: Writing in Britain 1066–1547*. Cambridge, forthcoming, 690–719.

Coughlan, Patricia, ed. *Spenser and Ireland: An Interdisciplinary Perspective*. Cork, 1989.

Cowen, Janet M. 'Chaucer's *Legend of Good Women*: Structure and Tone'. *SP* 82 (1985), 416–36.

Crane, Ronald S. 'The Reading of an Elizabethan Youth'. *MP* 11 (1913–4), 269–71.

—— 'The Vogue of *Guy of Warwick* from the Close of the Middle Ages to the Romantic Revival'. *PMLA* 30 (1915), 125–94.

Crane, Susan. 'Anglo-Norman Romances of English Heroes: Ancestral Romance?'. *Renaissance Papers* (1981–2), 601–8.

—— '*Guy of Warwick* and the Question of Exemplary Romance'. *Genre* 17 (1984), 351–74.

—— *Insular Romance: Politics, Faith, and Culture in Anglo-Norman and Middle English Literature*. Berkeley, 1986.

—— [See also Dannenbaum, Susan.]

Dannenbaum, Susan. '"Fairer bi one ribbe / Þan eni man þat libbe" (*King Horn*, C 315–16)'. *NQ* 28 (1981), 116–17.

—— [See also Crane, Susan.]

Davies, R. R. 'The Peoples of Britain and Ireland 1100–1400: II. Names, Boundaries and Regional Solidarities'. *TRHS* 5 (1995), 1–20.

Dean, Christopher. *Arthur of England: English Attitudes to King Arthur and the Knights of the Round Table in the Middle Ages and Renaissance*. Toronto, 1987.

Dichmann, Mary E. '"The Tale of King Arthur and the Emperor Lucius": The Rise of Lancelot', in Lumiansky, ed., *Malory's Originality*, 67–90.

Donaldson, E. Talbot. 'Malory and the Stanzaic *Le Morte Arthur*'. *SP* 47 (1950), 460–72.

Doyle, A. I., Elizabeth Rainey, and D. B. Wilson. *Manuscript to Print: Tradition and Innovation in the Renaissance Book*. Durham, 1975.

Doyle A. I. and M. B. Parkes. 'The Production of Copies of the *Canterbury Tales* and the *Confessio Amantis* in the Early Fifteenth Century', in M. B. Parkes and Andrew G. Watson, eds, *Scribes, Manuscripts & Libraries: Essays Presented to N. R. Ker*. London, 1978, 163–210.

Duff, E. Gordon. *A Century of the English Book Trade*. London, 1905.

——— *The English Provincial Printers, Stationers and Bookbinders to 1557*. Cambridge, 1912.

Duffy, Eamon. *The Stripping of the Altars: Traditional Religion in England c.1400–c.1580*. New Haven and London, 1992.

Eckhardt, Caroline D. 'Arthurian Comedy: The Simpleton-Hero in *Sir Perceval of Galles*'. *CR* 8 (1974), 205–20.

Edwards, A. S. G. ' "The Whole Book": Medieval Manuscripts in Facsimile'. *Review* 2 (1980), 19–29.

——— 'From Manuscript to Print: Wynkyn de Worde and the Printing of Contemporary Poetry'. *G-J* (1991), 143–8.

——— and Derek Pearsall. 'The Manuscripts of the Major Poetic Texts', in Griffiths and Pearsall, eds, *Book Production and Publishing*, 257–78.

——— and Carol M. Meale. 'The Marketing of Printed Books in Late Medieval England'. *Library* 6th ser. 15 (1993), 95–124.

Evans, Murray J. 'The Explicits and Narrative Division in the Winchester MS: A Critique of Vinaver's Malory'. *PQ* 58 (1979), 263–81.

——— 'The Two Scribes in the Winchester MS: The First Explicit and Malory's "Hoole Book" '. *Manuscripta* 27 (1983), 38–44.

——— 'Ordinatio and Narrative Links: The Impact of Malory's Tales as an "hoole book" ', in Spisak, ed., *Studies in Malory*, 29–52.

——— *Rereading Middle English Romance: Manuscript Layout, Decoration, and the Rhetoric of Composite Structure*. Montreal and Kingston, 1995.

Everett, Dorothy. 'A Characterization of the Middle English Romances', in her *Essays on Middle English Literature*, ed. Patricia Keen. Oxford, 1955.

Farness, Jay. 'Disenchanted Elves: Biography in the Text of *Faerie Queene* V', in Anderson, Cheney, and Richardson, eds, *Spenser's Life*, 18–30.

Fellows, Jennifer. 'Sir Bevis of Hampton in Popular Tradition'. *PHFCAS* 42 (1986), 139–45.

——— 'Editing Middle English Romance', in Mills, Fellows, and Meale, eds, *Romance in Medieval England*, 5–16.

——— 'St George as Romance Hero'. *RMS* 19 (1993), 27–54.

——— et al., eds, *Romance Reading on the Book: Essays on Medieval Narrative Presented to Maldwyn Mills*. Cardiff, 1996.

—— '*Bevis redivivus*': The Printed Editions of *Sir Bevis of Hampton*', in Fellows et al., eds, *Romance Reading*, 251–68.

Ferguson, Arthur B. *The Indian Summer of English Chivalry: Studies in the Decline and Transformation of Chivalric Idealism*. Durham, North Carolina, 1960.

—— *The Chivalric Tradition in Renaissance England*. Washington, 1986.

Fewster, Carol. *Traditionality and Genre in Middle English Romance*. Cambridge, 1987.

Fichter, Andrew. *Poets Historical: Dynastic Epic in the Renaissance*. New Haven and London, 1982.

Field, P. J. C. *Romance and Chronicle: A Study of Malory's Prose Style*. London, 1971.

—— 'The Source of Malory's *Tale of Gareth*', in Takamiya and Brewer, eds, *Aspects of Malory*, 57–70.

—— 'Malory and *The Wedding of Sir Gawain and Dame Ragnell*'. *Archiv* 219 (1982), 374–81.

—— *The Life and Times of Sir Thomas Malory*. AS 29. Cambridge, 1993.

—— 'Caxton's Roman War'. *Arthuriana* 5 (1995), 31–60.

Field, Rosalind. 'Romance as History, History as Romance', in Mills, Fellows, and Meale, eds, *Romance in Medieval England*, 163–73.

Finlayson, John. 'Definitions of Middle English Romance'. *CR* 15 (1980), 44–62, 168–81.

—— '*Richard, Coer de Lyon*: Romance, History or Something in Between?'. *SP* 87 (1990), 156–80.

Fletcher, Angus. *The Prophetic Moment: An Essay on Spenser*. Chicago and London, 1971.

Fletcher, Robert Huntingdon. *The Arthurian Material in the Chronicles, Especially Those of Great Britian and France*, expanded by Roger Sherman Loomis. 2nd edn. New York, 1966.

Flower, Robin. 'Laurence Nowell and the Discovery of England in Tudor Times'. *PBA* 21 (1935), 47–73.

Fox, Levi, ed. *English Historical Scholarship in the Sixteenth and Seventeenth Centuries*. Oxford, 1956.

Francis, F. C. *Robert Copland: Sixteenth-Century Printer and Translator*. Glasgow, 1961.

Frye, Northrop. *Anatomy of Criticism: Four Essays*. Princeton, 1957.

—— *The Secular Scripture: A Study of the Structure of Romance*. Cambridge, Mass., 1976.

Gerould, Gordon Hall. 'Forerunners, Congeners, and Derivatives of the Eustace Legend'. *PMLA* 19 (1904), 355–448.

—— 'The Hermit and the Saint'. *PMLA* 20 (1905), 529–45.

Giamatti, A. Bartlett. *The Earthly Paradise and the Renaissance Epic*. Princeton, 1966.

Goldberg, Jonathan. *James I and the Politics of Literature*. Baltimore and London, 1983.

Gransden, Antonia. *Historical Writing in England c.550–c.1307*. Ithaca, NY, 1974.

—— 'Propaganda and English Medieval Historiography'. *JMH* 1 (1975), 363–82.

—— 'The Growth of the Glastonbury Traditions and Legends in the Twelfth Century'. *Journal of Ecclesiastical History* 27 (1976), 337–58.

—— *Historical Writing in England ii: c.1307 to the Early Sixteenth Century*. Ithaca, NY, 1982.

Greenblatt, Stephen. *Renaissance Self-Fashioning: From More to Shakespeare*. Chicago and London, 1980.

Griffiths, Jeremy and Derek Pearsall, eds. *Book Production and Publishing in Britain 1375–1475*. Cambridge, 1989.

Grout, P. B. et al., eds. *The Legend of Arthur in the Middle Ages: Studies Presented to A. H. Diverres by Colleagues, Pupils and Friends*. AS 7. Cambridge, 1983.

Guddat-Figge, Gisela. *Catalogue of Manuscripts Containing Middle English Romances*. Munich, 1976.

Hadfield, Andrew. *Literature, Politics and National Identity: Reformation to Renaissance*. Cambridge, 1994.

—— 'From English to British Literature: John Lyly's *Euphues* and Edmund Spenser's *The Faerie Queene*', in Bradshaw and Roberts, eds, *British Consciousness*, 140–58.

Hamilton, A. C. *The Structure of Allegory in the Faerie Queene*. Oxford, 1961.

—— 'The Visions of *Piers Plowman* and *The Faerie Queene*', in Nelson, ed. (1961), 1–34.

—— ed. *Essential Articles for the Study of Edmund Spenser*. Hamden, Conn., 1972.

—— 'Our New Poet: "Well of English Undefyled"', in Hamilton, ed., *Essential Articles*, 488–506.

—— 'Elizabethan Romance: The Example of Prose Fiction'. *ELH* 49 (1982), 287–99.

—— gen. ed. *The Spenser Encyclopedia*. Toronto, 1990.

Hardman, Phillipa. 'A Mediaeval Library "*in Parvo*"'. *MÆ* 47 (1978), 262–73.

Harper, Carrie Anna. *The Sources of The British Chronicle History in Spenser's Faerie Queene*. Philadelphia, 1910.

Harris, Kate. 'Patrons, Buyers and Owners: The Evidence for Ownership and the Rôle of Book Owners in Book Production and the Book

Trade', in Griffiths and Pearsall, eds, *Book Production and Publishing*, 163–99.

Harris, Victor. *All Coherence Gone*. Chicago, 1949.

Helgerson, Richard. *Forms of Nationhood: The Elizabethan Writing of England*. Chicago and London, 1992.

Hellinga, Lotte. *Caxton in Focus: The Beginnings of Printing in England*. London, 1982.

—— 'Manuscripts in the Hands of Printers', in J. B. Trapp, ed., *Manuscripts in the First Fifty Years After the Invention of Printing: Some Papers Read at a Colloquium at the Warburg Institute on 12–13 March 1982*. London, 1983, 3–11.

Heninger, S. K., Jr. 'The Typographical Layout of Spenser's *Shepheardes Calender*', in Karl Josef Höltgen et al., eds, *Word and Visual Imagination*. Erlangen, 1988, 33–71.

Hibbard, Laura A. *Mediaeval Romance in England: A Study of the Sources and Analogues of the Non-Cyclic Metrical Romances*. New York, 1960.

—— [See also Loomis, Laura Hibbard.]

Hieatt, A. Kent. 'The Projected Continuation of *The Faerie Queene*: Rome Delivered?'. *SS* 8 (1990), 335–42.

—— 'Arthur's Deliverance of Rome? (Yet Again)'. *SS* 9 (1991), 243–8.

Hindman, Sandra, and James Douglas Farquhar. *Pen to Press: Illustrated Manuscripts and Printed Books in the First Century of Printing*. Maryland, 1977.

Holbrok, Ellen. 'Malory's Identification of Camelot as Winchester', in Spisak, ed., *Studies in Malory*, 13–27.

Hopkins, Andrea. *The Sinful Knights: A Study of Middle English Penitential Romance*. Oxford, 1990.

Hornstein, Lillian Herlands. 'Eustace-Constance-Florence-Griselda Legends', in Severs, gen. ed., *Manual*, 120–32.

Horton, Ronald Arthur. *The Unity of The Faerie Queene*. Athens, Georgia, 1978.

Hough, Graham. *A Preface to the Faerie Queene*. London, 1962.

Hudson, Anne. 'Epilogue: The Legacy of *Piers Plowman*', in John A. Alford, ed., *A Companion to Piers Plowman*. Berkeley, 1988, 251–66.

Huizinga, Johan. *The Waning of the Middle Ages*, tr. F. Hopman. London, 1924.

Hume, Anthea. *Edmund Spenser: Protestant Poet*. Cambridge, 1984.

Hume, Kathryn. 'Structure and Perspective: Romance and Hagiographic Features in the Amicus and Amelius Story'. *JEGP* 69 (1970), 89–107.

—— 'The Formal Nature of Middle English Romance'. *PQ* 53 (1974), 158–80.

Hurley, Margaret. 'Saints' Lives and Romance Again: Secularization of Structure and Motif'. *Genre* 8 (1975), 60–73.

Hynes-Berry, Mary. 'A Tale "Breffly Drawyne Oute of Freynshe"', in Takamiya and Brewer, eds, *Aspects of Malory*, 93–106.

Isaacs, Neil D. 'Constance in Fourteenth-Century England'. *NM* 59 (1958), 260–77.

Jacobs, Nicolas. '*Sir Degarré, Lay le Freine, Beues of Hamtoun* and the "Auchinleck Bookshop"'. *NQ* 29 (1982), 294–301.

—— 'The Second Revision of *Sir Degarre*: The Egerton Fragments and its Congeners'. *NM* 85 (1984), 95–107.

—— *The Later Versions of Sir Degarre: A Study in Textual Degeneration.* MÆ Monographs, n.s. 18. Oxford, 1995.

Jardine, Lisa. 'Encountering Ireland: Gabriel Harvey, Edmund Spenser, and English Colonial Ventures', in Brendan Bradshaw, Andrew Hadfield, and Will Maley, eds, *Representing Ireland: Literature and the Origins of Conflict, 1534–1660.* Cambridge, 1993, 60–75.

Jones, Timothy. 'Geoffrey of Monmouth, *Fouke le Fitz Warryn*, and National Mythology'. *SP* 91 (1994), 233–49.

Kaske, Carol V. 'The Dragon's Spark and Sting and the Structure of Red Cross's Dragon Fight: *The Faerie Queene*, i.xi–xii'. *SP* 66 (1969), 609–38.

Keen, Maurice. *Chivalry.* New Haven and London, 1984.

Keiser, George R. 'Lincoln Cathedral Library MS. 91: Life and Milieu of the Scribe'. *SB* 32 (1979), 158–79.

—— 'More Light on the Life and Milieu of Robert Thornton'. *SB* 36 (1983), 111–19.

Keith, W. J. '*Laȝamon's Brut*: The Literary Differences Between the Two Texts'. *MÆ* 29 (1960), 161–72.

Kempe, Dorothy. *The Legend of the Holy Grail.* EETS ES 95. London, 1905.

Kendrick, T. D. *British Antiquity.* London, 1950.

Kennedy, Beverly. *Knighthood in the Morte Darthur.* AS 11. 2nd edn. Cambridge, 1992.

Kennedy, Edward D. 'Malory's Use of Hardyng's *Chronicle*'. *NQ* n.s. 16 (1969), 167–70.

—— 'Malory and his English Sources', in Takamiya and Brewer, eds, *Aspects of Malory*, 27–55.

—— gen. ed., *A Manual of the Writings in Middle English: Fascicule 8,* 'Chronicles and Other Historical Writings'. Hamden, Conn., 1989.

King, Andrew. '"Well Grounded, Finely Framed, and Strongly Trussed Up Together": The "Medieval" Structure of *The Faerie Queene*'. *RES* (forthcoming).

King, John N. *English Reformation Literature.* Princeton, 1982.

—— *Tudor Royal Iconography: Literature and Art in an Age of Religious Crisis*. Princeton, 1989.
—— *Spenser's Poetry and the Reformation Tradition*. Princeton, 1990.
Klausner, David N. 'Didacticism and Drama in *Guy of Warwick*'. *MH* n.s. 6 (1975), 103–19.
Kratins, Ojars. 'The Middle English *Amis and Amiloun*: Chivalric Romance or Secular Hagiography?'. *PMLA* 81 (1966), 347–54.
Lagorio, Valerie M. 'The Evolving Legend of St Joseph of Glastonbury'. *Speculum* 46 (1971), 209–31.
—— '*The Joseph of Arimathie*: English Hagiography in Transition'. *MH* n.s. 6 (1975), 91–101.
Legge, M. Dominica. *Anglo-Norman Literature and its Background*. Oxford, 1963.
—— 'Anglo-Norman Hagiography and the Romances'. *MH* n.s. 6 (1975), 41–9.
Le Saux, Françoise H. M. *Laȝamon's Brut: The Poem and its Sources*. AS 19. Cambridge, 1989.
Leslie, Michael. *Spenser's 'Fierce Warres and Faithfull Loves': Martial and Chivalric Symbolism in The Faerie Queene*. Cambridge, 1983.
Levy, Fritz. *Tudor Historical Thought*. San Marino, 1967.
—— 'Spenser and Court Humanism', in Anderson, Cheney, and Richardson, eds, *Spenser's Life*, 65–80.
Lewis, C. S. *The Allegory of Love: A Study in Medieval Tradition*. Oxford, 1936.
—— *English Literature in the Sixteenth Century (Excluding Drama)*. Oxford, 1954.
—— 'The English Prose *Morte*', in Bennett, ed., *Essays on Malory*, 7–28.
—— *Spenser's Images of Life*, ed. Alastair Fowler. Cambridge, 1967.
Loades, D. M. *Politics and the Nation 1450–1660: Obedience, Resistance and Public Order*. Brighton, 1974.
—— ed. *John Foxe and the English Reformation*. Aldershot, 1997.
Loomis, Laura Hibbard. 'Chaucer and the Breton Lays of the Auchinleck MS'. *SP* 38 (1941), 14–33.
—— 'The Auchinleck Manuscript and a Possible London Bookshop of 1330–1340'. *PMLA* 57 (1942), 595–627.
—— [See also Hibbard, Laura.]
Loomis, Roger Sherman. 'Edward I, Arthurian Enthusiast'. *Speculum* 28 (1953), 114–27.
—— ed. *Arthurian Literature in the Middle Ages: A Collaborative History*. Oxford, 1959.
—— 'The Legend of Arthur's Survival', in Loomis, ed., *Arthurian Literature*, 64–71.

Luborsky, Ruth Samson. 'The Illustrations to *The Shepheardes Calender*'. *SS* 2 (1981), 3–53.

Lumiansky, Robert M. 'Arthur's Final Companions in Malory's *Morte Darthur*'. *Tulane Studies in English* 11 (1961), 5–19.

—— ed. *Malory's Originality: A Critical Study of Le Morte Darthur*. Baltimore, 1964.

McCabe, Richard A. 'The Masks of Duessa: Spenser, Mary Queen of Scots, and James VI'. *ELR* 17 (1987), 224–42.

—— *The Pillars of Eternity: Time and Providence in The Faerie Queene*. Dublin, 1989.

—— 'The Fate of Irena: Spenser and Political Violence', in Coughlan, ed., *Spenser and Ireland*, 9–25.

—— 'Edmund Spenser, Poet of Exile'. *PBA* 80 (1993), 73–103.

McCarthy, Terence. 'The Sequence of Malory's Tales', in Takamiya and Brewer, eds, *Aspects of Malory*, 107–24.

—— 'Malory and the Alliterative Tradition', in Spisak, ed., *Studies in Malory*, 53–85.

—— *An Introduction to Malory*. AS 20. Cambridge, 1991.

—— 'Malory and his Sources', in Archibald and Edwards, eds, *Companion to Malory*, 75–95.

McCoy, Richard C. *The Rites of Knighthood: The Literature and Politics of Elizabethan Chivalry*. Berkeley, 1989.

McKisack, May. *Medieval History in the Tudor Age*. Oxford, 1971.

Macquarrie, John. *Principles of Christian Theology*. 2nd edn. New York, 1977.

Macrae-Gibson, O. D. 'Wynkyn de Worde's *Marlyn*'. *Library* 6th ser. 2 (1980), 73–6.

Mahoney, Dhira B. 'The Truest and Holiest Tale: Malory's Transformation of *La Queste del Saint Graal*', in Spisak, ed., *Studies in Malory*, 109–28.

Mallette, Richard. *Spenser and the Discourses of Reformation England*. Lincoln, Nebraska, and London, 1997.

Mambelli, Giulano. *Gli annali delle edizione virgiliane*. Florence, 1954.

Mason, Emma. 'Legends of the Beauchamps' Ancestors: The Use of Baronial Propaganda in Medieval England'. *JMH* 10 (1984), 25–40.

Matthews, William. *The Tragedy of Arthur: A Study of the Alliterative 'Morte Arthure'*. Berkeley and Los Angeles, 1960.

Matzke, John E. 'The Legend of Saint George: Its Development into a *Roman d'aventure*'. *PMLA* 19 (1904), 449–78.

Meale, Carol M. 'Wynkyn de Worde's Setting-Copy for *Ipomydon*'. *SB* 35 (1982), 156–71.

—— 'The Middle English Romance of *Ipomedon*: A Late Medieval "Mirror" for Princes and Merchants'. *RMS* 10 (1984), 136–82.

—— 'Patrons, Buyers and Owners: Book Production and Social Status', in Griffiths and Pearsall, eds, *Book Production and Publishing*, 201–38.

—— 'The Morgan Library Copy of *Generides*', in Mills, Fellows, and Meale, eds, *Romance in Medieval England*, 89–104.

—— 'Caxton, de Worde, and the Publication of Romance in Late Medieval England'. *Library* 6th ser. 14 (1992), 283–98.

—— ed. *Readings in Medieval English Romance*. Cambridge, 1994.

—— ' "gode men / Wiues maydens and alle men": Romance and its Audiences', in Meale, ed., *Readings in Medieval English Romance*, 209–25.

—— ' "Prenes: engre": An Early Sixteenth-Century Presentation Copy of *The Erle of Tolous*', in Fellows, et al., eds, *Romance Reading*, 221–36.

—— ' "The Hoole Book": Editing and the Creation of Meaning in Malory's Text', in Archibald and Edwards, eds, *Companion to Malory*, 3–17.

Mehl, Dieter. *The Middle English Romances of the Thirteenth and Fourteenth Centuries*. London, 1968.

Mendyk, Stan A. E. *'Speculum Britanniae': Regional Study, Antiquarianism, and Science in Britain to 1700*. Toronto, 1989.

Mills, Jerry Leath. 'Spenser and the Numbers of History: A Note on the British and Elfin Chronicles in *The Faerie Queene*'. *PQ* 55 (1976), 281–7.

—— 'Prudence, History, and the Prince in *The Faerie Queene*, Book II'. *HLQ* 41 (1978), 83–101.

Mills, Maldwyn. 'The Composition and Style of the "Southern" *Octavian*, *Sir Launfal*, and *Libeaus Desconus*'. *MÆ* 31 (1962), 88–109.

—— '*Sir Isumbras* and the Styles of the Tail-Rhyme Romance', in Meale, ed., *Readings in Medieval English Romance*, 1–24.

—— Jennifer Fellows, and Carol Meale, eds. *Romance in Medieval England*. Cambridge, 1991.

Montrose, Louis Adrian. 'Celebration and Insinuation: Sir Philip Sidney and the Motives of Elizabethan Courtship'. *Renaissance Drama* n.s. 8 (1977), 3–35.

—— 'Renaissance Literary Studies and the Subject of History'. *ELR* 16 (1986), 5–12.

Moorman, Charles. 'Desperately Defending Winchester'. *Arthuriana* 5 (1995), 24–9.

Morgan, Margery M. 'Pynson's Manuscript of *Dives and Pauper*'. *Library* 5th ser. 8 (1953), 217–28.

Murrin, Michael. *The Veil of Allegory: Some Notes Toward a Theory of Allegorical Rhetoric in the English Renaissance*. Chicago, 1969.

—— *The Allegorical Epic: Essays in its Rise and Decline.* Chicago and London, 1980.

Nelson, William. *Fact or Fiction: The Dilemma of the Renaissance Storyteller.* Cambridge, Mass., 1973.

—— ed. *Form and Convention in the Poetry of Edmund Spenser.* New York and London, 1961.

Newell, W. W. 'William of Malmesbury on the Antiquity of Glastonbury'. *PMLA* 18 (1903), 459–512.

Nitze, W. A. 'The Exhumation of King Arthur at Glastonbury'. *Speculum* 9 (1934), 355–61.

Noguchi, Shunichi. 'The Winchester Malory'. *Arthuriana* 5 (1995), 15–23.

Nohrnberg, James. *The Analogy of The Faerie Queene.* Princeton, 1976.

Norbrooke, David. *Poetry and Politics of the English Renaissance.* London, 1984.

Oakley, Francis. *The Medieval Experience: Foundations of Western Cultural Singularity.* Medieval Academy Reprints for Teaching 23. Toronto, 1988.

O'Connell, Michael. 'History and the Poet's Golden World: The Epic Catalogues in *The Faerie Queene*'. *ELR* 4 (1974), 241–67.

—— *Mirror and Veil: The Historical Dimension of Spenser's Faerie Queene.* Chapel Hill, 1977.

O'Connor, John J. *Amadis de Gaule and Its Influence on Elizabethan Literature.* New Brunswick, N.J., 1970.

Olefsky, Ellyn. 'Chronology, Factual Consistency, and the Problem of Unity in Malory'. *JEGP* 68 (1969), 57–73.

Owst, G. R. *Preaching in Medieval England: An Introduction to Sermon Manuscripts of the Period, c. 1350–1450.* Cambridge, 1926.

—— *Literature and Pulpit in Medieval England: A Neglected Chapter in the History of English Letters and of the English People.* 2nd edn. Oxford, 1961.

Painter, George D. *William Caxton: A Quincentenary Biography of England's First Printer.* London, 1976.

Paradise, N. Burton. *Thomas Lodge.* New Haven, 1931.

Parker, M. Pauline. *The Allegory of The Faerie Queene.* Oxford, 1960.

Parker, Patricia A. *Inescapable Romance: Studies in the Poetics of a Mode.* Princeton, 1979.

Parkes, Malcolm B. 'The Literacy of the Laity', in David Daiches and Anthony Thorlby, gen. eds, *Literature and Western Civilization: The Medieval World.* London, 1973, 555–77.

—— 'The Influence of the Concepts of *Ordinatio* and *Compilatio* on the Development of the Book', in his *Scribes, Scripts, and Readers.* London and Rhio Grande, Ohio, 1991, 35–70.

—— *Pause and Effect: An Introduction to the History of Punctuation in the West*. Aldershot, 1992.

Pearsall, Derek. 'The Development of Middle English Romance'. *MS* 27 (1965), 91–116.

—— 'John Capgrave's *Life of St Katherine* and Popular Romance Style'. *MH* n.s. 6 (1975), 121–37.

—— 'The English Romance in the Fifteenth Century'. *Essays & Studies* n.s. 29 (1976), 56–83.

—— ed. *Manuscripts and Readers in Fifteenth-Century England: The Literary Implications of Manuscript Study*. Cambridge, 1983.

—— 'Middle English Romance and its Audiences', in Mary-Jo Arn and Hanneke Wirtjes, with Hans Jensen, eds, *Historical & Editorial Studies in Medieval & Early Modern English for Johan Gerritsen*. Groningen, 1985, 37–47.

—— ed. *Studies on the Vernon Manuscript*. Cambridge, 1990.

—— 'The Uses of Manuscripts: Late Medieval English'. *Harvard Library Bulletin* 4 (1994), 30–6.

Pevsner, Nikolaus and Alexandra Wedgwood. *The Buildings of England: Warwickshire*. Harmondsworth, 1966.

Phillips, James Emerson. *Images of a Queen: Mary Stuart in Sixteenth-Century Literature*. Berkeley and Los Angeles, 1964.

Plomer, Henry R. *Wynkyn de Worde and his Contemporaries*. London, 1925.

Pochoda, Elizabeth. *Arthurian Propoganda: Le Morte Darthur as an Historical Ideal of Life*. Chapel Hill, 1971.

Pope, M. K. 'The Romance of Horn and *King Horn*'. *MÆ* 25 (1956), 164–7.

Putter, Ad. 'Finding Time for Romance: Medieval Literary History'. *MÆ* 63 (1994), 1–18.

—— *Sir Gawain and the Green Knight and French Arthurian Romance*. Oxford, 1995.

Rambuss, Richard. 'Spenser's Lives, Spenser's Careers', in Anderson, Cheney, and Richardson, eds, *Spenser's Life*, 1–17.

Rance, Adrian B. 'The Bevis and Ascupart Panels, Bargate Museum, Southampton'. *PHFCAS* 42 (1986), 147–53.

Rathbone, Isabel E. *The Meaning of Spenser's Fairyland*. New York, 1937.

Rice, Joanne A. *Middle English Romance: An Annotated Bibliography, 1955–1985*. New York, 1987.

Richmond, Velma Bourgeois. *The Legend of Guy of Warwick*. New York and London, 1996.

Riddy, Felicity. *Sir Thomas Malory*. Leiden, 1987.

—— 'Glastonbury, Joseph of Arimathea, and the Grail in John Hardyng's *Chronicle*', in Abrams and Carley, eds, *Archaeology and History of Glastonbury*, 317–31.

—— 'Contextualizing *Le Morte Darthur*: Empire and Civil War', in Archibald and Edwards, eds, *Companion to Malory*, 55–73.

Rigg, A. G. *A Glastonbury Miscellany of the Fifteenth Century: A Descriptive Index of Trinity College, Cambridge, MS. o.9.38.* Oxford, 1968.

Robinson, J. Armitage. *Two Glastonbury Legends: King Arthur and St Joseph of Arimathea.* Cambridge, 1926.

Robinson, P. R. 'A Study of Some Aspects of the Transmission of English Verse Texts in Late Medieval Manuscripts'. B. Litt. thesis. University of Oxford, 1972.

Roche, Thomas P., Jr. *The Kindly Flame: A Study of the Third and Fourth Books of Spenser's Faerie Queene.* Princeton, 1964.

Rogers, Gillian. 'The Percy Folio Manuscript Revisited', in Mills, Fellows, and Meale, eds, *Romance in Medieval England*, 39–64.

Rossi, Joan Warchol. '*Briton moniments*: Spenser's Definition of Temperance in History'. *ELR* 15 (1985), 42–58.

Rouse, Mary A. and Richard H. Rouse. 'Backgrounds to Print', in their *Authentic Witnesses: Approaches to Medieval Texts and Manuscripts.* Notre Dame, 1991, 449–66.

—— '*Ordinatio* and *Compilatio* Revisited', in Mark D. Jordan and Kent Emry, Jr., eds, *Ad Litteram: Authoratative Texts and Their Medieval Readers.* Notre Dame, 1992, 113–34.

Rovang, Paul R. *Refashioning 'Knights and Ladies Gentle Deeds': The Intertextuality of Spenser's Faerie Queene and Malory's Morte Darthur.* Madison and London, 1996.

Ruff, Joseph R. 'Malory's Gareth and Fifteenth-Century Chivalry', in Benson and Leyerle, eds, *Chivalric Literature.*

Saunders, Corinne J. *The Forest of Medieval Romance: Avernus, Broceliande, Arden.* Cambridge, 1993.

Saunders, J. W. 'The Stigma of Print: A Note on the Social Bases of Tudor Poetry'. *Essays in Criticism* (1951), 139–64.

Scattergood, V. J. *Politics and Poetry in the Fifteenth Century.* London, 1971.

—— 'Literary Culture at the Court of Richard II', in V. J. Scattergood and J. W. Sherborne, eds, *English Court Culture in the Later Middle Ages.* London, 1983, 29–43.

Schlauch, Margaret. *Chaucer's Constance and Accused Queens.* New York, 1927.

Schulze, I. L. 'Elizabethan Chivalry and the Faerie Queene's Annual Feast'. *MLN* 50 (1935), 158–61.

Severs, J. Burke, gen. ed. *A Manual of the Writings in Middle English 1050–1500: Fascicule 1*, 'Romances'. New Haven, 1967.

Seymour, M. C. 'MSS Douce 261 and Egerton 3132A and Edward Banyster'. *Bodleian Library Record* 10 (1980), 162–5.

Sharpe, Kevin. *Sir Robert Cotton, 1586–1631: History and Politics in Early Modern England*. Oxford, 1979.

Shonk, Timothy A. 'A Study of the Auchinleck Manuscript: Bookmen and Bookmaking in the Early Fourteenth Century'. *Speculum* 60 (1985), 71–91.

Simons, John. 'Robert Parry's *Moderatus*: A Study in Elizabethan Literature', in Fellows et al., eds, *Romance Reading*, 237–50.

Sinfield, Alan. *Literature in Protestant England 1560–1660*. London, 1983.

Sklar, Elizabeth S. '*Arthour and Merlin*: The Englishing of Arthur'. *Michigan Academician* 8 (1975), 49–57.

Smith, Jeremy. 'Language and Style in Malory', in Archibald and Edwards, eds, *Companion to Malory*, 97–113.

Smithers, G. V. 'Story-Patterns in Some Breton Lays'. *MÆ* 22 (1953), 61–92.

Smyser, H. M. '*Charlemagne and Roland* and the Auchinleck MS'. *Speculum* 21 (1946), 275–88.

Southern, R. W. 'Aspects of the European Tradition of Historical Writing: 4, The Sense of the Past'. *TRHS* 5th ser. 23 (1973), 243–63.

Spearing, A. C. *Medieval to Renaissance in English Poetry*. Cambridge, 1985.

Speed, Diane. 'The Saracens of *King Horn*'. *Speculum* 65 (1990), 564–95.

—— 'The Construction of the Nation in Medieval English Romance', in Meale, ed., *Readings in Medieval English Romance*, 135–57.

Spisak, James W., ed. *Studies in Malory*. Kalamazoo, 1985.

Staines, David. '*Havelok the Dane*: A Thirteenth-Century Handbook for Princes'. *Speculum* 51 (1976), 602–23.

Stanley, E. G. 'Laȝamon's Antiquarian Sentiments'. *MÆ* 38 (1969), 23–37.

Stern, Karen. 'The Middle English *Prose Merlin*', in Alison Adams et al., eds, *The Changing Face of Arthurian Romance: Essays on Arthurian Prose Romances in Memory of Cedric E. Pickford*. AS 16. Cambridge, 1986, 112–22.

Stevens, John. *Medieval Romance: Themes and Approaches*. London, 1973.

Stewart, George R. 'English Geography in Malory's "*Morte D'Arthur*"'. *MLR* 30 (1935), 204–9.

Strohm, Paul. '*Storie, Spelle, Geste, Romance, Tragedie*: Generic Distinctions in the Middle English Troy Narratives'. *Speculum* 46 (1971), 348–59.
—— 'The Origin and Meaning of Middle English *Romaunce*'. *Genre* 10 (1977), 1–28.
Strong, Sir Roy C. *Portraits of Queen Elizabeth I*. Oxford, 1963.
—— *The Cult of Elizabeth: Elizabethan Portraiture and Pageantry*. London, 1977.
Summers, David A. *Spenser's Arthur: The British Arthurian Tradition and The Faerie Queene*. Lanham and Oxford, 1997.
Takamiya, Toshiyuki and Derek Brewer, eds. *Aspects of Malory*. AS 1. Cambridge, 1981.
Taylor, Andrew. 'The Myth of the Minstrel Manuscript'. *Speculum* 66 (1991), 43–73.
Taylor, John. *English Historical Literature in the Fourteenth Century*. Oxford, 1987.
Thomas, Henry. 'English Translations of Portuguese Books Before 1640'. *Library* 4th ser. 7 (1926), 1–30.
Thompson, John J. 'The Compiler in Action: Robert Thornton and the "Thornton Romances" in Lincoln Cathedral MS 91', in Pearsall, ed., *Manuscripts and Readers*, 113–24
—— *Robert Thornton and the London Thornton Manuscript*. Cambridge, 1987.
—— 'Collecting Middle English Romances and Some Related Book-Production Activities in the Later Middle Ages', in Mills, Fellows, and Meale, eds, *Romance in Medieval England*, 17–38.
—— 'Looking Behind the Book: MS Cotton Caligula A.ii, Part 1, and the Experience of its Texts', in Fellows et al., eds, *Romance Reading*, 171–87.
Treharne, Reginald F. *The Glastonbury Legends*. London, 1967.
Trounce, A. McI. 'The English Tail-Rhyme Romances'. *MÆ* 1 (1932), 87–108, 168–82; 2 (1933), 34–57, 189–98; 3 (1934), 30–50.
Tucker, P. E. 'Chivalry in the *Morte*', in Bennett, ed., *Essays on Malory*, 64–103.
Turville-Petre, Thorlac. '*Havelok* and the History of the Nation', in Meale, ed., *Readings in Medieval English Romance*, 121–34
—— *England the Nation: Language, Literature, and National Identity, 1290–1340*. Oxford, 1996.
Tuve, Rosemond. *Allegorical Imagery: Some Medieval Books and Their Posterity*. Princeton, 1966.
Vinaver, Eugene. *Malory*. Oxford, 1929, rpt. 1970.
Warnicke, Retha M. *William Lambarde, Elizabethan Antiquary, 1536–1601*. London and Chichester, 1973.

Warton, Thomas. *Observations on the Fairy Queen of Spenser.* 2nd edn. London, 1807.

Weatherby, Harold L. 'The True Saint George'. *ELR* (1987), 119–41.

Weiss, Judith. 'The Major Interpolations in *Sir Beues of Hamtoun*'. *MÆ* 48 (1979), 71–6.

Wells, William, ed. *Spenser Allusions in the Sixteenth and Seventeenth Centuries, 1580–1700.* SP, Texts and Studies 68–9 (1971–2).

White, Helen C. *Social Criticism in Popular Religious Literature of the Sixteenth Century.* New York, 1944.

Whiting, B. J. 'A Fifteenth-Century English Chaucerian: The Translation of *Partonope of Blois*'. *Medieval Studies* 7 (1945), 40–54.

Williams, Kathleen. *Spenser's Faerie Queene: The World of Glass.* London, 1966.

Wilson, R. H. 'Malory, The Stanzaic *"Morte Arthur"* and the *"Mort Artu"*'. *MP* 37 (1939–40), 125–38.

—— 'The Fair Unknown in Malory'. *PMLA* 58 (1943), 1–21.

—— 'Malory's Naming of Minor Characters'. *JEGP* 42 (1943), 364–85.

—— 'Malory's French Book Again'. *Comparative Literature* 2 (1950), 172–81.

—— 'Malory's Early Knowledge of Arthurian Romance'. *Texas Studies in Literature* 32 (1953), 33–50.

Windeatt, Barry. 'Chaucer and Fifteenth-Century Romance: *Partonope of Blois*', in Ruth Morse and Barry Windeatt, eds, *Chaucer Traditions: Studies in Honour of Derek Brewer.* Cambridge and New York, 1990, 62–80.

Withington, R. *English Pageantry.* Cambridge, Mass., 1918.

Withrington, John. 'Caxton, Malory, and The Roman War in *The Morte Darthur*'. *SP* 89 (1992), 350–66.

Wittig, Susan. *Stylistic and Narrative Structures in the Middle English Romance.* Austin and London, 1978.

Wogan-Browne, Jocelyn. '"Bet...to rede on holy seyntes lyves...":Romance and Hagiography Again', in Meale, ed. (1994), 83–97.

Worton, Michael and Judith Still, eds. *Intertextuality: Theory and Practices.* New York and Manchester, 1990.

Woudhuysen, H. R. *Sir Philip Sidney and the Circulation of Manuscripts, 1558–1640.* Oxford, 1996.

Wright, C. E. 'The Elizabethan Society of Antiquaries and the Formation of the Cottonian Library', in Francis Wormald and C. E. Wright, eds, *The English Library Before 1700.* London, 1958, 176–212.

Wright, Louis B. *Middle-Class Culture in Elizabethan England.* Chapel Hill, 1935.

Wright, T. L. 'On the Genesis of Malory's *Gareth*'. *Speculum* 57 (1982), 569–82.
Yates, Frances A. *The Art of Memory.* Chicago, 1966.
——*Astraea: The Imperial Theme in the Sixteenth Century.* London, 1975.

Index

Metham, John 96, 97
Merlin (English prose) 96, 99
Morte Arthur (stanzaic) 75–6, 122–3
Morte Arthure (alliterative) 13, 74,
   109–11, 122–3, 128, 184
Morte le roi Artu 76, 122–3

Nashe, Thomas 40

Octavian 22, 32, 78, 85–7, 99, 100
   and *Faerie Queene*, Bk I 149, 154–5
Oxford, Bodleian Library:
   MS Ashmole 45 38
   MS Ashmole 61 1–20
   MS Digby 185 97–8
   MS Douce 261 38
   MS Greaves 60 38
   MS Laud Misc. 108 42

Partonope of Blois 27, 96
Pearsall, Derek 95
Perceval 91–3, 99, 102
   and *Faerie Queene* Bk I 148, 151
Percy Folio MS 38
Piers Plowman-tradition 5
Plato/Platonic thought 186–7
Ponthus 97–9
printing of romance (sixteenth-century),
   see romance (Middle English), printing
   and sixteenth-century reception
Protestantism
   see Calvin, Jean; Spenser, *Faerie
   Queene*, Protestantism/Calvinism
providence 21, 22–5, 44–5, 47–8, 50,
   52, 54–6, 63–5, 69, 78–9, 88, 112,
   124–5, 177–80, 212–13
   and *Faerie Queene* Bk II 160, 172,
   180–8
   and *Faerie Queene* Bk V 196, 200
Puttenham, George 40
Pynson, Richard 30–3

Richard Coeur de Lion 42, 58–9, 197,
   200
Robinson, Richard 177–8
romance (Middle English):
   audiences/readership 25–9, 96, 99
   generic relations with historical
   writings and hagiography, 13–14,
   18–21, 24–5, 45, 69–73, 78–9,
   99–101, 112
   mirror 97–8, 100, 104, *see also* 'still
   there' topos

mode 21–5
printing and sixteenth-century
   reception 11, 29–41
   tradition 14–18, 102–3, 112–13
   see also manuscripts

Sidney, Sir Philip 39–40, 44, 167–8, 186
Sklar, Elizabeth S. 57
slandered women, see Constance-
   Florence figures
South English Legendary 65–6, 70
SPENSER, EDMUND:
   Faerie Queene:
      Adicia 203
      'Antiquitie of Faerie lond' 1,
      180–1, 183–8, 208
      Artegall 183, 189, 194–209
      Arthur 9–11, 173–5, 178, 183,
      185, 194–7, 209
      Arthurian/Tudor genealogy
      175–80, 183–5, 194–6, 210–11
      Astraea, 206
      Bon Font 206–7
      Bower of Bliss 166–7
      Burbon 203–4, 208
      Britomart 195–6
      'Briton moniments' 1, 180–5, 200,
      208
      Clarinda 204
      'Communist Giant' 199–201
      Despair, 127–8
      dragon-fight and *Bevis* 129–45
      Duessa 203, 207–8
      Eumnestes (memory) 1, 144–5,
      165–9, 180–7, 190, 192, 195, 213
      faerie land 161, 173–5, 190–1
      Gloriana 9–11, 174, 184, 185,
      195–6
      Grantorto 208–9
      Grille 188
      Guyon 142, 173–4, 183, 189,
      193–4
      history and national identity
      160–88, 189, 192, 212–13
      Ireland/colonialism 198–206
      Malengin 204–6
      Mercilla 205, 206–8
      Mutabilitie Cantos 212–13
      Phantastes 165–73, 181, 192, 213
      Pollente 202
      Protestantism/Calvinism 126–45,
      148–53, 156–9, 173, 177–80, 212
      Radigund 204, 207–8